PANTHER

OSPREY
PUBLISHING

PANTHER

GERMANY'S QUEST FOR COMBAT DOMINANCE

MICHAEL & GLADYS GREEN

First published in Great Britain in 2012 by Osprey Publishing,
Midland House, West Way, Botley, Oxford, OX2 0PH, UK
43-01 21st Street, Suite 220B, Long Island City, NY 11101, USA
Email: info@ospreypublishing.com
Osprey Publishing is part of the Osprey Group.
© 2012 Michael and Gladys Green

Every attempt has been made by the Publisher to secure the
appropriate permissions for material reproduced in this book.
If there has been any oversight we will be happy to rectify
the situation and written submission should be made to
the Publishers.

A CIP catalogue record for this book is available from the
British Library.

ISBN: 978 1 84908 841 1

Page layout by Ken Vail Graphic Design, Cambridge, UK
Indexed by Sandra Shotter
Typeset in Sabon and Franklin Gothic
Originated by PDQ Media, Bungay, UK
Printed in China through World Print Ltd.

13 14 15 16 17   11 10 9 8 7 6 5 4 3 2

Osprey Publishing is supporting the Woodland Trust, the UK's
leading woodland conservation charity, by funding the
dedication of trees.

www.ospreypublishing.com

FRONT COVER: Four of the five-man crew of a Panther Ausf. D
tank. *(Patton Museum)*

BACK COVER: A trio of parked Panther Ausf. D tanks
camouflaged with varying levels of foliage. *(Patton Museum)*

PAGE 2: A member of the German tank troops poses next to a
band-new Panther Ausf. A tank. *(Patton Museum)*

IMPRINT AND CONTENTS PAGE: An abandoned Panther Ausf. G
tank riled through by American soldiers. *(Patton Museum)*

CONTENTS

DEDICATION

To the late Jacques Littlefield, founder of the Military Vehicle Technology Foundation, for his dedication and persistence in the restoration of a Panther tank.

ACKNOWLEDGEMENTS

Special thanks are due to the staff of the Military Vehicle Technology Foundation, the Tank Museum at Bovington, the Virginia Museum of Military Vehicles, and the former Patton Museum of Armor and Cavalry for their assistance in completing this book. Individuals who made an extra effort in helping out on this book besides supplying pictures include David Fletcher, Chun-Lun Hsu, James D. Brown, Richard Cox, Michael Panchyshyn, Candace Fuller, and Randy Talbot.

A special note of thanks goes to Vladimir Yakubov and Yuri Pasholok, who provided information about the Red Army's reaction to the Panther tank. Yuri V. Desyatnik provided translations from the *Panther-Fibel* (Panther handbook) and information about German World War II radios.

INTRODUCTION

The German Panther tank was almost certainly the most elegant design of World War II. It embodied a balance of firepower, armor protection, and mobility unmatched by any other tank of the period. Yet, it was not the war-winner it might have been. The gulf between the potential of the Panther tank design and its performance on the battlefield will be explored in this book, as will how the vehicle functioned.

The basic requirements for the Panther tank were laid out as a result of lessons learned in the summer of 1940 in France and the autumn of 1941 in Russia. In a remarkable feat of engineering and production, the Germans fielded a number of light and medium tanks before the war in Europe, which served as the backbone of their doctrine of operational maneuver (*Bewegungskrieg*) or, as the West called it, *Blitzkrieg*. As robust as these designs were, however, their weapons proved unable to penetrate the armor on some of their opponents' tanks. To make matters worse, the armor protection levels on the German tanks proved inadequate for the job at hand.

This lesson was hammered home to the Germans in July 1941 when they first encountered the Red Army's T-34 medium tank. Though crudely manufactured in many ways, the Russian tank featured a highly efficient, sloped armor design, which gave excellent protection for its weight. The broad tracks and consequent low ground pressure, along with a suspension design "borrowed" from American J. Walter Christie's designs of the 1930s, also gave the T-34 tank outstanding tactical mobility. Though the initial encounter was painful for the *Panzertruppen* (German tank troops), it provided valuable knowledge needed to design the next generation of panzers.

The new panzers were not long in coming. By November 1941, the Germans were planning their response in the form of a tank that combined the armor protection and mobility of the T-34 medium tank, coupled with a main gun superior to any then fielded. An initial production order was placed in March 1942 for 250 examples of the new medium tank to be ready for use by May 12, 1943.

The resulting Panther medium tank was an engineering masterpiece that in many ways was years ahead of its adversaries. The thick, well-sloped armor featured interlocking mortise joints, which reinforced its welds. The powerful Maybach engine gave a relatively high horsepower-to-weight ratio, and the interleaved suspension gave good weight distribution along the wide track strands. The long, high-velocity, 75-mm main gun was a potent threat to almost any opponent it encountered on the battlefield.

Why then, was the Panther tank not the super weapon Adolph Hitler hoped it would be? A few reasons: First, the design was rushed into production and fielded before engineering development was complete. Panthers suffered from mechanical breakdowns to the extent that field commanders often noted that more of their Panthers were lost to mechanical failure than to enemy action. Second, the design, although elegant, was too expensive, complicated, and time-consuming to build in a wartime economy. The Germans built only a few thousand Panthers while the Americans and Russians were building tens of thousands of tanks to go up against it. Third, Hitler's preoccupation with ever larger and more impressive weapons diluted both the engineering and economic resources available to Germany. Too many *Wunderwaffen* (wonder weapons) competed for too few resources.

Thus the Panther tank, that most elegant of tank designs, accomplished little to turn the Allied tide. Although often a formidable opponent when confronted on the battlefield, the tank was not available in sufficient numbers to make a difference in the outcome of the war.

CHAPTER ONE

BACKGROUND

Before the German military invasion of the Soviet Union on June 22, 1941, code-named Operation Barbarossa, the medium tanks of the German tank troops had dominated the battlefields of Western and Eastern Europe. These tanks were designated the Pz.Kpfw. III and Pz.Kpfw. IV, both having entered into German Army service before the invasion of Poland on September 1, 1939, which marked the official beginning of World War II.

Assisting the Pz.Kpfw. III and Pz.Kpfw. IV medium tanks of the German tank troops in combat were the Pz.Kpfw. I and Pz.Kpfw. II light tanks. Like their medium tank counterparts, both light tanks had entered service before the beginning of World War II.

The abbreviation "Pz.Kpfw." stands for *PanzerKampfwagen* (armored fighting vehicle or tank). *Panzer* means armor or tank. The term "Panzer" will be used in place of Pz.Kpfw. throughout the remainder of the text.

Despite the fact that the early-model Panzer III and Panzer IV medium tanks were inferior in some design features to their early-war French and British counterparts, such as in armor protection and firepower, the German medium tanks had prevailed over their opponents due to the higher level of training their crews possessed and the tactics those same crews employed in combat.

The first post-World War I German tank was the two-man Panzer I light tank armed with twin turret-mounted 7.92-mm MG13 machine guns. Production began in July 1934 and ended in June 1937 with almost 1,500 units built. The restored Pz.Kpfw. I Ausf. A version pictured belongs to the German Army Tank Museum. *(Thomas Anderson)*

PANZER III TANK

Combat experience in France showed that the penetration capability of the armor-piercing (AP) projectiles fired from the 37-mm main gun on the original versions of the roughly 22-ton (20-mt)[1] Panzer III medium tanks was inadequate in dealing with its more heavily armored enemy counterparts such as the French Army 22-ton (20-mt) Somua S-35 medium tank, which was armed with a 47-mm main gun and 47 mm of armor at its thickest point

To rectify this firepower shortcoming, a 50-mm main gun began appearing on a later version of the Panzer III medium tank and was retrofitted to many earlier models of the vehicle. Despite the retrofitting, many of the Panzer III medium tanks that took part in the invasion of the Soviet Union in the summer of 1941 still mounted the original 37-mm main gun.

Hitler had wanted a longer and even more powerful version of a 50-mm main gun fitted to the Panzer III medium tank. Lengthening the barrel of tank guns results in higher projectile velocity and improves the penetrating

---

[1] All weights listed in tons are in U.S. short tons (2,000 lbs per ton) or metric tons (2,204.6 lbs per ton) unless otherwise noted.

power of the projectiles fired. The *Heereswaffenamt* (German Army Ordnance Department) ignored his orders, due to supply difficulties in obtaining a longer 50-mm main gun and their belief that the existing shorter 50-mm main gun was effective enough to deal with any future battlefield opponents. Battlefield encounters in the Soviet Union would find this belief to be in error. The longer version of the 50-mm main gun did not appear on the Panzer III medium tank until December 1941.

PANZER IV TANK

Instead of a high-velocity tank-killing weapon, the roughly 22-ton (20-mt) Panzer IV medium tank originally mounted a low-velocity 75-mm gun. This short and stubby main gun primarily was intended to fire high-explosive (HE) rounds at enemy antitank guns and defensive positions. This reflected the fact that the original mission of the Panzer IV in the German Army was as a fire-support vehicle for the Panzer I and Panzer II light tanks and the Panzer III medium tank and not a tank killer.

Despite the mounting of the low-velocity 75-mm gun on the early versions of the Panzer IV medium tank when the design requirements for the vehicle

This restored Panzer II Ausf. F light tank belonging to the German Army Tank Museum is in Afrika Korps colors. The three-man Panzer II was armed with a 2-cm (20-mm) Kw.K. 30 automatic cannon and a single 7.92-mm MG34 machine gun. Production began in 1937 and ended in December 1942 with about 1,700 units built. *(Thomas Anderson)*

were first being established in 1934, the German Army had considered arming it with a much longer, high-velocity, 75-mm main gun to deal with a new generation of better-armored French tanks. However, in the end, they decided that the existing tank-killing round fired from the low-velocity 75-mm gun would be sufficient, even though German military intelligence had discovered that the armor on some French tanks was actually thicker than anticipated.

As events transpired in France during the summer of 1940, it became clear that the low-velocity 75-mm gun on the early models of the Panzer IV medium tank were unable to penetrate the armor of the French Army 34-ton (31.5-mt) B1-bis heavy tank, which had armor up to 60 mm thick, or the British Army infantry-support 29-ton (27-mt) Matilda II tank, which featured armor up to 78 mm thick.

The German firm Fried.Krupp A.G. Essen (hereafter referred to as "Krupp") wasted no time in developing a high-velocity 75-mm main gun with a long barrel for the Panzer IV series medium tank that could penetrate the thick frontal armor on the British Army Matilda II infantry-support tank. Unfortunately, the German Army Ordnance Department insisted that no tank main gun could extend over the front of a tank's hull for fear that it might suffer damage by striking an object on the battlefield, such as a tree or building. Krupp reluctantly shortened the gun tube on their new 75-mm main gun, which in turn reduced the gun's penetrative abilities. Only one trial

TANK CLASSIFICATIONS

The classification of tanks as light, medium, or heavy is based on the vehicle's weight and varies between armies and the time periods during which they fought. One army's light tank could be another's medium tank while one army's medium tank could be another's heavy tank during different time periods.

Light tanks generally are considered as being reconnaissance vehicles, while medium tanks proved to be the workhorse of tank fleets from World War II through the 1950s. Heavy tanks originally were considered breakthrough vehicles and later evolved in World War II to offer the medium tanks long-range fire support.

Heavy tanks were phased out from the inventory of the world's armies in the 1960s because the medium tanks now had main guns with equal performance to those of the maintenance intensive heavy tanks. The former medium tanks became known as main battle tanks and, in the case of the American M1 Abrams tank series, weigh as much as a German World War II Tiger Ausf. B heavy tank.

The three-man French Army S-35 medium tank, armed with a turret-mounted 47-mm main gun and a single coaxial 7.5-mm Model 31 machine gun, was superior in almost all aspects of firepower, protection, and mobility when compared to its German Army medium tank counterparts in the summer of 1940. *(Michael Green)*

version of the gun was ever mounted on a Panzer IV medium tank. The shortsightedness of this decision would come back to haunt the German tank troops during the invasion of the Soviet Union.

MEETING THEIR MATCH

Advancing deep into the Soviet Union on their Panzer III and IV medium tanks in the summer of 1941, the elite tank troops of the German Army must have felt invincible as they pushed deep into the Russian countryside at up to 50 miles (80 km) a day, leaving large pockets of cut-off Red Army units to be mopped up by the follow-on infantry formations. The Red Army tanks they encountered along the way were generally obsolete models or in poor mechanical condition with untrained crews operating them.

The German Army had invaded the Soviet Union with about 3,000 tanks, of which 965 were Panzer IIIs and 439 were Panzer IV medium tanks of various models. The Red Army possessed a total of 24,000 tanks when the Germans invaded, the majority of them being insufficiently armored light tanks such as the 10.6-ton (9.6-mt) T-26 series with armor ranging between 6 mm and 25 mm thick. Almost 12,000 of these light tanks, in a variety of models, entered Red Army service between 1931 and 1940.

However, not everything went the German tank troops' way. A German Panzer unit ran into a large formation of Red Army tanks the day after the German invasion of the Soviet Union on June 23, 1941. The tanks they encountered included the 50-ton (45-mt) KV-1 heavy tank, armed with a 76.2-mm main gun, and the 57.5-ton (52-mt) KV-2 heavy tank armed with a 152-mm howitzer. The German tank troops were equipped both with impressed 11.6-ton (10.5-mt) Czechoslovakian light tanks designated the Panzer 35(t) armed with a 37-mm main gun and with the Panzer IV medium tank armed with a low-velocity 75-mm main gun.

Unfortunately, neither German tank gun proved able to penetrate the thick armor on the Red Army heavy tanks they ran into, despite repeated strikes from the front and flanks. Making matters even worse, once the Red Army tanks returned fire, they easily penetrated the thin armor on the German tanks. To avoid being annihilated by their opponents, the German tanks

Forming part of the impressive armored fighting vehicle collection of the French Army Tank Museum at Saumur is this up-gunned and up-armored Panzer III Ausf. F medium tank armed with a 5-cm (50-mm) Kw.K. L/42 main gun. Notice the weapon does not protrude over the front hull. *(Christophe Vallier)*

quickly sought to withdraw; however, not before one of the Red Army heavy tanks in a primal example of battlefield superiority took the time to run over one of the German tanks that had become immobilized in a marsh.

Ten days later, on July 3, 1941, elements of the German 18th Panzer Division engaged and destroyed a small number of Red Army 30-ton (28-mt) T-34 medium tanks. The commander of the Panzer division involved in this fracas quickly grasped the significance of this new medium tank design armed with 76.2-mm main gun and a well-sloped armor array, and provided General Heinz Guderian, then commander of *Panzergruppe II* (a German army command level higher than a corps but lower than an army), with two captured examples to inspect. Panzergruppe II consisted of three Panzer corps, with a total of 930 tanks.

Freiherr von Langermann, the general in charge of the 4th Panzer Division, wrote a report near the end of October 1941 detailing his impressions of his unit's encounter with the T-34 medium tank and KV-1 heavy tank. In that report, he lamented the absolute superiority of the Red Army tanks over the existing German medium tanks. He detailed how the Red Army tanks could accurately engage and destroy his own tanks at ranges at which they could not effectively return fire. According to General Langermann, a single projectile strike from the 76.2-mm main guns mounted on the Red Army tanks could tear apart his thinly armored medium tanks or cause their vehicle commander cupolas to fly off. To Langermann, the worst part of this surprising battlefield inferiority was the toll it would take on the morale of his tankers, who would quickly lose their offensive spirit and become much more cautious in combat.

Despite some setbacks during the opening months of the German invasion of the Soviet Union, the German tank troops, as a general rule, prevailed over the armored elements of the Red Army, even when the Soviets were equipped with the T-34 medium tank or KV-1 heavy tank. The poor state of training among the Russian tank crews and a lack of a suitable logistical system that could provide them with a sufficient amount of fuel and main gun ammunition left them at a disadvantage against the better-trained and better-equipped German tank troops.

Only when a larger number of T-34 medium tanks and KV-1 heavy tanks became available and finally massed together to engage the Germans at Mtsensk in October 1941, using German-type tank tactics, did the true fighting potential of these vehicles become painfully obvious to the German tank troops and their leaders. Up to that point in the war, the officers in command of Red Army tank formations had often shown a level of tactical

OPPOSITE
A Panzer IV Ausf. D medium tank armed with the 7.5cm (75mm) Kw.K L/24 short barreled gun heads a long convoy of vehicles. Behind the Panzer IV Ausf. D is either a Panzer IV Ausf. B or C due to its lack of a front hull mounted bow machine.
(Patton Museum)

incompetence that allowed the German tank troops to prevail in the majority of battlefield encounters.

The poor early-war leadership skills of the Red Army can largely be attributed to the pre-invasion purges of the Red Army officer corps by Joseph Stalin, who feared they might pose a threat to his dictatorship of the Soviet Union.

THE RESPONSE

Guderian alerted the German armaments ministry to the danger posed by the Red Army T-34 medium tank and KV-1 heavy tanks. In his memoirs, Guderian stated that the combat engagements that occurred at Mtsensk highlighted to him the clear superiority of the new generation of Red Army tanks to his own medium tanks. German General Friedrich Wilhelm von Mellenthin stated that, "We had nothing comparable."

On display at the French Army Tank Museum is this Renault B1 bis heavy tank. With its thick armor protection and heavy armament, it was more than a match for the German Panzer III and Panzer IV medium tanks during the battle for France in the summer of 1940. (*Christophe Vallier*)

Guderian could not have been that surprised by the technical superiority of the new Red Army tanks, as is recounted in his postwar memoirs, *Panzer Leader*. In that book, he recounted how a Russian military commission, which had visited Germany before the start of hostilities between the two nations, had been granted special access by Hitler to all the German tank schools and factories, with nothing to be hidden from them. During that visit, the Russian VIPs could not believe that the most impressive tank the Germans had in their inventory was the Panzer IV medium tank. These same Russian VIPs protested so much about being denied the right to see the newest German tanks in service that the German tank manufacturers and ordnance officers present could only conclude that the Red Army had in service far larger and more capable tanks than were currently known.

Unbeknownst to Guderian and the high command was the fact that the German Army military intelligence service had identified the T-34 medium tank before the German invasion of the Soviet Union. However, that information was never passed on to those in the German tank troops or those involved with maintaining the technical superiority of German tanks.

Another tank that posed a serious threat to the early-model German Panzer III and Panzer IV medium tanks during the battle for France in the summer of 1940 was the British Army's Matilda II. The only weapon in the German military inventory that could penetrate its thick frontal armor was the 8.8-cm (88-mm) Flak antiaircraft gun. (*Tank Museum, Bovington*)

In November 1941, weapons experts from the German armaments ministry and their civilian counterparts from private industry inspected captured examples of the Red Army T-34 medium tanks and KV-1 heavy tanks. The ministry experts were impressed by the extensive use of sloped armor on the T-34 medium tank and the large-caliber 7.62-mm main gun on both tanks. Other impressive features noted on the Red Army tanks included their large road wheels and wide tracks. German General Field-Marshal Paul Ludwig Ewald von Kleist stated that the T-34 medium tank was "The finest tank in the world."

On arrival of the weapons experts from the German armament ministry in Russia, Guderian addressed them with a speech. He told them that the most immediate need was to upgrade the existing medium tanks so that they possessed a main gun able to penetrate the armor of the T-34 medium tank and the KV-1 heavy tank at a range from which their opponents could not return effective fire.

Guderian went on to tell the weapons experts what he wanted on a next-generation medium tank. The list included thicker armor, an improved suspension system with wider tracks, and a more powerful engine. He also stressed that the next-generation medium tank must have a high horsepower-to-weight ratio to provide it the ability to easily drive off-road in all seasons.

In his speech to the weapons experts from the German armament ministry, Guderian rated the KV-1 heavy tank as a bigger threat to his beloved tank troops than the T-34 medium tank. This emphasis on the KV-1 heavy tank instead of the T-34 medium tank reflected the fact that the German tank troops initially found the KV-1 heavy tank a bigger threat than the T-34 medium tank. It was the German infantry who believed the more numerous T-34 medium tank was a larger threat to them. German General Günter Blumentritt stated that, "This tank [T-34] adversely affected the morale of the German infantry."

The T-34 medium tank would become the most numerous tank in the Red Army inventory by 1943. The KV-1 heavy tanks, besieged by design shortcomings, dwindled in importance for the Red Army and eventually were relegated to the infantry support role. Production of the KV-2 heavy tank ended after the German invasion of the Soviet Union, with only 250 having been built between 1940 and 1941. As a stop-gap measure to deal with the T-34 medium tank and the KV-1 heavy tanks, the German Army fielded a version of the Panzer IV medium tank armed with a long-barrel, high-velocity 75-mm main gun in March 1942.

NEW MEDIUM TANK REQUIREMENTS

Based on their evaluation of captured Red Army tanks, the German armaments ministry staff quickly settled on a design and manufacturing plan to field a new medium tank for the German tank troops to eventually replace the Panzer III and IV medium tanks within the Panzer divisions. The armaments ministry staff issued their directives on November 25, 1941, only a few days after their return from the Soviet Union inspection trip.

The new medium tank would require a high-velocity 75-mm main gun. The gun chosen was a *Rheinmetall-Borsig*-designed weapon (hereafter referred to as "Rheinmetall") designated the 7.5 cm K.w.K. 42 L/70. Without a muzzle brake fitted, the gun was 17 feet long (5.25 m). With a muzzle brake fitted, the gun was 18 feet long (5.53 m). By way of comparison, the 120-mm main gun on the newest version of the American M1 Abrams tank series is 18.5 feet (5.64 m) long and does not have a muzzle brake.

The abbreviation "K.w.K." stood for *Kampfwagenkanone*, or tank gun, and in German ordnance designators, it was followed by the number assigned to that particular weapon. The "L/70" refers to the 70-caliber length of the of the gun tube measured from the muzzle to the rear face of the breech. The term "caliber" defines the bore diameter of a gun. In large guns, design nomenclature also may refer to barrel length as a multiple of the caliber, thus a 7.5-cm L/70 denotes a gun with a 7.5-cm bore diameter that is 70-caliber long, or 7.5 cm × 70 = 525 cm (17 feet).

Other requirements for the new medium tank set by the armaments ministry staff included a gross vehicle weight of 34 to 39 tons (31 to 35 mt) a top speed of 35 mph (56 km/h), and armor thicknesses of 60 mm on the upper front plate (called the glacis by tankers) and 40 mm on the sides of the vehicle.

In late November 1941, the German firms of Daimler-Benz AG and MAN (Maschinenfabrik Augsburg-Nuernberg AG) were commissioned to design the chassis for the new medium tank. The German Army Ordnance Department, which included an automotive design office, referred to as the *Waffenpruefamter 6*, shortened to "Wa Pruef 6," encompassed all new tank development projects and set the technical requirements for the new medium tank. Daimler-Benz and MAN submitted proposals for final approval by the German Army Ordnance Department, following a presentation to be given in Berlin on March 3, 1942.

German production tanks traditionally had featured rear-mounted gasoline-powered engines and front transmissions. In a departure from this tradition, Daimler-Benz's final prototype featured a rear-mounted, liquid-cooled diesel engine close-coupled to the transmission, similar to the power-train configuration of the T-34 medium tank. This in turn required that the turret be placed farther forward than other German tanks of the period. The suspension system consisted of large interleaved road wheels supported by external lower-hull coil springs, which is typically described as a Christie-style suspension system after American inventor John Walter Christie, who first devised the arrangement. In many ways, the Daimler-Benz prototype was a rough German copy of the T-34 medium tank.

The final MAN prototype chassis reflected more conventional German design features, with its rear-mounted, liquid-cooled, gasoline-powered engine and front transmission. A disadvantage of this arrangement was that the engine and drive sprockets (connected to the transmission) were at opposite ends of the tank's hull. This made it necessary to have a drive shaft that ran from one end of the vehicle's hull to the other. This took up valuable space inside the hull and in turn pushed up the height of the tank's turret since the turret basket floor must clear the drive-train enclosure.

Belonging to the U.S. Army Ordnance Museum is a Red Army KV-1 heavy tank. In service it was armed with a turret-mounted 76.2-mm main gun and three 7.62-mm machine guns. Maximum frontal armor thickness on the KV-1 was 106 mm. The five-man KV-1 was a potent foe for the German tank troops in the summer of 1941. *(Patton Museum)*

The steel turret basket in the Panther formed part of the tank's internal structure. It was a circular structure attached to the bottom of the vehicle's turret and rotated with the turret. The turret basket floor was the platform for the standing loader and seated gunner.

Although the first-generation of the American-designed and -built M4 medium tank series (hereafter referred to as the Sherman tank) had a full turret basket, the T-34 medium tank had none at all. The vehicle commander (who also doubled as the loader) and gunner sat on small, padded metal seats attached to the turret ring. The main gun rounds were stored in thin, pressed metal boxes located in the hull floor and covered with a large rubber mats that could be rolled up when access to the main gun rounds was required.

The placement of the turret on the MAN prototype chassis at the center of the vehicle minimized the gun-barrel overhang, again following traditional German tank design practice up to that time. The only major break with tradition was the employment of sloped armor plates. Like the T-34 medium tank, the prototype MAN chassis also featured much wider steel tracks than seen on prior German medium tanks.

Forming part of the impressive collection of the U.S. Army Ordnance Museum is this four-man T-34 medium tank armed with a turret-mounted 76.2-mm main gun and two 7.62-mm machine guns. It began appearing in Red Army service in 1940 and was a rude surprise to the German Army in the summer of 1941. *(Michael Green)*

CONTRACTS GO OUT

Unlike the U.S. Army, for which both the turret and chassis of contracted tanks were designed and built by the same firm, the German Army divided the process, with one firm awarded the contract to design and build the turret and another firm the chassis. The contract for the design of the turret for the German tank troops' new medium tank went to the German firm of Rheinmetall.

The Rheinmetall turret design featured a 100-mm-thick cast steel rounded gun shield (mantlet) that extended almost across the width of the turret front. The side and rear armor plates of their hexagonal-shaped turret were 45 mm thick, sloped at 25 degrees. The armor side plates bent inward near the back of the turret to meet the edges of a comparatively narrow rear armor plate.

Hitler took a personal interest in the evaluation of the Daimler-Benz and MAN prototypes for the new medium tank chassis. He was impressed with the Daimler-Benz prototype, especially the diesel engine, placing an initial

Notice the wide tracks of this Red Army KV-1 heavy tank in this frontal view. It was these wide tracks that provided it with off-road mobility far superior to the narrow tracks on the German Panzer III and Panzer IV medium tanks. Top speed of the KV-1 was 21.8 mph (35 km/h). *(Patton Museum)*

order for two hundred units in March 1942. This greatly frustrated Wa Pruef 6, which had not yet completed its careful evaluation based on the needs of the German tank troops.

Two basic requirements were established for the new medium tank. It had to be placed into production quickly in order to be ready for service in large numbers by no later than the summer of 1943. It also had to be so superior in individual capability that it would be able to offset the Red Army's numerical advantage in tanks.

The German Army Ordnance Department eventually picked the MAN chassis design on May 11, 1942, in the belief that the MAN chassis could be placed into production more quickly than that of Daimler-Benz. The problem that Daimler-Benz had was the fact that the chosen Rheinmetall turret did not fit on their chassis. Although they insisted they could quickly design and build a suitable turret for their chassis, the German Army Ordnance department deemed the risk of running behind schedule too high.

Hitler's approval of the decision to favor the MAN design over that of Daimler-Benz took place on May 14, 1942. MAN was informed of the decision the next day. At the same time, the order for two hundred Daimler-Benz chassis was cancelled.

In his book *Panther vs T34: Ukraine 1943*, author Robert Forczyk suggests that there were other influences on the selection of the MAN chassis over that of Daimler-Benz. He points the finger at Heinrich Ernst Kniepkamp, the senior engineer at Wa Pruef 6.

Kniepkamp had worked for MAN prior to becoming a government employee, and his main passion in life seemed to be to incorporate torsion bar suspension systems into new tanks. Once Hitler began expressing his favor for the Daimler-Benz chassis, which did not include a torsion bar suspension system, over that of the MAN chassis, which did, Kniepkamp and his boss, Oberst Sebastian Fichtner, began to spread disparaging remarks about the Daimler-Benz design in order to discredit it in the eyes of Hitler and the German Army.

Kniepkamp and others in Wa Pruef 6 also leaked Daimler-Benz proprietary design information regarding their tank chassis to MAN in order to allow MAN to improve their odds of winning the contract.

Forczyk goes on to suggest that Karl-Otter Saur, the principal deputy to Albert Speer, Hitler's *Reichsminister* (civilian minister of armament) and the civilian head of the German Ministry for Armaments and War Production, also influenced the selection of the MAN chassis design by his insistence to

OVERLEAF
Belonging to the Russian Army Tank Museum at Kubinka is this nicely restored German Panzer IV Ausf. G medium tank. It is armed with a long barrel, high-velocity 7.5-cm (75-mm) KwK. 40 L/43 main gun that was capable of a fair degree of accuracy at 1,093 yards (1,000 m). *(R. Bazalevsky)*

Abandoned during the German military advance into Russia in the summer of 1941 is this six-man Red Army KV-2 heavy tank. The large, unwieldy vehicle was armed with a 152-mm howitzer mounted in a large box-shaped turret that raised the vehicle's height to 12 feet 11 inches (3.93 m). *(Patton Museum)*

his boss that the new medium tank had to be in service by December 1942, a goal that he knew Daimler-Benz could not meet due to the need to come up with a new turret and get the diesel engine ready for series production.

HITLER'S INPUT

Hitler had insisted that the glacis plate on the new production MAN chassis be thickened to 80 mm from its original design specification of 60 mm. This would in turn push the weight of the series production vehicle to 48 tons (43.5 mt), with a resulting strain on automotive components not designed to bear such a load.

The same day that Hitler approved the MAN design, the German Army went ahead and ordered one experimental chassis for delivery by August 1942 and a complete experimental chassis with mounted turret to be delivered by September 1942. Series production would need to start sometime before the end of 1942.

During a meeting on June 4, 1942, Hitler had expressed his doubts about whether the upgrading of the glacis plate on the Panther to 80 mm would suffice on the battlefields of 1943. He really wanted to see the glacis plate on the Panther thickened to 100 mm. This would not come to pass because the vehicle chassis and drive train could not handle the extra weight that would be imposed by the addition of more armor.

VEHICLE DESIGNATIONS

The official designation of the new medium tank was Pz.Kpfw. V Panther Ausf. D (Sd.Kfz. 171). The prefix "Pz.Kpfw. V" was phased out of use in February 1944 on Hitler's order. In most German wartime reports, the new medium tank went by "Panzer V" or just "Panther." American and British military reports generally referred to it as the "Mark V."

The name "Panther" came from the Panther Commission, the small group of tank designers and engineers that helped set the requirements for the vehicle. "Ausf." is the abbreviation for the German word *Ausfuehrung* and refers to a specific model of a vehicle. It was used only in ordering parts for the respective models. It had no meaning for the actual combat users, all models of the Panther being expected to perform the same combat missions, without any regard to the model of the vehicle being employed.

The abbreviation "Sd.Kfz." stands for *Sonderkraftfahrzeug*, which means "special motor vehicle" and refers to the vehicle's ordnance inventory number.

MODELL DB

A wooden mockup of the Daimler-Benz proposed tank that would meet the Panther specifications. This particular mockup is seen with an interleaved road wheel arrangement. Notice the similarity to the Red Army T-34 medium tank, which Daimler-Benz studied and also copied. The overhang of the high-velocity 75-mm cannon is another copied T-34 feature. *(Tank Museum, Bovington)*

PRODUCTION BEGINS

By autumn 1942, MAN had presented the German Army with the two preproduction Panther tank chassis they had requested: one without a turret and one with the specified Rheinmetall turret. The two prototype Panther tanks were employed for driving trials and demonstrations for the organizations concerned with the design and production of the vehicle in early November 1942. The contingent from MAN stated that they were pleased with the automotive performance of their new vehicle.

Despite a series of technical problems cropping up during the testing of the two prototype Panther tanks, the German Army went ahead and ordered the vehicle into full series production in November 1942. This occurred without the standard testing process that had occurred with German tanks designed before World War II. Kinks in the vehicle's design that usually were fixed in testing now meant costly and time-consuming retrofitting after production had begun.

Four firms initially were chosen to build a total of 1,000 units of the Panther Ausf. D tank, later dropped down to 850 units (minus 12 units converted into armored recovery vehicles) just before the first series

The only surviving complete Panther Ausf. D tank is located in the town of Breda, in the Netherlands. Notice the pistol port on the left side of the tank's turret. Also visible is the circular communication port on the left side of the turret that was dispensed with beginning in July 1943. *(Pierre-Olivier Buan)*

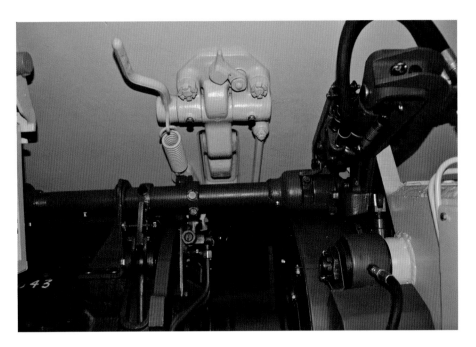

This is the view that the radioman on the Panther Ausf. D tank and early production Panther Ausf. A tanks had of the hinged armored letter-box flap from his seat. The insides of German tanks were painted for most of the war with the Ivory (Elfenben) color seen here. *(David Marian)*

production vehicle came off the assembly line. The firms were MAN, Daimler-Benz, MNH (Maschinenfabrik Niedersachsen of Hanover), and Henschel und Sohn, Kassel (hereafter referred to as "Henschel"). These four firms had met on June 2, 1942, to discuss the Panther Ausf. D tank production goals. MAN and Daimler-Benz planned to have the first series production vehicles coming off the assembly lines in late 1942, while MNH and Henschel would not begin building Panther Ausf. D tanks until July 1943. On June 18, 1942, it was decided that MNH and Henschel should begin production of the Panther Ausf. D tanks by January 1943.

As events unfolded, it turned out that neither MAN nor Daimler-Benz could deliver the first series production Panther Ausf. D tanks until January 1943. Daimler-Benz and MNH delivered their first series production vehicles in February 1943. The number of Panther Ausf. D tanks built per month was to increase to 305 in December 1943, with two other firms scheduled to join in the production program: Demag in June 1943 and Nibelungenwerk in September 1943.

Unlike the other firms engaged in Panther tank production, which assembled both the turrets and chassis of their vehicles, Henschel only did the chassis and outsourced the assembly of the turret to the German firm of Wegmann. Wegmann then shipped the completed turrets to Henschel for the final mounting of the turret on the Panther tank chassis.

A close-up view of the glacis plate on a Panther Ausf. D tank. On the right of the picture is the hinged armor flap (closed in this picture), which protected the driver's direct-vision viewing port. On the left is the partially opened hinged armored flap that protected the radioman's weapon's port. *(Virginia Museum of Military Vehicles)*

According to Walter J. Spielberger, author of *Panther and Its Variants*, rough estimates based on the hours of labor involved in building a vehicle showed that four Panther tanks could be built for the cost of five Panzer III medium tanks. At a reported cost of 117,100 *Reichmarks*, the new Panther tank (without weapons and radios) was just slightly more expensive than a Panzer IV medium tank and less than half the cost of a Tiger Ausf. E heavy tank, which is reported as having an average cost of 250,800 Reichmarks or more.

A demonstration of the new Panther Ausf. D tank took place in February 1943 under the observation of Speer. Upon the conclusion of the demonstration, General Heinrich Eberbach, inspector of Panzer troops for the army, had an officer from the demonstration unit relate to Speer some of the problems they found with the vehicle, which included engine fires, fuel pump failures, and transmission breakdowns. Despite these problems and others, those in charge believed that the issues with the early series production Panther Ausf. D tanks were well within reason for a new and untried design.

Notwithstanding Eberbach's positive slant on the teething problems encountered with the first batch of new production Panther Ausf. D tanks, the number of design shortcomings found with the vehicle continued to grow. In addition, between April and June, 1943, poor quality control by some of the builders led to a situation where a need arose to have new tanks straight off the factory floor modified and inspected before being accepted by the German Army. Field units being equipped with the Panther Ausf. D tanks also were authorized to make minor improvements to their vehicles.

The rush to build the Panther Ausf. D tanks was necessary to support Hitler's and the German military high command's plan to launch a massive summer offensive against the Red Army, codenamed Operation *Zitadelle* (Operation Citadel). The armored spearhead of that operation was to be the Tiger Ausf. E heavy tank that had first rolled off the production lines in August 1942 and the new Panther Ausf. D tank.

In *Panzer Leader*, Guderian recounted how, during a meeting on May 4, 1943, he had tried to talk Hitler out of placing too much faith in the new

Four of the five-man crew of a Panther Ausf. D tank posed for the cameraman in this picture. Notice that the hinged armored flap that protected the driver's direct-vision viewing port is open in this photograph. Except for the loader, all the Panther tank crewmen pictured are wearing their headsets and throat microphones. (*Patton Museum*)

PzKpfw V, Ausf D (SdKfz 171)
"Panther" Early Production

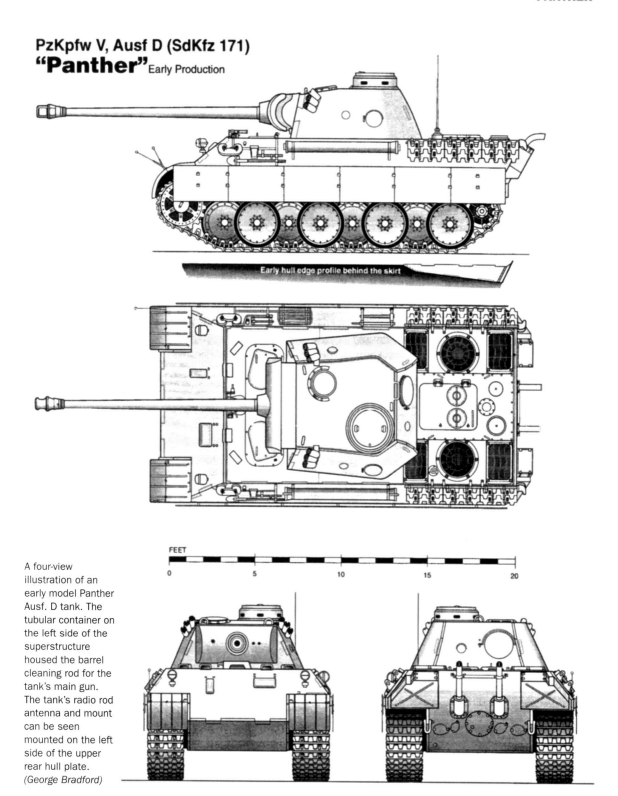

Early hull edge profile behind the skirt

FEET

0   5   10   15   20

A four-view illustration of an early model Panther Ausf. D tank. The tubular container on the left side of the superstructure housed the barrel cleaning rod for the tank's main gun. The tank's radio rod antenna and mount can be seen mounted on the left side of the upper rear hull plate. *(George Bradford)*

Panther tanks as the battle-winning weapon he thought they would be for Operation Zitadelle:

> " ... I pointed out that the Panthers, on whose performance the Chief of the Army General Staff was relying so heavily, were still suffering from the many teething troubles inherent in all new equipment and it seemed unlikely that these could all be put right in time for the launching of the attack. "

Through intense effort, the German Army managed to have two hundred Panther Ausf. D tanks ready for service by July 5, 1943, for the start of Operation Zitadelle. What Hitler and the German Army did not know was that Russian factories had already ramped up to build a thousand T-34 medium tanks per month. Only 850 Panther Ausf. D tanks entered German military service between January and December 1943 (along with several hundred Panther Ausf A. tanks).

On display at a French Army base is this Panther Ausf. A tank. This particular vehicle was captured by the French Army's 2nd Armored Division in September 1944. The French Army employed Panther tanks postwar till 1952 until replaced by American tanks supplied under a military assistance program (MAP). *(Pierre-Olivier Buan)*

COMPARATIVE DIMENSIONS

The Panther Ausf. D tank was 29 feet (8.86 m) long with the main gun pointed over the front hull of the vehicle. The vehicle's hull was 22 feet (6.87 m) long. With thin armored side skirts fitted to either side of the hull, the tank was 11 feet 2.64 inches (3.42 m) wide. Without the thin armored side skirts fitted, the tank was 10 feet 8.74 inches (3.27 m) wide. The Panther Ausf. D tank was 10 feet 2.04 inches (3.10 m) tall with the vehicle commander's hatch in the open position. Combat loaded, the Panther Ausf. D tank weighed in at about 50 tons (45.5 mt).

The T-34 medium tank was, by comparison to the Panther Ausf. D tank, fairly small. With its main gun pointed over the front hull, it was 22 feet 2 inches (6.75 m) long, with the hull being about 20 feet (6.09 m) long.

The tank was 8 feet 6 inches (2.6 m) tall and had a width of about 11 feet (3 m). Combat loaded, the T-34 medium tank was about 30 tons (28 mt).

By way of comparison to the Panther Ausf. D tank and the T-34 medium tank, the Tiger Ausf. E heavy tank was 27 feet and 9 inches (8.45 m) long with its main gun pointed over the front hull. The hull was 20 feet 9 inches (6.32 m) long. With mudguards fitted, the vehicle was 12 feet 3 inches (3.70 m) wide. Height came in at 9 feet 10 inches (3 m) tall. Combat loaded, the Tiger Ausf. E heavy tank weighed about 62 tons (56 mt).

An American soldier looks into one of the two storage boxes mounted on the rear hull plate of this Panther Ausf. D tank. Despite being replaced in service by the Panther Ausf. A tank and then the Panther Ausf. G tank, examples of the original model of the Panther tank series could be found soldiering on until the war in Europe ended in May 1945. *(Patton Museum)*

THE RESULTS ARE IN

The combat debut of the Panther Ausf. D tank during Operation Zitadelle proved to be a major disappointment for the German Army. During the first few days of fighting, the number of operational Panther Ausf. D tanks had dropped to ten vehicles by the evening of July 10, 1943, out of the original two hundred vehicles. Those not lost to mechanical breakdowns met destruction at the hands of the enemy. Contributing to these losses was the lack of training for the Panther tank units, which had been unable to do so because almost all their vehicles were undergoing rebuilding prior to Operation Zitadelle.

On July 10, 1943, Guderian, now the German Army inspector of armored troops, visited the Panther tank units that had taken part in the fighting during Operation Zitadelle. A week later, he sent a report about his findings to the chief of staff of the German Army. In that report, Guderian listed only 38 Panther tanks fit for combat on the evening of July 11, 1943, with 131 being in need of repair and another 31 being unrepairable. He also mentioned the fact that eighty-one Panther tanks had been taken out of service due to combat damage, which attested to the heavy fighting that had taken place.

Since the combat debut of the Panther tank during Operation Zitadelle had been less than overwhelming and resulted in some unhappiness among the senior leadership of the German Army and the troops on the ground, Guderian took great pains in his report to remind his superiors that, in light of the toughness of the Red Army defenses encountered and the extensive minefields that had to be traversed during the fighting, the Panther tank had done very well considering it was an untested design with numerous mechanical deficiencies that would be corrected in the near future.

Despite the numerous issues that marred the combat debut of the Panther tank during Operation Zitadelle, some positive attributes about the Panther stood out on the battlefield. One of these was the long-range accuracy and lethality of the vehicle's 75-mm main gun. Another was the tank's frontal armor array, which had survived direct hits from the Red Army's ZiS-3 76.2-mm towed antitank guns, the F34 76.2-mm main gun mounted on the T-34 medium tank, and a version of the same gun on the KV-1 heavy tank designated the ZiS-5.

A Panther tank unit commander who took part in Operation Zitadelle wrote a report on July 17, 1943, that described his impressions of the Panther Ausf. D tank. He reiterated what Guderian reported to his superiors, that

Pictured on display at Beltring, England, during the annual War and Peace Show is this nonoperational Panther Ausf. A tank belonging to the Cadman Brothers' collection. The tank was acquired in trade by them from the French Army Tank Museum. Notice that this vehicle's main gun is missing its muzzle brake. (*Christophe Vallier*)

A member of the German tank troops in his black uniform poses next to a brand-new factory fresh Panther Ausf. A tank. The single hole on the right side of the gun shield shows that the vehicle was built after October 1943, when the gunner's original binocular gun sight was replaced by a monocular gun sight. *(Patton Museum)*

despite being a new vehicle with a number of mechanical shortcomings that had to be addressed, the Panther tank was a good vehicle. Due to its superior main gun, his regimental unit had knocked out 263 enemy tanks in combat, with some KV-1 heavy tanks being knocked out at ranges up to 3,281 yards (3,000 m) and almost all T-34 medium tanks engaged being destroyed at ranges from 1,640 yards to 2,187 yards (1,500 to 2,000 m). He also pointed out in his report that the sides of the Panther tank were not proof against penetration by Red Army 76.2-mm armor-piercing (AP) projectiles, as were the flanks of the Tiger Ausf. E heavy tank, which also saw use during Operation Zitadelle.

PANTHER II TANK

In late 1942, even before the first preproduction Panther Ausf. D tanks appeared, Hitler's continued desire to see a more heavily armored Panther tank fielded resulted in developmental work on a new version of the vehicle, originally designated the Panther 2 tank, and redesignated the Panther II tank after April 1943.

PATTON MUSEUM'S PANTHER II TANK

During an interview with the authors, Charles Lemons, retired curator of the former Patton Museum of Armor and Cavalry, described the background of the Panther II tank that had long formed an important part of the museum's collection:

"Our former Panther II arrived at Aberdeen Proving Ground (APG), Maryland (home of the U.S. Army Ordnance School), after the war in Europe ended. The description of the tank at that time was very brief, simply noting that it had arrived without a turret. Instead, it had a number of large flat metal rings fitted on top of the chassis to simulate the missing weight of a turret. The engine was not operable, apparently having been sabotaged at the German development facility where it was found and had to be rebuilt in order to test the vehicle. Once it was operable, the tank was taken for a test ride and after going a couple of miles, a large spur gear on the right-hand side broke, disabling the vehicle again. Repair was considered but instead the vehicle was parked. In order to use the vehicle for exhibit, APG fitted it with a late-model Panther Ausf. G turret and placed it on the display line for the U.S. Army Ordnance Museum, formerly located at APG.

When the Smithsonian Institute requested some examples of American and foreign vehicles for a proposed ground vehicle museum, the Panther II was one of those transferred to their care. The proposed museum never got off the ground and the Panther II remained at APG until it was transferred back to the U.S. Army and eventually ended up at the Patton Museum of Cavalry and Armor at Fort Knox.

When it arrived it was obvious that the tank was a test vehicle, as it had only a driver's station installed. The Panther Ausf. G turret, however, was complete except for the gun counterweight. The Panther II hull is made of mild steel and is easily dented, as evidenced from the damage on the front of the hull caused by movement by caterpillar tractor. The track is Tiger II narrow transport track, but the transmission and running gear appear to be custom built for the vehicle. The torsion bars are much bigger than the normal Panther. The engine was, once again, inoperable — this time from being left outside for too long.

Someone at the Patton Museum decided that they needed an operational Panther and attempted to combine their incomplete Panther Ausf. G with the Panther II. They tore the Ausf. G completely apart, only to find that the only thing that fit was the engine — everything else was too large. You see, the exterior of the Panther II is the same size as a normal Panther, but the armor was thickened 20-mm on the sides and front. Turns out it was thickened to the inside and none of the ammunition storage or radio racks would fit inside. The engine for the Panther Ausf. G did fit and was rebuilt to run in the Panther II.

As was mentioned before, during its testing at APG, a spur gear in one of the final drives had been broken. The Patton Museum spent some money and had a new one fabricated and installed. The Panther II was used for several years as a demonstration vehicle, but exhibited the same problems that most Panthers had — especially concerning the engine. The carburetors on the engine were partially melted when the engine backfired during movement and caught them on fire. Since we were down to one set of carburetors, it was decided to retire the vehicle from active use around 1980. That is how I saw it when I arrived at the museum in 1986. The Panther II was shipped to Fort Benning, Georgia, in December 2010, where it will eventually form part of the planned National Armor and Cavalry Museum."

This Panther Ausf. A tank is seen on display at the Canadian War Museum in Ottawa, Ontario. A 100-mm-thick cast armor cupola is visible on the turret roof, which featured seven replaceable periscopes. Also seen on the turret roof is the armored bracket for the loader's periscope and an armored turret ventilator cover. *(Paul Hannah)*

At first it was envisioned that the proposed Panther II tank would differ from the original Panther design only in the thickness of its armor and the associated weight gain imposed by the added armor.

Compared to the 80-mm-thick armor on the glacis of the Panther Ausf. D tank, sloped at an angle of 55 degrees, and the 40-mm-thick side hull armor plates sloped at 35 degrees, the proposed Panther II tank was intended to feature a 100-mm-thick glacis plate sloped at 55 degrees, with hull side plates 60-mm thick and sloped at 35 degrees.

As developmental work on the concept of the Panther II tank evolved, the vehicle became envisioned by February 1943 as a way in which to rationalize production of different tank types by having the yet-to-be-built Panther II tank, with the yet-to-be-built Tiger Ausf. B heavy tank, share as many parts as possible between the two vehicles (the first series production Tiger Ausf. B tanks did not come off the assembly line until February 1944). The interoperability between these systems included automotive components such as the engine, steering gear, transmission, and steel-rimmed, rubber-cushioned road wheels.

As a result, a decision was made to rush the Panther II tank into series production as quickly as possible. Documents uncovered by researcher

Thomas L. Jentz showed that preliminary plans for the Panther II tank called for series production to start in September 1943. A realization in May 1943 forced a decision to curtail production of the Panther II tank, as it would cause a slowdown in production of existing tanks. This was considered unacceptable. However, series production of the original Panther series tanks would continue incorporating modifications and improvements developed for the Panther II tank.

No complete Panther II tank was ever built. A turret design for the Panther II tank never made it off the drawing board, and only a single experimental chassis was completed. This chassis was found by the U.S. Army at the conclusion of the war in Europe and returned to the United States for technical evaluation.

MODEL DIFFERENCES

Most tanks go through a constant upgrading process of modifications, both big and small, throughout their service life based on combat experience. This is caused by the development of new technology and the need to maximize production efficiency as builders become familiar with the design. Often, modifications are made to a vehicle based on the input of the user

Belonging to the Military Vehicle Technology Foundation is this restored Panther Ausf. A tank. The large size of the Panther tank is evident by comparing it to the former Czech Army T-54 medium tank in the background. The Panther Ausf. A tank consisted of a new upgraded turret on a Panther Ausf. D chassis. *(Christopher Hughes)*

community, which quickly finds out under adverse conditions what works and what doesn't in the field.

Because of the haste in which the Panther tank was fielded, it underwent a constant stream of modifications from the start of series production, many of these being invisible upon exterior viewing of the vehicle. The designations for the various versions of the Panther tank tend only to reflect the largest of changes, which resulted in three different models of the tank seeing service during World War II.

An interesting comment regarding the problems of continuous modification of a tank's design and pushing updated models into field use comes from the concluding chapter in a U.S. Army booklet titled *German Tank Maintenance in World War II* and published by the U.S. Government Printing Office:

> " If, for instance, a tank regiment was equipped with three basic models of tanks, each of which came in three or four modified types, the maintenance system could not possibly function properly. The Germans would have done better to retain one standard model, as the Russians did with their T34, and forget about improvements, than to constantly introduce new and improved versions for which no spare parts were available. In general, a few weeks after a new shipment of tanks arrived at the Russian front, most of the vehicles were dead-lined and many became a total loss, simply because parts whose installation would have required only a few hours were missing. "

Some newer versions of the Panther tank might appear with parts from a previous model due to a shortage of new parts or because the factories building them tried to exhaust their inventory of older parts.

PANTHER AUSF. A TANK

Production of the replacement for the Panther Ausf. D tank began in September 1943. The new Panther Ausf. A tank consisted of a Panther Ausf. D tank chassis fitted with a redesigned turret. By the time production of the Panther Ausf. A tank ended in May 1944, German industry had produced approximately 2,200 units.

One of the most obvious visual differences long used to distinguish between the Panther Ausf. D tank and its successor, the Panther Ausf. A tank, was a new *Panzerfuehererkuppel* (vehicle commander's cupola) located on top of the Panther tank turret. The Panther Ausf. D tank had a drum-shaped cupola about 10 inches (25 cm) tall, similar in outline to those fitted to the Panzer III and Panzer IV medium tanks. It had six direct-vision slots (protected by ballistic glass) arranged around the circumference for the vehicle commander to observe outside the tank. The vehicle commander could close the vision slots from within the tank by rotating a steel ring around the exterior of the cupola.

The Panther Ausf. A tank came with a cast-armor cupola for the vehicle commander with seven hooded periscopes arranged around its exterior circumference. The improved visibility offered by this arrangement was popular with the German tank troops. The cupola on the Panther Ausf. A tank also had a fixed ring for mounting a machine gun to use against enemy infantry or low-flying enemy aircraft. Some Panther Ausf. D tanks also featured a fixed ring of a different design around the outer circumference of the vehicle commander's cupola.

Just to show that blanket statements regarding the identification of any German tank are useless, Jentz points out in *Panzer Tracts No. 5-2 Panzerkampfwagen "Panther" Ausfuehrung A* that historical evidence shows that the drum-shaped cupola common to the Panther Ausf. D tank also appeared on some production units of the Panther Ausf. A tank.

A harder to spot but more reliable external feature to distinguish the Panther Ausf. A tank from its predecessor, the Panther Ausf. D tank, was

Pictured is an abandoned Panther Ausf. G tank rifled through by American soldiers, as is evident by the clothing and open boxes surrounding it. Extending horizontally along the side of the long one-piece superstructure hull plate is a rail employed for mounting thin, soft, steel protective plates (not mounted on this vehicle) and referred to as *Schuerzen*. *(Patton Museum)*

On interior display at the French Army Tank Museum is this Panther Ausf. A tank. This second version of the Panther tank series had a new variable-speed turret power traverse system compared to the single-speed turret power traverse system found on its predecessor, the Panther Ausf. D tank. *(Michael Green)*

The absence of a driver's armored visor port on the glacis plate of this Panther tank marks it as a Panther Ausf. G tank. This particular vehicle is on display in Grandmenil, Belgium. The Panther Ausf. G tank was essentially a Panther Ausf. A tank turret mounted on a new redesigned and upgraded chassis. *(Andreas Kirchhoff)*

the addition of a fixed periscope on the turret roof for the vehicle's loader, beginning in November and December 1943.

Another important external visual difference between the Panther Ausf. D tank and Panther Ausf. A tank began appearing on the Panther Ausf. A tank in November and December 1943. It consisted of an armored spherical-bow machine gun mount in the right-hand corner of the vehicle's glacis plate, through which an MG34 machine gun was fired. Aiming, firing, and loading of the machine gun was the duty of the Panther tank radioman. Because the new machine gun position incorporated a self-contained sighting device, the builders of the Panther Ausf. A tank deleted the fixed forward-looking radioman's periscope seen on the Panther Ausf. D tank and earlier Panther Ausf. A tanks. A second fixed overhead periscope for the Panther Ausf. A tank radioman, looking out to the right-hand side of the tank, was retained.

Prior to the appearance of the spherical-bow machine gun mount on the Panther Ausf. A tank glacis, the radio operator on the Panther Ausf. D tank and early production Panther Ausf. A tanks had a small rectangular observation slot in the right corner of the glacis. When the observation slot was not in use, the radioman covered it with a hinged armored hatch cover. If required, the radioman could fire a weapon stored within the tank through

A key identifying feature of the Panther Ausf. G tank is the long, one-piece superstructure hull plates clearly seen on one side of this vehicle on display in Houffalize, Belgium. Notice the broken suspension system on this particular vehicle, which caused the idler assembly to drop to the ground from its normal position on the tank. *(Andreas Kirchhoff)*

47

DISGUISED PANTHER TANKS

During the Battle of the Bulge, which ran from December 16, 1944, until late January 1945, the U.S. Army found that the German Army had taken the time to modify a small number of Panther Ausf. G tanks to look like American M10 tank destroyers. The examination of captured examples of those Panther tank adapted to resemble American M10 tank destroyers appeared in an issue of the *U.S. Army's Tactical and Technical Trends, Number 57* of April 1945, and is reprinted here.

"1) In the recent breakthrough in Belgium four enemy Panther tanks were knocked out in the Malmedy area. These tanks were carefully and cleverly disguised as M10 gun motor carriages with the upmost attention given to details. The most interesting and important feature of this attempted deception is the amount of work entailed in order to imitate the appearance of our M10. The time, work, and materials involved, as well as the technical knowledge of our M10s required, definitely point to fourth or fifth echelon alterations. However, it is believed that the work was done by enemy maintenance units rather than at a factory.

2) Inside the one tank which was not blown were found items of GI clothing, viz. helmet, overcoat and leggings.

3) Since the Panther does not at once lend itself to be easily disguised as an M10, some changes were necessary. In order to prepare the Panther for the alteration the following work was done: The distinctive cupola was removed from the turret. In its place two semi-circular hatch covers were hinged to the turret top in order to cover the opening. Extra water cans, gas cans, the rammer staff container and accessories stowed on the outside of the tank were removed.

4) The tank was then camouflaged or disguised with sheet metal. The sheet metal used on the turret and upper bow was 3/22" thick and that on the sides of the hull was 9/64" thick. The lower part of the false bow was thicker; possibly made of double plates. To accomplish the camouflaging, the work might have been divided into four parts, the turret, bow, rear and sides.

5) The turret was disguised by having five pieces of sheet metal. Two pieces were cut to shape to resemble the distinctive sides of the M10 turret. These pieces were then flanged on the edges, bent to shape, and stiffened with small angle iron. The gun shield was carefully formed from another sheet to the exact shape of the M10 gun shield, this being particularly well done. A hole was made to the right of the gun hole in the shield for the coaxial MG34 [machine gun]. It might be noted that there is no similar hole in the shield of the M10. Finally the rear of the turret was made of two pieces of sheet metal, one piece to represent the bottom slant surface of the rear, and one piece to represent the counterweight. The pieces representing the sides and rear were joined together and braced with angle iron and the whole was attached to the turret. The false gun shield was attached to the Panther gun shield. All of the lifting rings, brackets, extra-armor studs, etc. found on the turret of the M10 were carefully duplicated and welded to the false turret. To heighten the deception, U.S. stars were painted on both sides and also on the top of the turret.

6) The false bow was made of approximately four pieces of sheet metal. These pieces were cut and formed to shape to imitate as closely as possible the contours and shape of the bow of the M10. Much care was taken as to

detail since the Panther bow is to an extent bulkier than the M10 bow. The false bottom of the bow was shaped with an effort to give the characteristic appearance of the front drive sprocket housing of the M10. The top of the false bow was carefully shaped and the various components pieces attached to the front of the tank. All of the brackets, lifting rings, towing cables, etc. were welded to the false bow to give it, on the whole, a very similar appearance to the M10 bow. A square opening was cut in the false bow to permit the use of the bow MG34. However, a cover for this opening was made and attached with a small chain, and this cover could be removed to fire the gun. The bow, like the rest of the tank, with painted OD [olive drab] and a U.S. star was painted to complete the deception. The markings of the 5th Armored Division, 10th Armored Regiment and vehicle number were painted on.

7) The false rear was made of sheet metal to give the appearance of the rear of the M10. The only distinctive difference was the cutting of two holes to permit the twin exhaust elbows of the Panther to protrude.

8) Since the sides of the M10 have shirting armor which appears to go lower than the side armor of the Panther and is beveled in at the bottom, an attempt was made to simulate this. A long flat strip of sheet metal was attached to the sides parallel to the ground. At right angles to this strip a vertical sheet strip was attached in order to give the appearance of low shirting armor.

9) The false vehicle numbers of the four tanks knocked out were B4, B5, B7 and B10. This may or may not indicate the use of at least ten similarly disguised tanks.

10) The characteristics which were not disguised and could not be camouflaged were: The distinctive Panther bogie [road wheel] suspension (we now have a somewhat similar suspension in the M18 Motor Gun Carriage). The muzzle brake on the 7.5 cm [75-mm] KwK 42 (we have some muzzle brakes) and the wide and distinctive tracks of the Panther.

11) It is believed that had the enemy employed these disguised tanks in the proper tactical situation and at the proper time, much damage might have resulted. "

the open observation slot and direct the weapon's fire by using his two fixed overhead periscopes.

The Panther Ausf. A tank was supposed to have been fitted with reinforced road wheels having twenty-four rim bolts instead of the sixteen rim bolt road wheels of the Panther Ausf. D tank, which were failing. The twenty-four rim bolt road wheels first appeared in August 1943, a month before series production of the Panther Ausf. A had begun. The sixteen rim bolt road wheels would continue appearing on Panther Ausf. A tanks until roughly March 1944. Some of the earlier sixteen rim bolt road wheels were strengthened with rivets by the factories building them. Pictorial evidence shows that the inventory of sixteen rim bolt road wheels lasted long enough for some of them to appear on the follow-on Panther Ausf. G tank.

One of the unseen but important interior improvements to the Panther Ausf. A tank turret was the replacement of the single-speed turret traverse drive with a variable-speed turret traverse drive, which in theory would allow the gunner to acquire targets in his sight more quickly.

Other unseen internal changes within the Panther Ausf. A tank turret included redesigned seals for both the turret race and the gun shield and the addition of simplified elevating gear for the main gun. There also were changes to the loader's and gunner's seats, as well as the gunner's foot pedals for using the hydraulic traverse to turn the vehicle's turret.

According to a report written by Guderian on March 5, 1944, the constant improvements to the Panther tank series resulted in some positive feedback from the user community. He wrote that one Panther tank-equipped unit on the Eastern Front stated that they felt their tank was far superior to the Red Army T-34 medium tanks. They went on to report that all the early mechanical difficulties that had so bedeviled the early production units of the Panther tank had been ironed out of the design. As proof, they offered the fact that service life of the tank's engine had gone up to 435 to 621 miles (700 to 1,000 km). In addition, the same Panther tank-equipped unit reported that final drive breakdowns had ended and that transmission and steering gear failures were now within an acceptable range, which is damning with faint praise.

PANTHER AUSF. G TANK

The replacement for the Panther Ausf. A tank was the Panther Ausf. G tank, consisting of a Panther Ausf. A turret on a newly improved chassis that incorporated production simplifications from the design work done for the Panther II tank. The Panther Ausf. G tank chassis was up-armored in some areas and thinned in other areas to maintain the vehicle's weight.

Production of the Panther Ausf. G tank began in March 1944 and ended in April 1945, as the victorious Allied armies swept through the country occupying German factories. Captured German documents indicated that at least 2,953 Panther Ausf. G tanks made it across the assembly lines before production ceased, making it the most numerous model of the Panther tank.

Key external spotting features for the Panther Ausf. G tank chassis included large, tapering superstructure plates on either side of the vehicle's hull, which replaced the two-piece hull superstructure plates of previous models. On the glacis of the Panther Ausf. G tank, the driver's direct-vision visor port and his two overhead fixed periscopes, as were fitted on the Panther Ausf. D and Ausf. A tanks, were done away with and replaced with a single overhead 360-degree rotating and tilting periscope.

Taken out for a rare public appearance is this restored Panther Ausf. G tank belonging to the German Army Evaluation Center. The *Zimmerit* seen on this vehicle was first introduced in September 1943 and discontinued on German tanks built after late September 1944 when an unfounded belief arose that it would catch fire when struck by a large projectile. *(Andreas Kirchhoff)*

PzKpfw V, Ausf G (SdKfz 171)
"Panther"

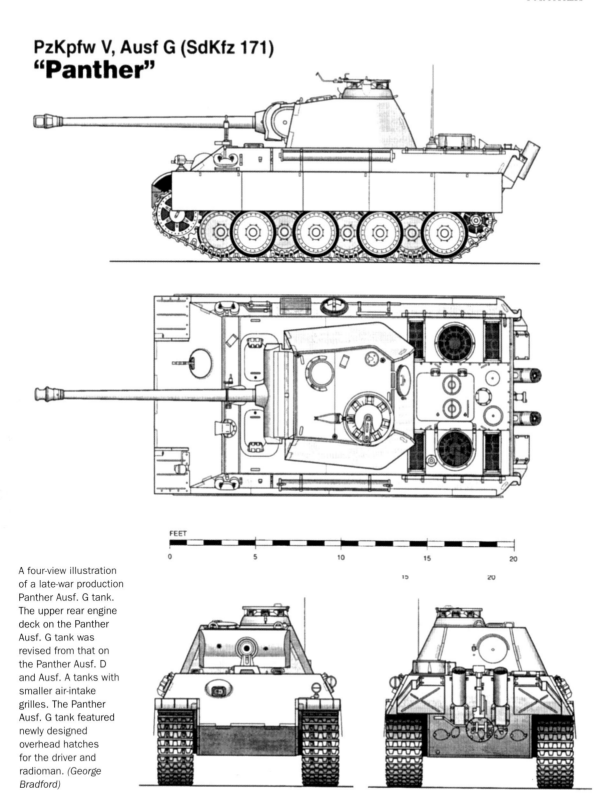

FEET

0   5   10   15   20

15   20

A four-view illustration of a late-war production Panther Ausf. G tank. The upper rear engine deck on the Panther Ausf. G tank was revised from that on the Panther Ausf. D and Ausf. A tanks with smaller air-intake grilles. The Panther Ausf. G tank featured newly designed overhead hatches for the driver and radioman. *(George Bradford)*

Some production units of the Panther Ausf. G tank would have their cylindrical gun shields replaced with a newer version that boasted a pronounced chin on the bottom portion. The chin was intended to prevent incoming projectiles from being deflected downward into the driver's and radioman's positions, as had happened when some enemy projectiles had struck the lower portion of the cylindrical gun shield design.

Harder to spot external changes to the Panther Ausf. G tank included new simplified overhead armored hatches for the driver and radioman that could be jettisoned if blocked. There also was a revised tool and equipment storage

Immobilized on a stone fence, a Panther Ausf. G tank sits forlornly in the air. No doubt the driver never heard the end of it from the vehicle commander about the situation the tank found itself in. Only those who have driven a large tank while straining to look through a small dirty periscope can understand how something like this could happen. *(Patton Museum)*

arrangement on the exterior of the vehicle. In addition, new tools and equipment were added to the Panther Ausf. G tank. These included longer steel tow cables and a larger wooden block used as a base for the jack mounted on the rear hull plate. On the top of the vehicle's turret roof, three small mountings were added to provide anchor point for the mounting of a portable 4,409-pound (2 mt) jib boon.

On the rear hull of the Panther Ausf. G tank, there were new welded armored guards for the twin exhaust pipes. The twin exhaust pipes themselves originally were covered by sheet metal guards, and later, a more complex flame suppressor device was attached to each exhaust pipe to prevent the glowing exhaust pipes or flaming exhaust plumes from giving away the location of the vehicle at night.

The upper rear engine deck of the Panther Ausf. G tank was revised with smaller air intake grills. The most noticeable feature of the revised rear engine deck on the Panther Ausf. G tank was the eventual addition of a raised fan tower for the *Kampfraumheizung* (crew compartment heater) that could be easily spotted in many pictures of the tank.

One of five Panther Ausf. G tanks modified prior to the Battle of the Bulge to roughly look like U.S. Army M10 tank destroyers. The intention being to fool American troops into not firing at the vehicles until the German tankers could gain a battlefield advantage. Notice the American markings on the vehicle. *(Patton Museum)*

CHAPTER TWO

FIREPOWER

During the early part of World War II, German tanks were valued for mobility first, firepower second, and protection third. Encounters in France in 1940 and with the Red Army T-34 medium tanks and the KV heavy tanks in 1941 convinced the Germans to rearrange their tank design priorities. Firepower became first, protection second, and mobility last. The Panther tank was a product of those revised design parameters.

It is important to understand that not all tank guns for a given caliber are created equal. The size and type of ammunition fired by a tank's main gun is just a single element contributing to its overall lethality. The length of its barrel, the materials used in its construction, and the weapon's integration with other elements of the vehicle's fire-control system, such as the optical sighting system, remain critical design factors. These factors all came together successfully in the Panther tank, which is what made it so deadly on the battlefield.

The 75-mm main gun mounted on the three versions of the Panther tank to see service in World War II was considered one of the finest tank guns for its size in that conflict. It was more potent than the 88-mm main gun on the Tiger Ausf. E heavy tank and was copied postwar by the French for mounting on their new light tank designated the AMX-13, which first appeared in service in 1953.

The slightly shorter French adaptation of the Panther 75-mm main gun, which was designated the CN 75-50, later appeared on refurbished Israeli Sherman medium tanks, referred to as the M50 beginning in 1956, and went on to see combat that same year in the Sinai Campaign. It also would see service with Israeli army reserve tank units in the 1967 Six Day War and the 1973 Yom Kippur War.

After the 1973 Yom Kippur War, the Israeli army retired its M50 tanks, which went on to serve with Christian militia units in southern Lebanon up through the 1982 Israeli invasion of that country. This makes for an impressive longevity for any tank gun and speaks highly of its battlefield value.

TANK AMMUNITION TERMINOLOGY

The 75-mm main gun on all the various versions of the Panther tank fired one-piece (fixed) rounds in which the projectile was spin-stabilized in flight by the rifling engraved into the gun's barrel. The term "fixed" meant that the metal cartridge case containing the primer and propelling charge was attached to the projectile.

German tank cartridge cases, as with those of its opponents during World War II, were typically made of brass. Due to a shortage of brass, the Germans began using steel cartridge cases late in the war.

Most modern tank main guns are now smoothbore cannons and fire fin-stabilized projectiles instead of spin-stabilized projectiles, as was done during World War II.

The projectile is the part of a round that is expelled at very high velocity from a gun bore by the extremely fast burning of the propelling charge and the gaseous energy it produces. Projectiles are metal cylinders with pointed cones to obtain the desired flight characteristics of stability and minimum air resistance.

A 1950 U.S. Army report titled *The Vulnerability of Armored Vehicles to Ballistic Attack* contains this passage regarding the importance of shape in projectiles:

“The shape of the projectile also has a great influence on its ability to penetrate resistant objects. Although a long, streamlined nose may be particularly desirable to increase terminal velocity, a more blunt nose will not break off or shatter as easily on impact, thereby providing better penetration and perforation. Actually, the shape may have to be a compromise between streamlining and bluntness to obtain velocity and penetration. "

At the rear portion of spin-stabilized projectiles are circular metal bands that engage the rifling in a gun barrel and impart spin to the projectile as it travels down the barrel, thus helping to stabilize it in flight. The circular metal bands also prevent the gaseous energy generated by the burning propellant from leaking past the projectile as it travels down the gun barrel.

The fixed rounds for the Panther tank were loaded manually into the main gun as a single unit, which allowed for a reasonable rate of fire depending on the strength and endurance of the tank's loader. German manuals indicate an average of six to eight rounds per minute. American manuals for the Sherman tanks indicate that a loader should be able to insert up to twenty rounds in the breech of his main gun for at least the first minute or so of combat. Few surviving Sherman tank loaders remember being able to achieve this goal in combat, with twelve rounds per minute being more realistic.

Extending out from either side of the breech end of the 75-mm main gun on this prototype Panther tank turret is the recoil guard. To the left of the main gun breech is the gunner's binocular gun sight. On either side of the turret walls are the interior components of the armored pistol ports. *(Virginia Museum of Military Vehicles)*

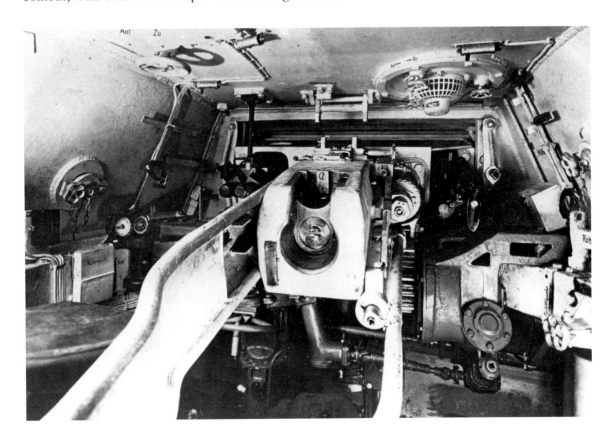

The long length of the 75-mm main gun on the Panther tank is clearly evident in this picture of an Ausf. A model belonging to the collection of the French Army Tank Museum. The German designation for the gun was the 7.5-cm Kw.K. 42 L/70. It was capable of first-round hits at ranges in excess of 1,093 yards (1,000 m). *(David T. Lin)*

Tanks or tank destroyers whose rounds became too heavy for their loaders to manually lift them were supplied with semifixed ammunition, in which the projectile was loaded first and then the metal cartridge case containing the primer and propelling charge second. This naturally slowed down the rate of fire, but allowed for a larger projectile to be fired, something the Red Army accepted on the IS-II Josef Stalin heavy tank armed with a 122-mm main gun and the Germans with their *Jagdtiger* (Hunting Tiger) tank destroyer armed with a 128-mm main gun.

MUZZLE VELOCITY

Higher muzzle velocities offer a number of advantages to the lethality of a tank gun. Muzzle velocity is the speed at which a projectile leaves the bore of a gun. Because the projectile is subjected to external forces (e.g., gravity, cross-wind), a higher velocity means a shorter amount of time in flight and an increased probability of obtaining a hit. Higher muzzle velocity also

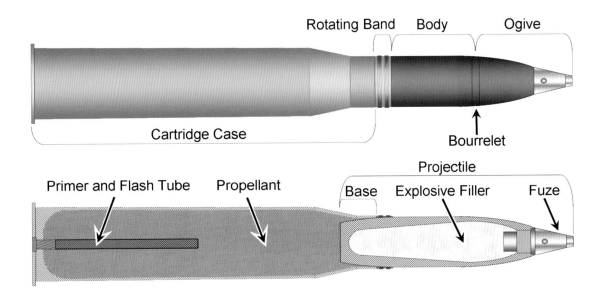

reduces the requirement for precise range estimation and simplifies the gunner's problem of lead estimation against moving targets. Higher muzzle velocity also provides a much flatter trajectory (flight path) for projectiles. This was revealed during post-World War II testing of Panther tanks by the American military at Aberdeen Proving Ground, Maryland, in 1946, in which it was shown at 1,000 yards (914 m) that the 75-mm main gun on the Panther tank could place all of its shots within a 12-inch (31-cm) circle. Tests conducted at the same location the prior year on captured Panther tanks had demonstrated that the fired projectiles had such a flat trajectory that the gunner did not even have to change his elevation settings until he began engaging enemy targets at ranges greater than 2,000 yards (1.8 km).

A U.S. Army report dated July 26, 1946, and prepared for the Command and General Staff School located at Fort Leavenworth, Kansas, titled *Characteristics for Tank Guns* described the problems American tanks had due to the fact that little emphasis had been given to equipping most of them with main guns that possessed the same high-velocity flat trajectory characteristics of late-war German tank main guns:

> Experience has shown that the ability to get a hit with the first round is often the decisive factor and that flat trajectory is necessary if this is to be accomplished. In tank against tank combat the one getting the first hit usually wins. German tanks and SP [self-propelled] guns were able to get a hit with the first round because of

This illustration shows all the components necessary to fire a generic fixed high-explosive (HE) main gun tank round. These components are the projectile (which includes a fuse), the propellant, the primer, and the cartridge case. In fixed rounds, all components are firmly contained by the cartridge case. *(James D. Brown)*

their flat trajectory. Our tanks had to fire several rounds to get a hit and were subject to being destroyed or having the target obscured during the process. **"**

The same report listed other advantages that would come from mounting high-velocity main guns on American tanks. Higher muzzle velocities would increase the range and penetration of AP projectiles. Direct hits by high-velocity AP projectiles, even if they do not penetrate a tank's armor, can disable a vehicle or force it to withdraw. It also may result in the crew abandoning their tank. German tankers had seen this occur on the Eastern Front. Other positive traits listed for high-velocity main gunfire were the adverse effect it would have on the enemy's morale and the positive effect that it would have on the morale and confidence of American tank crews if they could expect to get a hit with the first round.

STANDARD ARMOR-PIERCING ROUND

The primary method by which one tank killed another tank during World War II was with kinetic-energy (KE) AP projectiles. Kinetic energy is the product of mass and projectile speed (squared) at the time of impact (striking velocity) divided by two. An effective KE projectile has to be tough enough to survive target impact so it can penetrate the armor array of another tank.

The standard AP round for the Panther's 75-mm main gun was designated the *Panzergranate* (armor-piercing round) 39/42 (Pzgr.39/42) and weighed 31 pounds (lbs) (14kg). The complete round was 35 inches (90 cm) long. The full-bore steel projectile portion of the round weighed about 16 lbs (7.3 kg). Full-bore meant the projectile was flush with the interior walls of a tank's barrel.

Like all German tank main gun rounds, at the rear of the projectile portion of the Pzgr. 39/42 round was a tracer element to allow the crew to observe the trajectory of their shots as they headed toward their target or targets. This provided them with a method by which subsequent fire corrections could be made.

A small, high-explosive (HE) element was contained within the Pzgr. 39/42 projectile, which was insensitive enough to permit penetration through an enemy tank's armor without premature detonation, with the aid of a base-detonating fuse. The purpose of the HE was to increase the damage to the interior of a target vehicle after penetration.

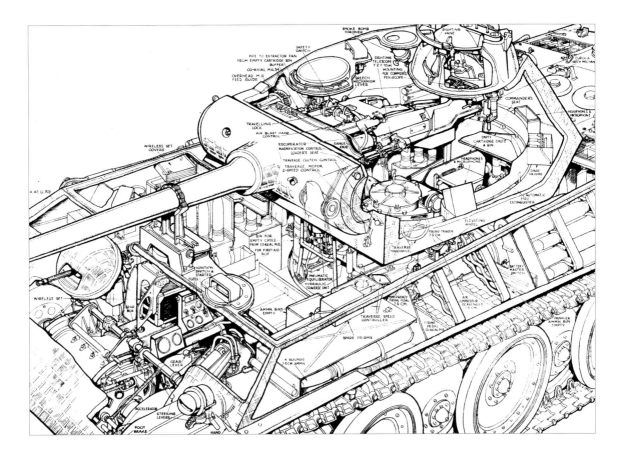

The Pzgr. 39/42 round had a strong curved penetrative cap fitted over the blunt nose of a standard steel AP round, which helped to relieve initial stress on impact by spreading the impact energy over a larger area and for a longer period of time. The mostly undamaged projectile was thus able to penetrate the armor of an enemy tank. The penetrative cap also assisted in turning the projectile into the sloping armor of an enemy tank, reducing the chance of ricochet and thus improving the odds of penetration.

Because the somewhat blunt penetrative nose of an AP projectile reduced its flight stability, the Pzgr. 39/42 had a thin metal windshield, or ballistic cap, fitted over the penetration cap. The resulting shape provided better flight stability and reduced aerodynamic drag. The windshield cap collapsed upon impact with the target.

In American military terminology, the Pzgr. 39/42 round would be classified as an armor-piercing capped with tracer (APC-T) round and in British military terminology as a armor-piercing capped/ballistic cap (APCBC) round. It also could be described as an APCBC-HE round.

A ghosted illustration shows the interior layout of a Panther Ausf. G tank. Visible are both the horizontal and vertical main gun storage arrangements. As with the tanks of all the major combatants of World War II, access by the loader to the vehicle's main gun ammunition often depended on what direction the tank's turret was turned. (*Patton Museum*)

On the right side of the picture is a Panther tank's Pzgr. 39/42 armor-piercing capped tracer (APC-T) main gun round. On the left side of the picture is the M61 APC-T round for the 75-mm main gun mounted on the first-generation M4 Sherman medium tank. The Panther tank's AP round came with a high-explosive filler, which the Sherman's AP round did not receive until late in World War II. (David Marian)

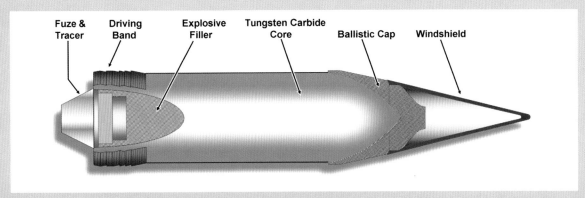

Visible in this illustration are the various components that made up a fixed generic armor-piercing capped (APC) main gun projectile employed by both the Allies and the Germans during World War II. In British military terminology, it would be classified as an armor-piercing capped ballistic cap (ABCBC) main gun round. *(James D. Brown)*

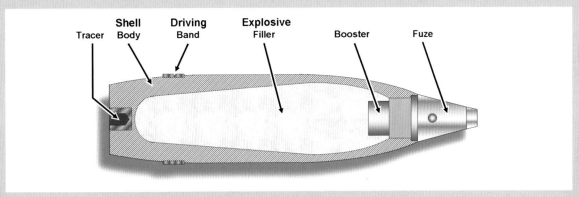

The various components of a generic high-explosive (HE) main gun projectile are visible in this illustration. HE projectiles consist of a steel body filled with a high-explosive element. The fus-e sets off the explosive filler, which causes fragmentation and blast in the area of impact or detonation. *(James D. Brown)*

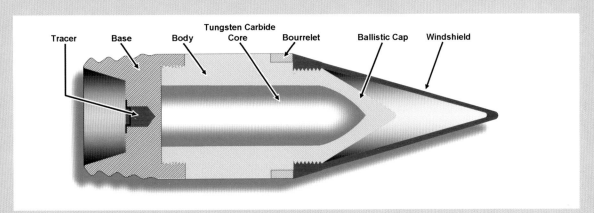

This illustration shows a generic armor-piercing round with a sub-caliber penetrator, which was very similar to the Pzgr. 40/42 main gun round employed by Panther crews to kill heavily armored targets like the Red Army IS-2 heavy tank. In American parlance, this round was known as High Velocity Armor Piercing (HVAP), whereas in British terminology it was known as Armor-Piercing, Composite Rigid (APCR.) *(James D. Brown)*

Taken from a British Army wartime report is this overhead illustration of the main gun ammunition storage arrangement for a Panther Ausf. G tank. Missing in this illustration are the three main gun rounds stored horizontally under the tank's turret basket on the right side of the hull. *(Tank Museum, Bovington)*

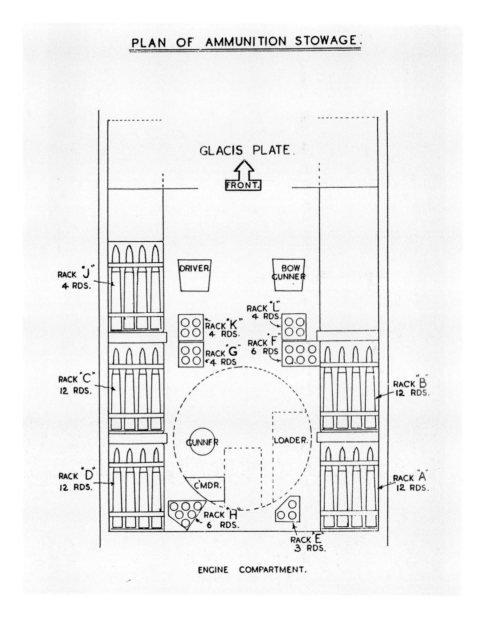

PLAN OF AMMUNITION STOWAGE.

GLACIS PLATE.

FRONT.

RACK "J" 4 RDS.

DRIVER

BOW GUNNER

RACK "L" 4 RDS.

RACK "K" 4 RDS.

RACK "F" 6 RDS

RACK "G" 4 RDS

RACK "C" 12 RDS.

RACK "B" 12 RDS.

GUNNER

LOADER.

RACK "D" 12 RDS.

RACK "A" 12 RDS.

CMDR.

RACK "H" 6 RDS.

RACK "E" 3 RDS.

ENGINE COMPARTMENT.

The first-generation Sherman tank armed with a 75-mm main gun typically fired the M61 APC-T 75-mm round. The projectile portion had a hollow cavity within it for the fitting of a high-explosive element; however, production difficulties prevented insertion into the projectile until late in World War II. The second-generation Sherman tank was armed with a 76-mm main gun and typically fired the M62 APC-T round, the projectile portion containing a HE filler. The standard AP rounds for the Red Army's first-generation T-34 medium tanks also contained a small HE filler.

ARMOR PENETRATION ABILITIES

The muzzle velocity of the Pzgr. 39/42 projectile was 3,068 feet/second (935 m/s) when it left the end of the very long Panther tank barrel. In contrast, the 75-mm main gun on the first-generation Sherman tank, with its much shorter, 10-foot (3.05-m) barrel, could manage only 2,030 ft/sec (617 m/s) with a 15-lb (6.8-kg) M61 APC-T projectile. The standard M62 APC-T projectile fired from the almost 14-foot (4.27-m) barrel of the 76-mm main gun on second-generation Sherman tanks had a muzzle velocity of 2,600 ft/sec (792 m/s). The 10-foot, 5-inch (3.2-m) main gun on the first-generation T-34 medium tank fired a 14-lb (6.35-kg) BR-350A APC projectile that achieved a muzzle velocity of 2,231 ft/sec (680 m/s).

The very high muzzle velocity of the Panther tank main gun APC-T round allowed the projectile, in theory, to penetrate up to 138 mm of armor sloped

From the loader's position on a Panther Ausf. D tank looking to the rear of the turret, one can see the recoil guard in the foreground, the closed loader's hatch on the left, a pistol port in the middle, and the tank commander's communication port on the right. (*Virginia Museum of Military Vehicles*)

at 30 degrees at a range of 109 yards (100 m). At 547 yards (500 m), it supposedly could punch through 124 mm of armor sloped at 30 degrees, and at 1,094 yards (1 km), it was supposed to penetrate 111 mm of armor sloped at 30 degrees. When engaging targets out to a range of 1.24 miles (2,000 m), the Pzgr. 39/42 projectile, in theory, could slice through 89 mm of armor sloped at 30 degrees.

According to German penetration tables, a Pzgr. 39/42 APC-T projectile could cleanly penetrate the turret front and glacis on the first-generation Sherman tank at a range of 1,094 yards (1,000 m). The side and rear of a first-generation Sherman tank could be easily penetrated at 3,828 yards (3,500 m).

From a March 27, 1945, report titled *A Report on United States vs. German Armor* (prepared for General of the Army Dwight D. Eisenhower, Supreme Commander Allied Expeditionary Force) comes this extract by Sergeant Leo Anderson of an encounter his unit had with a couple of Panther tanks:

Some things I have seen in combat that were disturbing and disgusting to any tanker. Many times I've seen our tanks engage German tanks in tank duels. Their tanks have the ups on us. Their guns and armor are far better than ours. On this particular occasion, just north of Wurselen, Germany, our column was advancing toward its objective when suddenly we began to draw direct fire from German tanks. At once we located two Mark V [Panther] tanks at about 2,800 to 3,000 yards [2.6 km to 2.7 km]. At once our tank destroyers and tanks opened fire on them. The gunners had the eye to hit but our guns didn't have the power to knock them out. I saw our tank destroyers and self-propelled get several direct hits on the Kraut tanks, but the projectiles just bounced off the Jerries. The Jerries' guns didn't fail they knocked out three of our tank destroyers and one Sherman tank at 2,800 [2.6 km] to 3,000 yards [2.7 km]. If our tanks had been as good as the German tanks they would never have scored a hit. "

From the same wartime report appears this passage by Corporal Raoul O. Barrientes, a Sherman tank gunner who recounted his run-in with a Panther tank:

" … We were hit by a Jerry tank, of unknown type, probably a Mark V [Panther], in the track. It broke the track. The second shot hit the front plate just above the bow

Looking into the bottom of a Panther Ausf. A tank hull, one can see the arrangement for three horizontally stored main gun rounds stored under the vehicle's turret basket, which is not fitted here. The loader would access the round through a hatch in the bottom of the turret basket floor. *(Michael Green)*

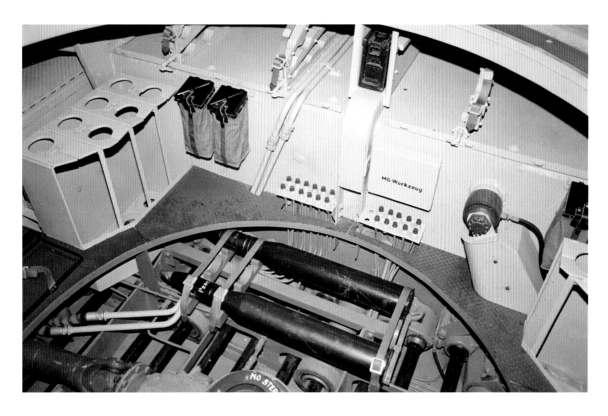

The Panther tank's main gun and its fire-control system was optimized for the destruction of enemy tanks at long range. Here we see members of the crew of a Panther Ausf. A using a pair of binoculars to spot distant targets. Allied tankers were impressed with the extremely high quality of German-made optical instruments. *(Patton Museum)*

gun, piercing the sandbags and the armor plate and exploded inside. There were about two feet of sandbags in front of the armor plate. The third shot hit the turret gun shield, piercing it, and entering the turret. The fourth and fifth hit in the same place and each pierced the gun shield and entered the turret. The tank was set on fire and burned completely. **"**

When employed against the second-generation version of the Red Army T-34 medium tank, introduced into service in early 1944 and designated the T-34-85 tank, the lethal range dropped only a bit when the Panther tank used its Pzgr. 39/42 APC-T round due to the thicker turret armor on the T-34-85 tank. With the introduction of the T-34-85 tank into Red Army service, the Germans designated the original first-generation T-34 medium tank armed with the 76.2-mm main gun as the T-34/76 to distinguish it from the T-34-85, which weighed 35 tons (32 mt) combat loaded.

The Panther tank's Pzgr. 39/42 APC-T projectile could penetrate the T-34-85 tank turret gun shield at 1,312 yards (1,200 m). Punching a hole through the tank's well-sloped glacis plate meant the Panther tank had to be within 328 yards (300 m). The side turret armor on the T-34-85 tank could be penetrated at a range of 2,953 yards (2,700 m), and the side superstructure

This close-up picture shows the small hinged loader's ingress and egress armored hatch on the rear wall of a Panther Ausf. G tank turret. It was also used by the tank's loader to eject spent main gun cartridge cases from the interior of the vehicle lest the propellant fumes built up within the tank's fighting compartment. *(David T. Lin)*

A close-up interior shot of the replaceable loader's overhead periscope in a Panther Ausf. G tank turret. This overhead periscope first appeared on the Panther Ausf. A tank. Being fixed in position meant the loader's vision to the right side of the vehicle was extremely restricted by the relatively narrow field of view offered by his overhead periscope. *(Chun-Lsu Hsu)*

armor at 3,171 yards (2,900 m). The lower hull side armor of the T-34-85 tank was penetrated at 3,828 yards (3,500 m).

It was more difficult for the Panther tank's Pzgr. 39/42 APC-T projectile to penetrate the thick armor on the Red Army IS-II heavy tank, introduced into service in early 1944. It could only punch a hole in the turret front at 875 yards (800 m) and in the thicker gun shield at 437 yards (400 m). To penetrate the glacis, the Panther tank had to be within 656 yards (600 m). Both the side turret armor on the IS-II heavy tank as well as the side superstructure armor were penetrated at 1,750 yards (1,600 m). The lower hull side armor was penetrated at 2,187 yards (2,000 m).

ENHANCED ARMOR-PIERCING ROUND

To improve the odds of the Panther tank taking on Soviet heavy tanks in combat, Panther tank crews sometimes had access to what the U.S. Army referred to as a hyper-velocity armor-piercing (HVAP) round. In the British Army, the same round would be referred to as an armor-piercing, composite rigid (APCR) round. In German military service, the round was designated the Panzergranate 40/42 (Pzgr. 40/42). It was 34.5 inches (87.6 cm) long and weighed 25 lbs (11 kg). The muzzle velocity of the Pzgr. 40/42 was 3,675 ft/sec (1,120 m/s).

Unlike the full-bore Pzgr. 39/42 projectile with its steel body and small high-explosive element, the Pzgr. 40/42 projectile consisted of a subcaliber tungsten core centered within a lightweight metal carrier that matched the diameter of the Panther tank gun bore. The metal carrier traveled to the target along with the projectile and was stripped away upon impact, leaving the very dense and hard subcaliber core to penetrate the armor of an enemy tank.

The advantage of the Pzgr. 40/42 projectile was that the subcaliber core concentrated its penetrative energy on a smaller area of the target, making it more effective in penetrating armor. The disadvantage was the aerodynamic drag created by the lightweight metal carrier that traveled to the target, which lowered the projectile muzzle velocity going downrange and meant its penetrative powers dropped off at longer ranges.

First-generation Sherman tanks armed with a 75-mm main gun were never issued a HVAP round. The American second-generation Sherman tanks armed with a 76-mm main gun began receiving small numbers of M93 HVAP rounds beginning in August 1944. It had a muzzle velocity of 3,400 ft/sec (1,036 m/s).

Red Army T-34/76 tankers had access to small numbers of tungsten-core subcaliber rounds after October 1943, designated the BR-350P, which boasted a muzzle velocity of 3,165 ft/sec (965 m/s). The letter "P" in the ammunition designation stood for *polkaliberniy* (subcaliber). In the summer of 1944, the T-34-85 tankers were provided with a small number of a tungsten-core subcaliber rounds designated the BR-365P, which had a muzzle velocity of 3,937 ft/sec (1,200 m/s). The 15-foot, 3-inch (4.66 m) main gun on the T34-85 tank fired its standard BR-365 APC projectile at 2,599 ft/sec (792 m/s).

In theory, a Pzgr. 40/42 subcaliber projectile could penetrate up to 194 mm of armor sloped at 30 degrees at a range of 109 yards (100m). At

547 yards (500m), it could punch through 174 mm of armor sloped at 30 degrees, and at 1,094 yards (1 km), it would penetrate 149 mm of armor sloped at 30 degrees. When engaging targets out to a range of 2,188 yards (2 km), the Panther tank gun firing the Pzgr. 40/42 round could slice through 106 mm of armor sloped at 30 degrees.

The British took the next big step in AP ammunition development during World War II by deciding that it made more sense for the lightweight metal carrier, referred to as a "sabot," which surrounded the subcaliber core projectile in an APCR round, to be disposed of upon leaving the barrel of a gun. This in turn would reduce wind resistance and increase velocity and penetration by up to 25 percent. This new type of ammunition was referred to in British military parlance as an armor piercing discarding sabot (APDS) round, and the lightweight metal carrier was peeled off by wind resistance as it left a barrel in flight.

The APDS round first appeared in British Army service in late 1944 on a variety of tanks and tank destroyers. It was not widely adopted into military service for use on the tanks of other nations until after World War II. The U.S. Army did not adopt the APDS round until the late 1950s, with the introduction of the M60 main battle tank armed with a British-designed 105-mm main gun. The Soviet Army developed an APDS round for the 100-mm main gun on their T-55 medium tank in 1967.

HIGH-EXPLOSIVE ROUND

The Panther tank's main gun also was capable of firing the *Sprenggranate* (high-explosive fragmentation round) 42 (Sprgr. 42), a high-explosive (HE) round that weighed 25 lbs (11 kg) and was 37 inches long (94 cm). The projectile portion of the round had a muzzle velocity of 2,300 ft/sec (701 m/s), which allowed the Panther tank to engage unarmored targets (trucks) and enemy personnel well beyond the range of the vehicle's own machine guns.

Other potential targets for the Sprgr. 42 included enemy towed antitank guns and defensive positions. Most German tankers identified emplaced towed enemy antitank guns as more of a threat to them than enemy tanks, since they were harder to spot and typically got in the first shot.

The first-generation Sherman tank had two different versions of the M48 HE round. There was the normal version, which weighed 18.8 lbs (8.5 kg) and had a muzzle velocity of 1,470 ft/sec (448 m/s). The second version was a supercharged HE round that weighed 19.56 lbs (8.9 kg) and had a muzzle velocity of 1,885 ft/sec (574 m/s). As can be deduced, the supercharged HE round went farther the normal HE round by 2,300 yards (2.10 kg).

The T-34/76 main gun could fire the older generation F-354 HE round or the OF-350 HE-fragmentation round, which weighed 13.7 lbs (6.23 kg) and had a muzzle velocity of 1,521 ft/sec (680 m/s). For the T-34-85, there was the 35.9-lb (16.3-kg) O-365 HE-fragmentation round with a muzzle velocity of 1,774 ft/sec (793 m/s).

Although large-caliber HE rounds typically are not used for killing tanks, they can still do a great amount of damage at certain vulnerable locations. U.S. Army postwar testing showed that the blast from a large-caliber HE projectile, which creates a high-pressure wave front, can inflict a great deal of damage to the hull roofs of tanks as well as the joints between the turrets

The breech end of a Panther tank's 75-mm main gun. Also visible is the gun mount that provides a platform for not just the main gun but also for the coaxial machine gun on the right side of the main gun. The main gun's hydraulic recoil mechanism is to the left of the coaxial machine gun.
(Michael Green)

and hull roofs. A blast from a large caliber HE projectile on a turret wall could bow the roof of a tank and bend the traversing gear rings, preventing the rotation of a vehicle's turret. Testing also showed that the blast from a large-caliber HE projectile exploding on or near a vehicle commander's cupola typically would cause considerable damage.

A close-up view of the muzzle brake on a Panther Ausf. A tank. Also visible is the rifling at the end of the barrel and the baffles that help direct propellant gases rearward. The muzzle brake screwed onto the end of the barrel and was fixed in place with setscrews. *(David Marian)*

OPPONENT'S COMMENTS

An American military report from the Ordnance Section of the Headquarters European Theater of Operations United States Army and dated July 24, 1944, describes the types of main gun ammunition carried onboard a captured Panther Ausf. A tank and the number of rounds carried:

> Two types of ammunition were carried in the tank. Forty rounds of APCBC/HE/T and thirty-two rounds of HE. The armor piercing ammunition was of two types. The two types appeared to be similar in construction to the Pzgr. 39 as used in the 7.5 cm Pak 40 [towed antitank gun] … All rounds had double rotating bands.

In the March 27, 1945, U.S. Army report titled *United States Armor vs. German Armor*, U.S. Army Private Arel B. McMahan, a gunner on a Sherman tank, compared American and German tank ammunition and guns:

> "My opinion, as a gunner, of how our equipment compares to that of the Germans is: AP is not as good as the German because of lower powder charge. Our HE is better than theirs for we have less duds and the shrapnel breaks up better. WP smoke is the best and at least as good as the Germans. The Germans have the best tank gun for range and muzzle velocity; with longer barrels on our small guns we would have as good a gun as theirs. "

PANTHER AUSF. D AND AUSF. A TANK MAIN GUN AMMUNITION STORAGE

The Panther Ausf. D and Ausf. A models were designed to carry seventy-nine unprotected main gun rounds in the hull. By way of comparison, the early-production first-generation Sherman tanks with cast-armored hulls carried ninety unprotected main gun rounds, while those with welded armored hulls carried ninety-seven unprotected main gun rounds.

The U.S. Army began providing armor-protected storage for the main gun rounds in its Sherman tanks beginning in August 1943. This slightly dropped the main gun ammunition storage capacity of both the cast- and welded-armored hull Sherman tanks. Depending on the version of the T-34/76, the Russian vehicle was designed to carry either seventy-seven or one hundred unprotected main gun rounds for its 76.2-mm main gun.

The second-generation Sherman tanks armed with a 76-mm main gun carried seventy-one protected main gun rounds while the Red Army T-34-85 tank had authorized storage space for fifty-five unprotected main gun rounds.

Of the seventy-nine unprotected main gun rounds stored in the Panther Ausf. D and Ausf. A, forty were stored horizontally in metal racks located on either side of the vehicle's superstructure, eighteen on the right side and twenty-two on the left side. Four of the horizontally stored main gun rounds on the left side of the tank, next to the driver's position, could be accessed only by the driver, who would hand back each round to the loader when the turret was at roughly the 9 o'clock position.

Another thirty-six main gun rounds in the Panther Ausf. D and Ausf. A tanks were stored in open-topped vertical metal racks that sat on the hull floor, not the turret basket floor. The rounds were divided among six vertical rack assemblies, with the largest containing eight main gun rounds and the smallest holding only three main gun rounds. Of the six main gun round vertical assemblies, the loader could access only four of them (containing a total of twenty-two rounds), depending on which way the turret was pointed, although he might have received assistance from other members of the crew if time permitted.

Of the remaining two main gun round vertical assemblies in the Panther Ausf. D and Ausf. A tank hulls, one contained six rounds and was located behind the driver's seat. The other held eight rounds and was located directly behind the radioman's seat. These rounds could be accessed only by the crewmen who sat in front of them and passed to the loader during lulls in combat. The British Army referred to these main gun round vertical assemblies as replenishment storage. They differed from the other four in the vehicle because they had a hinged steel plate mounted on top of them to prevent the crew's feet from damaging them as they entered and left the vehicle.

Three more main gun rounds for the Panther Ausf. D and Ausf. A tanks were stored horizontally in a bin under the turret floor plates and could be accessed only by the loader when the turret was directly pointed over the front hull.

According to a British military report dated December 1944, a captured German tanker stated the following regarding the main gun ammunition storage in Panther Ausf. A tanks:

> "Standard instructions are that 120 rounds for the 7.5 cm [75-mm] gun and 3,500 rounds for each MG [machine gun] should be stowed in the Panther before going into action. It is left to the crew to decide on the proportion of AP and HE shells to be carried; normally the proportion should be 50 percent of each. [The] prisoner of war carried 9,000 rounds of MG ammo for his two MGs. Stowage space is provided for 79 rounds of 7.5 cm [75-mm] ammo. The extra 41 rounds are added by removing the racks from ammo-boxes and by carrying some rounds in the spent cartridge box ... under the recoil guard. No rounds are carried on the floor."

The authorized storage for 7.92-mm machine gun rounds in the Panther Ausf. D and Ausf. A tanks was 5,100 rounds.

PANTHER AUSF. G TANK MAIN GUN AMMUNITION STORAGE

The Panther Ausf. G tank had factory-installed storage space for eighty-two unprotected main gun rounds in its hull. Fifty-two were stored horizontally in the superstructure, twenty-four on the right side, and twenty-eight on the left side. As with previous versions of the Panther tank, four of the main gun rounds stored on the left side of the tank, located next to the driver's position, could be accessed only by the driver.

The main gun round ammunition storage arrangement in the Panther Ausf. G tank was similar in location and access to that found in the Panther Ausf. D and Ausf. A tanks. The main difference was the addition of three more main gun rounds stored in each of the four hull panniers accessible to the vehicle's loader and lowering the number of main gun rounds stored in the vertical assemblies from six individual racks storing a total of thirty-six rounds down to twenty-seven distributed among six racks in the Panther Ausf. G.

The main gun rounds stored horizontally in the Panther Ausf. G tank superstructure originally were covered by thin 3-mm sheet metal dust covers. These were dropped from production units in September 1944.

As with the main gun round vertical assemblies distributed in the Panther Ausf. D and Ausf. A tanks, there was one located behind the driver's seat in the Panther Ausf. G tank and another behind the radioman's seat. These both were much smaller than those found in the earlier versions and held only four main gun rounds each. Of the remaining Panther Ausf. G tank four main gun round vertical assemblies, a total of only nineteen rounds were accessible to the loader, depending on which way the turret was turned.

Like the Panther Ausf. D and Ausf. A tank, the Panther Ausf. G tank had three main gun rounds stored horizontally in a hull bin under the turret basket floorboard. These were accessible only by the loader when the turret was directly pointed over the front hull.

A British Army document titled *Military Operational Research Report No. 61 Study No. 11 Motion Studies of German Tanks*, prepared by Captain G. Tunnicliffe in 1947, described the four horizontal main gun storage racks accessible by the loader, called panniers by the British, in the Panther Ausf. G tank:

"Racks A, B, C, and D are the four pannier racks which are accessible from the turret. Each rack held 12 rounds, stowed horizontally. The four rounds in the bottom

OPPOSITE
All versions of the Panther tank featured a front hull roof mounted hinged barrel clamp, seen here on a Panther Ausf. A. Below the barrel clamp is the upper portion of an armored housing for the front hull ventilator. The upper armored housing for the front hull ventilator differed in shape on the Panther Ausf. G. *(Christopher Hughes)*

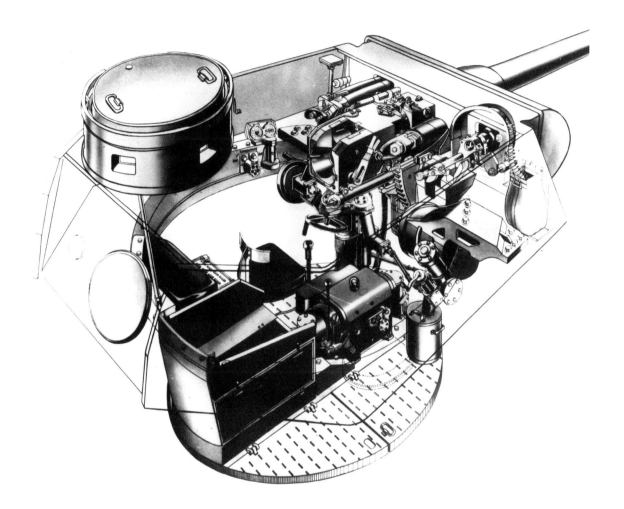

A ghosted illustration of a Panther Ausf. D tank turret shows all the various features found within. Notice the size of the spent cartridge case bin in relation to the rest of the turret. In Allied medium tanks, cartridge cases merely dropped to the turret basket or hull floor and rolled around until they could be disposed of. (Patton Museum)

layer are stowed bases rear, the three rounds in the next layer base forward, the three rounds in the next layer bases rear, and the top layer of two rounds is stowed base forward .... Each layer is supported by two steel arms, each of which is hinged and springs upwards when the layer of rounds is removed from it. This facilitates access to the layer below. "

The British were not impressed by main gun round vertical storage assemblies distributed around the hull floor of the Panther Ausf. G, as noted in this passage from the same report:

"There are four vertical storage racks accessible to the loader; they are rack E, F, G and H and contain a total of 19 stowed rounds, all stowed base down. The racks are similar in design, and are built of sheet metal .... The rounds are held by base cups and double top flaps which hinge inwards and which, when closed, hold the rounds rigid. Each pair of flaps is locked by a toggle switch .... A further bad feature was that when the flaps were opened and the first round removed, there was no support for the remaining rounds and they were liable to fall over. When this happened, they were not only difficult to find and reach but would have also jammed the turret had it been suddenly traversed. "

The Panther Ausf. G tank had authorized storage space for 4,800 rounds of 7.92-mm ammunition for its machine guns.

PANTHER TANK LOADER

The Panther tank *Ladeschutze* (loader) tended to be the junior member of the five-man crew as the job was considered an entry-level position. Unlike the American-designed and -built Sherman tanks, where the loader was on the left side of the main gun, the loader for the Panther tank was on the right side of the main gun and shoved a round into the breech with his left hand, while the gunner and vehicle commander sat on the left side of the main gun.

The Motion Studies of German Tanks written in 1947 described the loader's position in the Panther tank:

"A seat was optional. As the height of the turret is only 5 feet 3 inches (1.6 m), a loader of normal height must stoop. The combination of these factors was certain to result in fatigue, especially if the vehicles were on the move for long periods. "

The same document offered the British Army conclusions on the loader's position on the Panther Ausf. G tank:

"Loading times are reasonably fast because the loader has adequate floor space in which to maneuver the rounds, and also because the rounds are convenient to grip and handle. Also the deflector guard [recoil guard] rear plate being mounted well back from the breech and the absence of any top rail of the loader's side of the deflector guard allows the loader adequate room to insert the round into the chamber. "

The Panther tank's loader entered and exited the turret through an 18-inch (45.7-cm) diameter circular hatch located at the rear of the turret.

Located underneath and behind the breech end of the Panther tank's main gun was a spent cartridge case bin, something not seen on any other tank in World War II. Ejected main gun cartridge cases would hit the back end of the recoil guard and drop down through the spring-loaded flaps visible in this picture and into the bin. *(Michael Green)*

The spent cartridge case bin and the breech end of the main gun and the recoil guard surrounding it made it difficult for him to enter or leave his position through the vehicle commander's cupola and vice versa for the vehicle commander and gunner.

The loader's rear turret hatch was also the way in which he disposed of spent cartridge cases, once the spent cartridge case bin had become full. It was also one path by which the loader would reload the main gun racks within his vehicle with outside assistance. The hatch could be opened, closed, and locked from inside or outside of the turret. It presumably would be kept closed but not locked when the tank was in combat.

THE PANTHER TANK GUN

The *Rohr* (gun tube) is the most important component of tank main guns. It contains and guides a projectile during the critical firing phase. The gun tube on the Panther tank was a one-piece steel forging weighing about 2,390 lbs (1.1 mt) with muzzle brake and breech.

The large, 69-pound (31-kg) muzzle brake mounted on the end of the Panther gun tube helped to retard recoil by redirecting propellant gases rearward. Two sets of baffles applied a forward pull on the gun tube, lessening the amount of recoil as the gun barrel slammed back into the Panther turret. To minimize the amount of dust kicked up by the muzzle blast, the baffles were located in the sides of the muzzle brake. The muzzle blast was

Mounted in the hull of a Panther Ausf. A tank is an incomplete turret basket. Visible is the spent cartridge case bin and just in front of it is the light gray compressor that provided the air for the tank's bore evacuator system. Also visible is the gunner's seat on the left and loader's seat on the right, minus their seat cushions. *(Michael Green)*

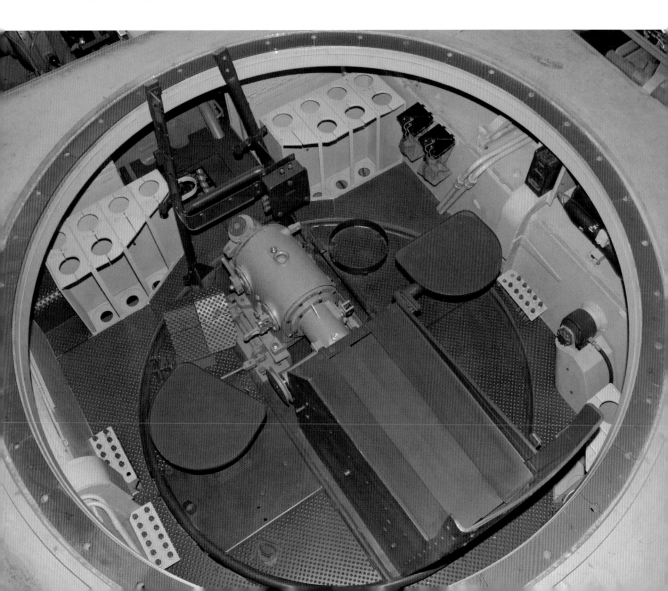

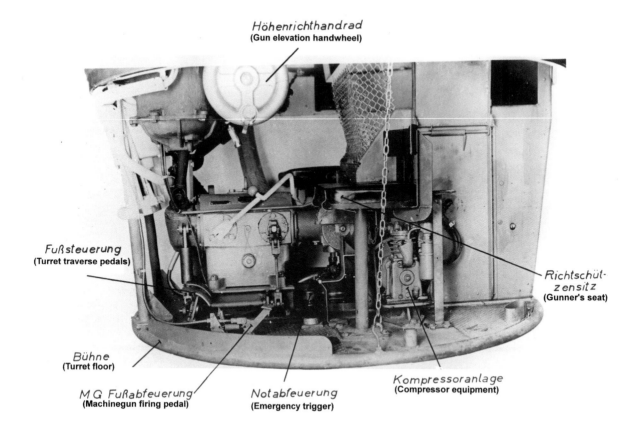

Höhenrichthandrad
(Gun elevation handwheel)

Fußsteuerung
(Turret traverse pedals)

Richtschüt-
zensitz
(Gunner's seat)

Bühne
(Turret floor)

M.G. Fußabfeuerung
(Machinegun firing pedal)

Notabfeuerung
(Emergency trigger)

Kompressoranlage
(Compressor equipment)

Some of the various components and parts that made up the lower portion of a Panther tank turret basket are labeled in this photograph. Notice at the upper portion of the picture a wire mesh, which was intended to keep ejected spent main gun cartridge cases aimed into the spent cartridge case bin. *(Patton Museum)*

thus directed sideways, which reduced obscuration of the chosen target. The Panther tank gun could not be fired without the muzzle brake fitted. Modern tanks no longer use muzzle brakes because fin-stabilized main gun projectiles would catch on the muzzle brake when exiting the barrel of a tank gun.

The breech is a mechanism housed within the confines of a tank's turret and located at the end of the gun tube. It opens by means of a breech-opening lever to allow insertion of a round, be it fixed or semifixed into a chamber. The breechblock is that part of the breech mechanism that slides downward to open and upward to close. The breech action on the Panther gun was semiautomatic, meaning the 80-lb (36.3-kg) breechblock remained locked in the open position after a cartridge case was ejected. This allowed the loader to quickly insert another round into the chamber of the gun. The chamber tapered down into a forcing cone at its forward end, which allowed the copper rotating bands on a projectile to be engaged gradually by the gun tube rifling.

As the primer within a cartridge case was detonated when the Panther tank gunner pulled on an electrically powered hand trigger, the propellant that surrounded it within the cartridge case ignited within the gun chamber. The sudden expansion of propellant gases down the gun tube propelled a projectile with resulting opposite rearward reaction, called recoil. Absorbing this powerful force was the muzzle brake and the recoil mechanism in the Panther tank turret that allowed the gun to move rearward within its gun mount during firing.

The turret-mounted hydraulic recoil mechanism in the Panther tank, located on the lower right-hand side of the gun tube, acted as a cushion between the gun and the gun mount (also known as a cradle), allowing the gun tube to move rearward up to almost 17 inches (43 cm) while the gun mount and vehicle remained stationary. A 56.5-lb (26-kg) hydro-pneumatic counter-recoil system, located on the lower left side of the gun barrel, would then return the gun assembly to its original firing position (referred to as the battery) and hold it there until fired again.

Taken inside a Panther Ausf. G tank turret, one can see the flexible metal tubing that ran from the spent cartridge case bin up to the overhead turret electric ventilator. Also visible is the traverse and elevation gear for the Panther's main gun. Missing in this photograph are the recoil guard and the coaxial 7.92-mm MG34 machine gun. *(Patton Museum)*

From the Panther handbook, which was aimed at enlisted men, comes these warnings about taking care of the main gun:

"Never shoot without a muzzle cover! Before shooting, remove the cover! If your cover is icy, you must remove it even if it's disposable! At the right time, but also not too soon! You need to remove camouflage branches from the muzzle. Before shooting you much look inside, whether or not the barrel rifling is full of dirt! Remove (at night by your portable flashlight) ice crust, residue, powder muck; and when there is a pause in the battle, unload the cannon when the barrel is hot .... The muzzle brake is there for a reason. It catches nearly three-quarters of the recoil. When your muzzle brake is loose or lost, in this case do not shoot."

MAIN GUN SUPPORTING COMPONENTS

The Panther tank gun mount had a trunnion on either side of it, which functioned as an axis around which the gun mount and the gun tube rotated in elevation and depression. The trunnions rested in bearings on the inside of the front of the vehicle's turret. Due to the excessive weight bias toward the muzzle end of the Panther tank gun and for ease of elevation, the vehicle had a hydro-pneumatic equilibrator mounted within the turret to compensate for any imbalance.

The main gun on the Panther Ausf. D tank had a maximum elevation of 20 degrees and a maximum depression of 8 degrees. The main gun on the Panther Ausf. A and Ausf. G tanks had a maximum elevation of 18 degrees and a maximum depression of 8 degrees.

A U.S. Army report dated November 1944 noted that the hydro-pneumatic equilibrator in the Panther differed from other German tanks:

"The equilibrator mechanism departs from conventional German design. It makes use of a hydro-pneumatic cylinder mounted to the [turret] basket wall and fastened to the gun by four cables through a system of pulleys. The cylinder is charged with air to 85 atmos."

Another U.S. Army report issued in April 25, 1945, stated the following about the Panther equilibrator mechanism: "The small size and simplicity of this equilibrator would seem to warrant its investigation for possible use with American long caliber gun tubes used in tanks and gun motor carriages."

When not in combat, the Panther tank's main gun was braced centerline by a *Rohrstuetze* (hinged barrel clamp) that was mounted centrally on the front of the vehicle's hull plate directly above the driver's and the radioman/bow gunner's compartment. When not needed, the barrel clamp would be folded down on top of the front hull armored ventilation fan cover. There was also an internal travel lock for the Panther tank's main gun on the interior roof of the turret.

BORE EVACUATOR SYSTEM

To prevent the buildup of propellant gases in the turret of the Panther tank during the firing of the main gun or coaxial machine gun, an electrically operated turret scavenging exhaust fan was located above the loader's

Visible in this picture to the right is the padded tank commander's seat. In front of the tank commander's seat is the hinged metal platform (folded up in this picture) that he could fold down to stand on in order to look out over the top of his cupola. Also visible in this image is the gunner's padded seat and controls. *(Chun-Lun Hsu)*

At the very top of the picture can be seen a portion of the azimuth indicator ring, graduated from 1 to 12 o'clock, on a Panther Ausf. A tank. The vertical shaft to the left of the tank commander's seat connected the azimuth indicator ring to the teeth of the turret ring. Notice the tank commander has no backrest. *(Michael Green)*

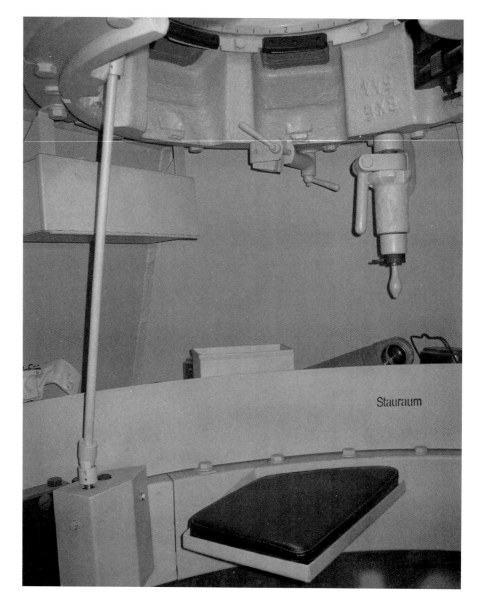

position. Also, a bore evacuator scavenging unit was mounted at the very rear face of the breech, powered by a small air compressor located underneath the breech of the Panther main gun. The bore evacuator scavenging unit directed a blast of air directly down the gun tube every time the weapon was fired and the breech block opened upon the counter-recoil stroke.

A description of the bore evacuator scavenging unit in the Panther tank appeared in a U.S. Army report dated February 1945:

"The gun scavenging unit consisted of a compressor, compressor tank, release valve and two ports of entry into the chamber of the gun through the breech ring.

The compressor was driven by a V-belt from a power take-off on the turret traversing mechanism. The air is fed into the compressor tank located in the cartridge case box by a flexible hose. A pressure relief valve on the tank prevents the tank from being charged to excess pressure although the exact pressure at which release was obtained was not determined. This feature serves to protect the air-lines and also the driving belt on the compressor from over-load.

Metal tubing is used to carry the compressed air to the air release valve which charges the air into the chamber .... The design of this valve is such that when ejection of the cartridge case is complete, a blast of air from the compressor tank is directed into the chamber from both sides of the breach ring to expel the gases left in the chamber and tube."

The Panther tank bore evacuator system differed from that of most postwar tanks which consist of a cylindrical object mounted on the exterior of a tank's main gun barrel. However, the U.S. Army did employ a compressed air scavenging system on two Cold War tanks, the M551 Sheridan light tank and the M60A2, both of which were fitted with a 5.98-inch (152-mm) short-barreled rifled tube capable of firing either a shaped charged projectile or a Shillelagh antitank missile.

Those who have not served in World War II-era tanks often fail to comprehend the effects of the fumes generated by firing the vehicle's weapons. From a U.S. Army report dated 1951–52 and titled *Men in Tanks: Conditions of Stress in Tank Crews, and Techniques of Stress Reduction* comes this passage explaining the impact of fumes based on surveys among tankers who had seen combat:

"Many secondary comments were made with respect to gun fumes. They affect vision, both because of actual blocking and due to smarting of the eyes. Fumes interfere with respiration with the tank closed, and in the opinion of many affect gunner accuracy. The large percentage of individuals stated

With the introduction of the Panther Ausf. A tank, the two-dial azimuth indicator found on the Panther Ausf. D tank was dispensed with and replaced by the single-dial azimuth indicator seen here. It was graduated from 1 to 12 o'clock and was located to the left of the gunner's position on the turret ring. *(Michael Green)*

Visible is the front end of the 100-mm thick cast-armored cupola that appeared on the Panther tank with the introduction of the Panther Ausf. A model. Notice the small sighting vane mounted directly in front of one of the replaceable periscopes. It was employed by the tank commander to line up the main gun with a target. (*Andreas Kirchhoff*)

a need for an efficient blower system fits into these comments consistently. Some ten individuals stated that the bore evacuator made a considerable difference in this respect. "

Neither the Red Army nor U.S. Army medium tanks employed a bore evacuator during World War II. Many a World War II American tanker still remembers the sting of the propellant fumes after firing a few rounds through the Sherman tank's main gun. The first American tanks to mount a bore evacuator were the postwar M26A1 Pershing medium tank and the M46 Patton medium, both of which saw service in the Korean War. The first Russian tank to receive a bore evacuator was the T-54B medium tank in 1956.

SPENT CARTRIDGE CASE BIN

Located just behind and below the Panther tank's main gun breech was a large metal bin affixed to the turret basket floor that was intended to store at least six spent cartridge cases as they were ejected from the breech upon the counter-recoil stroke. This spent case cartridge bin first appeared on the Panther Ausf. D tank in April 1943 and was continued through on the Panther Ausf. A and Ausf. G tanks.

As the spent Panther tank cartridge cases hurled straight out the back of the open breech, they would impact on a deflector shield incorporated into the main gun recoil guard and drop into the bin through two hinged doors. The deflector shield was fitted with a spring that would grip the base of the spent cartridge case and ensured that it dropped squarely into the bin below.

The spent cartridge case bin had two spring-loaded flaps along its length that opened downward when the cartridge case dropped into it. When sprung shut, they sealed the bin and prevented the escape of residue propellant gases

A photo of the rear of the tank commander's cupola on a Panther Ausf. G tank where the tank commander's overhead armored hatch has been swung to the open position. The small handle directly behind the cupola was one of several used when lifting the Panther tank's turret off the vehicle's chassis. *(Andreas Kirchhoff)*

The drum-shaped cupola of a Panther Ausf. D tank is seen in this close-up picture. It had six direct-vision open ports rather than periscopes. If enemy fire threatened the tank commander, he could rotate a 60-mm-thick armored ring, mounted inside his cupola, to close the vision ports. *(Patton Museum)*

from fouling the air of the turret. The bin was connected to the overhead turret electric ventilation by flexible metal tubing that drew out the residue propellant gases.

An official description of how the turret scavenging unit worked on the Panther appeared in a February 1945 U.S. Army report:

“When the smoking cartridge case is ejected rearward, the base strikes the rear of the shoulder-guard and is delayed by a spring catch so that it drops mouth first through a trap door into the cartridge case box on the floor. To the bottom of this box is attached a flexible steel tubing of perhaps four-inch diameter which leads to an exhaust fan, operated by a small electric motor, drives the gases from the box out through the turret roof. In circumstances when powder fumes or dust becomes excessive in the fighting compartment, a small trap on the fan housing at the turret roof may be opened to clean the fighting compartment.”

THE VEHICLE COMMANDER

If the tank was considered a living creature, then the vehicle commander would be its brains. On German tanks of World War II, the vehicle commander was typically referred to in German as the *Panzerkommandant* (tank commander) or sometimes as the *Panzerfuehrer* (tank leader). In a platoon of five Panther tanks, the platoon leader typically would be a *Leutnant* (lieutenant), with the other four tanks being generally commanded by *Feldwebelen* or *Unteroffizieren* (noncommissioned officers).

Within the Panther tank, the vehicle commander guided his crew with the help of an intercom system consisting of both a headphone set and throat microphone. The headphone set for both the U.S. Army and Red Army tankers was incorporated into specialized tankers' helmets. Both also used throat microphones like the Germans, although the vehicle commander in the Sherman tank normally used a hand-held microphone.

Up through July 1943, the Panther Ausf. D tank sported a small, hinged communication port located next to the vehicle commander on the left side

An overhead picture of the turret of a Panther Ausf. D tank showing the tank commander's drum-shaped cupola. Also visible is the standard antenna mount base just behind the turret. This vehicle also features the communication port seen on early production Panther Ausf. D tanks. *(Virginia Museum of Military Vehicles)*

PANTHER TANK AMBUSH

In April 2006, Edward Monroe-Jones interviewed Erwin Bachmann at his residence in Goettingen, Germany. The interview was conducted in response to a description of action in Herrlisheim in January 1945 by Ernst Storch. Storch and Bachmann were two of the last soldiers to be received by Adolph Hitler at the Reich Kanzlei in April 1945. Bachmann's account of the Herrlisheim event appears below as he described it:

"I was a young and somewhat naïve Waffen SS Obersturmfuehrer [First Lieutenant] working at the headquarters of Obersturmbannfuehrer [Lieutenant Colonel] Ernst Tetsch who commanded Die Erste Abteilung [a battalion with less than five companies] of the 10th Waffen SS Panzer Division. In January of 1945, we had established a beachhead on the west bank of the Rhein River from Gambsheim to Druisenheim. Between these two villages was Offendorf, where our headquarters lay. The American 12th Armored Division had attacked our hastily constructed defenses to the southwest of Offendorf. On January 16, 1945 our 88-mm guns decimated the attacking Shermans and prevented the Americans from advancing into Offendorf. On the following day the Americans attacked Herrlisheim, a small town only two miles northwest of Offendorf. They attacked with infantry and Sherman tanks in substantial numbers despite the punishment of the previous day.

We had infantry in Herrlisheim fighting alongside the 553rd Volksgrenadiers. We were desperately short of tanks, but had a few in Offendorf waiting to strike when needed. I sat in Offendorf performing administrative duties, but I was itching to get into action. When I heard that 3rd Company commander had been killed, I suggested with some temerity that I should drive to Herrlisheim and take over command of the company.

My impulsive offer surprised Tetsch, but not so much as myself. I had been born in 1921 and raised in Rostok, then had gone to Junkerschule, the military training institute. I did well, but still never considered myself a real soldier. To my surprise, Tetsch agreed and assigned a BKrad [motorcycle with sidecar] and driver to me. Rottenfuehrer [Sergeant] Sauerwein swung his leg over the motorcycle and I jumped into the sidecar. We shot up Rue de Offendorf and slowed when at the outskirts of town. We looked for 3rd and 4th companies, but couldn't find anyone. We chugged in low gear up the street toward the city center, all the while craning our necks, looking for some sign of life. We came to a fork in the road. To the left was a church with tall steeple. Farther to the west I could hear rifle fire coming from one of the houses. Straight ahead was a street which seemed to dead end in about 60 meters [66 yards]. To my right was the right side-street of the fork, but it had a curve and I couldn't see beyond the bend.

I dismounted from the BKrad and walked up the street. It was the Rue Chateauneuf la Fôret, but I took no notice of the geography at the time. Armed with only my officer's pistol I started to round the bend for a better look. A machine gun rang out and bullets ricocheted off the cobblestones around me. I ran back to the BKrad where Sauerwein was waiting. I told him that there were at least two Shermans up the street. I grabbed a *Panzerfaust* and a few hand grenades, then shouted for Sauerwein to turn around and get back into Offendorf to bring up the two lead Panther tanks. I watched momentarily as the BKrad sped back down the Offendorf road, then I crept back up the Rue Chateauneuf la Foret. I peeked around the corner and saw several American soldiers standing in a cross street only about 30 meters [32 yards] from my position. Dashing across the street and into a protected space formed by a brick wall and corner of a house, I again observed the Americans. From this location I could see the nose of a Sherman tank. I knelt down on one knee and brought the Panzerfaust to my shoulder. I tried to remain calm as I went through the simple firing procedure. Sighting along the barrel I pulled the trigger. The whoosh of the rocket startled me and I jumped back into the protection of the house and wall. I thought I heard the shell explode against a tank, but I wasn't sure. Remaining still, I listened for the enemy reaction. All seemed quiet from the American Sherman tanks.

Then I heard the squeaking of tank tracks from behind. Only a few minutes had passed since I had sent Sauerwein on his way. It would have been impossible for the Panthers to have come up from Offendorf in so short a time. Again I looked out from my hidden position, this time to my rear. Amazingly, two Panthers came to a stop where I had left Sauerwein and the BKrad. I dashed back to them.

Scharfuehrer Heinz Berger in the right-hand Panther jumped down and cupped an ear trying to listen to my directions. Scharfuehrer Hans Muelradt in the left-hand tank stayed in his turret. I told Berger to cut his engine and hand signaled Muelradt to do the same. The big Maybachs throttled back and died. Berger explained that they had been in a small orchard outside of town when they saw the BKrad zip by them on its way back to Offendorf. Having observed the same motorcycle go into Herrlisheim with an officer in its sidecar less than a half hour before, they decided to investigate. It had taken them only a few minutes to find the fork in the road where we now stood.

While the tank commander talked, I was only half listening. I was formulating a plan to attack whatever tanks may have been on that road running perpendicular to the two streets diverging from the fork. There was no time to lose. The Americans would shortly launch an attack of their own, if they knew just how puny the German forces were. I told Berger to take his tank up the right hand street (Rue Chateauneuf la Foret) and when he got far enough around the street's bend to see the Americans, he was to open fire on whatever might present itself. I would stay with Muelradt's Panther and when we heard the shooting we would move up the left-hand street, called the Rue de L'Eglise. We would then charge the Americans from behind when they were engaged with Berger coming at them on the opposite end.

The two tank commanders jumped up into their turrets and started their engines. Both roared into life simultaneously and as soon as I waved my hand, Berger drove his tank up Rue Chateauneuf la Foret. Meanwhile, I waved Muelradt on ahead. The tank crept up Rue de L'Eglise with me at its side with my pistol as my only weapon. Muelradt's tank was only half way up the short street when we heard Berger's cannon and his coaxial machine gun. Immediately, Muelradt accelerated and before I caught up, he had blasted the engine housing of a Sherman standing at the intersection. When I arrived, the tank was burning, but the crew members had not been injured. The Panther tank's cannon swung in its turret to the next Sherman. As I took stock of the situation, an American officer waved something white.

Simultaneously, Berger's tank at the front of the Sherman column swung around and faced the Americans. I quickly told Muelradt to radio Berger and tell him to hold fire. I walked out into the center of the east-west Rue de L'Eglise and looked down the column of American tanks. There were six of them not including the burning tank. The Americans were penned in and their guns were useless in their tight column disposition. It had taken only a few seconds for the commander of the American tanks to see the hopelessness of his situation. He waved what looked like a white undershirt, then stepped forward to greet his captors. I went forward to speak to him as he made hand signals, instructing the Americans to get down from their tanks.

The American lieutenant spoke rapidly in English, none of which I understood. As he did so, the crew members were assembling in the middle of the street, while I waved my pistol as menacingly as I could. The man un-holstered his Colt .45 automatic and threw it on the ground in front of him. I pointed to the side arm on the ground and instructed the Americans in German to lay down their arms. The American tankers complied. Muelradt got down from his tank to assist me in the roundup. He brandished his Schmeiser submachine gun even though he was outnumbered 60 to one. Walking up the street toward Berger's tank, he scowled at the Americans and shouted at them to form a double rank knowing full well that the Americans couldn't understand what he was saying. His attention was diverted behind him to the side utility yards next to the row of houses. He gaped at what he saw, turned and flew back to my side. He pointed to the side yards of the houses on the opposite side of the street. For the first time, we saw six other Shermans. Slowly walking away from them, were the American crew members, who, only minutes before had been enjoying their second cold meal of the day. I turned back to the American lieutenant and asked, "Is there anything else?" One of the American tankers spoke some German and interpreted. The American officer who understood German pointed over his shoulder to the side yard and said, 'Only the prisoners.'

Muelradt again dashed up the street and saw a group of German soldiers standing in a utility yard. He motioned for the German infantrymen to follow him. They approached me and stood at attention. Muelradt counted them and reported that these were twenty from the 553rd Volksgrenadier Division. I took charge of the group and ordered them to pick up the American weapons and to keep them as their own.

This was a strange situation, one that wasn't covered at Junkerschule. I considered what to do with the windfall of American tanks at a time when Germany had so few of its own. Through the American interpreter I ordered the American tank drivers to separate themselves from the other American tank crew members. The drivers stepped to the front of the American prisoners. I told them that they were going to drive their tanks to Offendorf. As motivation I would place a German soldier armed with a pistol behind each driver. The former German prisoners, now in charge of their former captors, volunteered to a man for the opportunity to ride in a Sherman. Berger selected the youngest and most eager of the group. The reluctant American drivers and their eager German escorts hopped up onto the high-sided tanks and disappeared down the turret hatches. The tanks in the street started their engines first. I made sure that all twelve of the captured tanks were ready. I then walked to the other side of the street and signaled Muelradt who yelled that the side yard tanks were ready. About four in the afternoon, the men of Tetsch's headquarters were startled to see all those Shermans being escorted into captivity by only two Panthers.

For this small contribution I received the German Cross in Gold and a handshake from Adolf Hitler.

of the turret. It allowed him to talk to ground personnel without having to leave the armored confines of his tank.

As a platoon or company leader, the Panther tank vehicle commander had the added responsibility of directing the tanks and crews of other vehicles in combat with a Fu 5 (radio) operated by the radio operator, located in the right front of the vehicle's hull. The 6-foot, 6.7-inch (2-m) *Stabantenne* (rod antenna) for the front hull mounted Fu 5 was located on the left side of the upper rear hull plate, just behind the turret.

Every Panther also came equipped with a set of signal flags and a flare gun when use of the radio was forbidden.

In contrast to the German medium and heavy tanks, which had their radios in the front hull, American and British tanks had their radios in the turret for easy access by the vehicle commander or loader. The Red Army T-34/76 tank had the radio in the front hull like the German medium and heavy tanks. The T-34-85 tank had the radios moved to the turret.

VEHICLE COMMANDER'S POSITION

The vehicle commander's station for the Panther tank was located toward the rear of the turret on the left side of the main gun, directly above and behind the gunner's position. He could sit on a nonadjustable padded seat fixed to the interior turret ring. Although there was no backrest for the tank commander when seated, he could lean back against the rear turret wall in reasonable comfort.

When the Panther vehicle commander wished to look out over the top of his cupola, he would stand on a small fold-down metal platform that was hinged to the left side of the spent cartridge case bin. The fold-down platform for the Panther tank commander to stand on was described in the 1947 British military document *The Motion Studies of German Tanks:*

" His alternative position is standing on a footrest which is hinged to the empty-round bin and which springs upward when not in use. The footrest has a roughed surface and is 11 inches [28 cm] long, 9 inches [23 cm] wide and 2 inches [50 mm] high. When standing on the footrest, the commander can observe with his head and shoulders outside the turret. The position is comfortable, but when the vehicle is on the move, the commander's feet are liable to slip off the plate. "

One of the seven replaceable periscopes and fasteners that were mounted in the thickly armored cast-armor cupola that appeared with the introduction of the Panther Ausf. A tank appears in this picture. A portion of the azimuth indicator ring can be seen just above the periscope. *(Michael Green)*

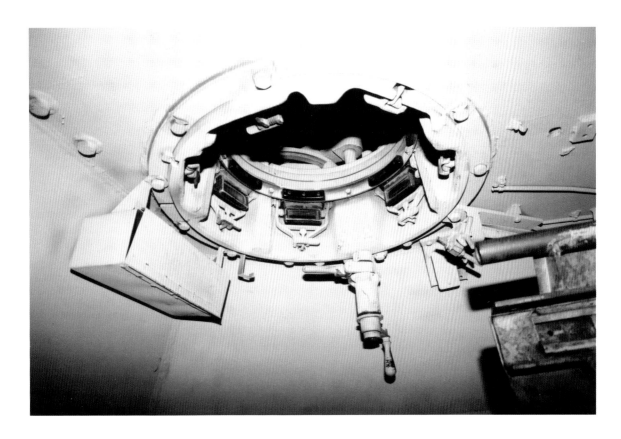

Not all Panther tanks had the small fold-down metal platform attached to the spent cartridge case bin for the vehicle commander to stand on when he wished to look out over the top of his cupola. A Panther Ausf. A tank restored by the Military Vehicle Technology Foundation never had the metal platform fitted. Instead, when the vehicle commander wished to see out over the top of his cupola, he would stand on two small metal footrests located alongside and behind the gunner's seat.

The commander's station on both first- and second-generation Sherman tanks was on the right side of the main gun. This tradition of placing the vehicle commander of American tanks on the right side of the main gun was continued after World War II all the way through the current M1 series of main battle tanks. The first postwar indigenously designed German Army tank, the Leopard 1, had the vehicle commander and gunner on the right side of the main gun. This arrangement continued with the latest version of the Leopard 2. Like the Panther tank series, the vehicle commander's station for the T-34/76 and T-34-85 tanks was located on the left side of the main gun.

From the loader's position in a Panther Ausf. G tank turret can be seen the interior portion of the tank commander's cupola. The periscope fasteners seen here are of an improved type that began appearing in July 1944. The object protruding downward from the cupola is the hand crank and lever for opening the commander's overhead armored hatch. *(Chun-Lun Hsu)*

The vehicle commander on the first- and second-generation Sherman tanks had two seats, the upper folding seat for looking out over the top of his tank's turret and the bottom folding seat for looking out of his overhead hatch periscope. The Sherman tank did not receive a proper cupola until the improved second-generation version began appearing in service in 1944. The Red Army T-34/76 tank received a cupola in early 1943, while the improved T-34-85 tank was designed with a cupola from the beginning.

VEHICLE COMMANDER'S CUPOLA

When seated, the Panther tank vehicle commander had all-around vision through the vision blocks or periscopes arranged around the interior of the cupola. A description of the original drum-style cupola installed on the Panther Ausf. D tank appears in a British wartime report based on information supplied by the Red Army:

> "The commander has a raised cupola, about 10¼ inches [28 cm] high and with a single circular hatch. The commander is provided with six horizontal vision slots around the cupola. These are closed by rotating a steel ring around the cupola. The ring is operated by a hand wheel situated directly in front of the commander."

The Motion Studies of German Tanks issued in 1947 described the new cupola that appeared with the introduction of the Panther Ausf. A tank:

> "The commander is provided with two vision devices. The first is a set of seven four-inch (102-mm) wide episcopes [periscopes] mounted in the fixed cupola in the roof above his position. An open sight is mounted on the roof in front of the center episcope. The episcopes provide all-around vision for the commander when seated; he has, therefore, no need to expose his head outside the turret. He can turn his head and observe to the rear of the vehicle while remaining seated."

TARGET ACQUISITION

The open sight mounted in front of the vehicle commander's center cupola periscope allowed him to make a rough indication to the gunner of the location of the intended target or targets.

PANTHERS IN THE CITY

In this interview with Werner Otte, Oberschuetze (Private, First Class) and gunner, 12th Waffen SS Panzer Division, conducted by Edward Monroe-Jones in September 2008, Otte recounted his memories of combat on the Panther tank:

"In July of 1944 we fought the British Shermans in and around Caen [France]. Our Panther, Panzer V, was a great tank with a few weaknesses. For example, the sloping frontal armor resisted shells which bounced off us with a terrible bang. But many of the internal brackets were poorly welded and broke off the tank turret/body when we were hit. These pieces of metal flew around the interior of the tank and caused injuries. We swore at the welders and when the tank went in for repair we took torch in hand and put them in proper order.

We had a 75-mm '*ueber lang*' main cannon. It was a reliable gun with huge muzzle velocity, but was difficult to keep clean. After each engagement we had to find a hiding place for our tank, then depress the gun, remove the tools and work from the exterior of the tank until the tank commander was satisfied that the barrel was clean. After each swipe he inspected the rag and shook his head until finally the rag was as clean coming out as it had been going in.

The Maybach engine was very reliable. We pampered our engine with frequent lubricating oil changes and bathed the air cleaner filter every chance we had. When other crews rested, our engine deck cover was up and we were leaning into the engine compartment. The engine and drive train gave us good service even in the most difficult of conditions.

Parts were a problem. As repairs were made the new parts were for more advanced Panzer Vs. They did not always fit and the repair technicians had to modify the new parts to fit our Panther.

Shermans were very fast, much faster than our tank and they had the luxury of rubber padded tracks. This made them quiet in the streets of Caen. Our tracks were wider which meant we had to be more careful when maneuvering in the tight spaces of the city. Rubble-filled streets are not conducive to tank warfare, especially the Panther. Most of the time we found a wall or half-destroyed building in which to conceal our tank. When the Shermans came they did so in column, coming toward us in narrow streets. We thought the crews must be poorly trained and inexperienced. When several Shermans appeared, our tank commander simply pointed to the last tank in column for our first shot. I responded, '*Ziel erkannt!*' (Target identified). Then the tank commander called out, '*Feur frei!*' (Fire at will) and I squeezed the trigger. Then I swung the barrel to the lead tank and did the same. We were always amazed that the British never seemed to catch on to this simple ploy. With the trailing tank and lead tank destroyed it was easy to pick off the rest. Sometimes we waited while the crews in the trapped tanks abandoned the scene.

It isn't the quality of the tank that is most important in a tank battle. It's the quality of training of the crew. Good crews can make up for inferior weapons. We were a good crew, but in the end we had to abandon our tank for lack of fuel. I was lucky to be captured shortly after that."

Another method by which the vehicle commander on the Panther Ausf. D and early production Ausf. A tanks could (up until March 1944) indicate to his gunner the direction to a target was by way of an azimuth indicator ring around the interior upper circumference of his cupola. It had gradations labeled 1–12 to indicate the position of the turret relative to the hull. A description of

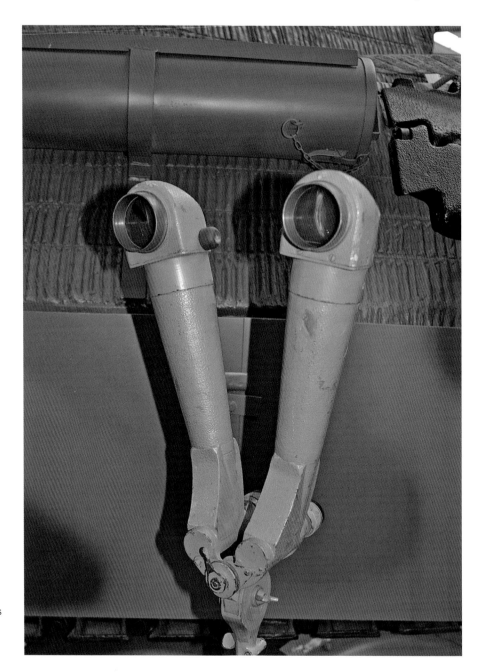

To improve their ability to determine the range to targets and to observe fire, Panther tank commanders could use an S.F.14Z Gi scissor telescope. An example of that sighting device is shown here. Neither Red Army nor U.S. Army tank commanders had access to such an optical device. *(David Marian)*

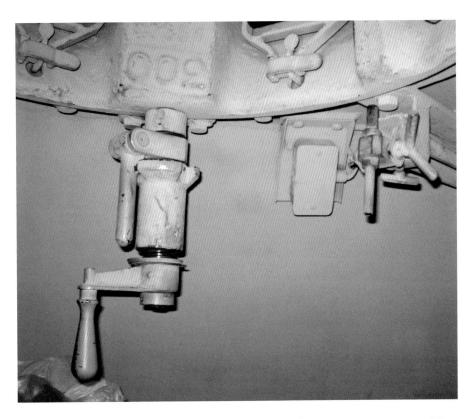

On the upper right-hand side of this picture can be seen the pivoting bracket for mounting an S.F.14Z Gi scissor telescope (not fitted here) in a Panther Ausf. G tank. The other handle is for opening or closing the cupola overhead hatch. German tank commanders tended to fight with their heads out above the level of the cupola for better situational awareness. (Chun-Lun Hsu)

how this system worked in conjunction with the gunner's turret position indicator appears in *PzKpfw V Panther*, written by Bryan Perrett:

❝The gunner was also equipped with a two-dial turret position indicator, driven by a pinion from the turret rack and located on his left. The left-hand dial was divided 1–12 with 64 subdivisions each of 100 mils, the right-hand dial being divided into mils with 100 subdivisions. The indicator did have a use during semi-indirect shooting, but had originally been intended for use in conjunction with a 1–12 clock scale recorded around the inside of the commander's cupola on a toothed annular ring. This scale worked on the counter-rotation principle. When the turret was traversed a pinion which also engaged the teeth of the turret rack [ring] drove the scale in the opposite direction but at the same speed, so that the figure 12 remained in constant alignment with the hull's centre line, looking directly forward. This enabled the commander to determine the bearing of his next target and inform the gunner accordingly. The gunner would then traverse onto the bearing ordered, using his turret position indicator, and find the gun approximately 'on' for line. Such a device was essential on the earliest models of the Panther [Ausf. D], in which the commander was forced to peer through the direct-vision blocks of the

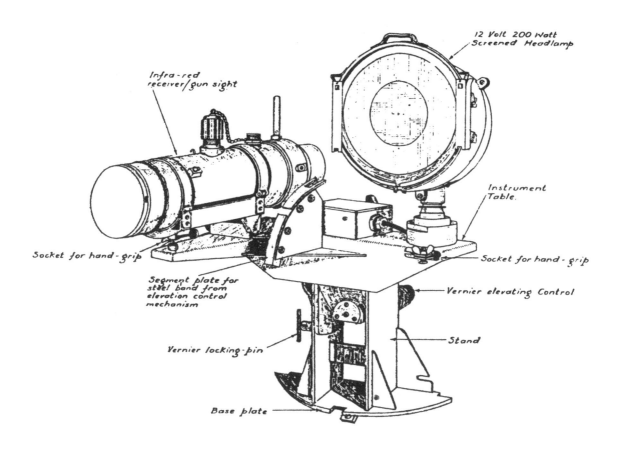

Infra-red
receiver/gun sight

12 Volt 200 Watt
Screened Headlamp

Instrument
Table.

Socket for hand-grip

Socket for hand-grip

Segment plate for
steel band from
elevation control
mechanism

Vernier elevating Control

Vernier locking-pin

Stand

Base plate

A line illustration from a World War II British Army report shows the mounting arrangement on the tank commander's cupola of a Panther Ausf. G tank for an infrared searchlight and scope that the German military designated as the FG 1250. The battery and generator for the device was located in the right rear of the tank's fighting compartment. *(Tank Museum, Bovington)*

rudimentary cupola. However, with the arrival of improved cupolas [with the introduction of the Panther Ausf. A] containing episcopes [periscopes] his head was naturally lower and he had a direct view of the turret position indicator, thus removing the necessity for the cupola clock scale. "

A simplified single dial turret position indicator for the gunner appeared on the Panther Ausf. A in September 1944.

The second generation of Sherman tanks provided the vehicle commander with a lever that allowed him to override the gunner's power turret traverse system and move the turret under power to the direction that he desired. This was a feature the Germans considered adding to the never-fielded Panther Ausf. F tank. Modern American tanks, such as the M1A2 and M1A2 SEP Abrams tanks, provide the vehicle commander the opportunity both to power traverse the turret in his direction of choice and to fire the main gun from his position.

VEHICLE COMMANDER'S OPTICS

To improve their view of the battlefield while turret-down, Panther tank vehicle commanders sometimes had access to the T.S.R.1 *Sehstab*, a tall thin periscope, roughly 5 feet (1.5 m) long, mounted in an adjustable socket inside the cupola. American soldiers who examined captured examples concluded that its purpose was to allow observation of fire by the tank commander without having his view obscured by the effects of muzzle blast and to improve vision from concealed positions.

There was also a pivoting bracket attached directly under the vehicle commander's cupola on Panther Ausf. A and Ausf. G tanks that permitted the mounting of a scissor-type telescope designated the S.F.14Z Gi. A British wartime military report described their impression of it, as it was found on not just the Panther, but the Tiger Ausf. E and Tiger Ausf. B heavy tanks:

> "An adjustable mounting is incorporated in the tanks to hold a scissors telescope. This instrument is fitted primarily for observation of fire. The S.T.T. [School of Tank Technology] report on Tiger states the telescope gives the commander an excellent means of aligning the gun into a target the gunner cannot see.
>
> The existing instrument is removable. When fitted, it restricts access to the turret since it projects through the cupola. Although not bulky, it is inconveniently situated and the mounting appears crudely designed. The telescope has the undoubted advantage, however, of allowing the commander to observe fall of shot accurately without exposing his head outside the turret."

INFRARED-EQUIPPED PANTHERS

Beginning with Panther Ausf. A tanks built from April 3, 1944, the vehicle commander's azimuth indicator ring was deleted from production vehicles by order of Wa Pruef 6. Eight days later they rescinded the order and told the factories to reintroduce it on production vehicles for the mounting of a special device, which later turned out to be an infrared searchlight and imaging converter designated as the FG 1250.

As events transpired, the FG 1250 originally considered for fitting on the Panther Ausf. A tank ended up mounted in very small numbers of Panther Ausf. G tanks beginning in late 1944 for training purposes.

The external components of the FG 1250 were mounted on a metal bracket that attached to the inner lip of the vehicle commander's cupola and were slaved to the main gun. Power for the FG 1250 came from a battery-powered electrical generator mounted inside the tank's hull in place of some main gun rounds.

The FG 1250 had a range of 656 yards (600 m) on a clear night. The intention was that the infrared-equipped Panther tanks would work with a halftrack equipped with a much larger and more powerful infrared searchlight to improve ability to spot potential targets at longer ranges.

While there were some minor actions involving infrared-equipped Panther tanks during the last few weeks of the war in Europe, their contribution was too little and too late for the German war effort. However, the developmental work done by the Germans on mounting infrared equipment on tanks was copied by the victors in World War II and appeared in widespread service beginning in the early 1960s on both American and Soviet tanks.

PANTHER TANK GUNNER

The *Richtschuetze* (gunner) in the Panther tank sat on the left side of the turret basket on a padded seat with a backrest. His seat was below and directly in front of the vehicle commander. His main route for entering or exiting the turret was the vehicle commander's cupola.

All of the Sherman tanks had a three-man turret crew, consisting of vehicle commander, gunner, and loader. The T-34/76 tank had a two-man turret crew with the vehicle commander doubling as the loader. It was not until the introduction of the T-34-85 tank in 1944 that a loader appeared and freed the vehicle commander from that task.

A description of the gunner's position on a Panther Ausf. G tank and a conclusion appeared in the 1947 British military document titled, *The Motion Studies of German Tanks*:

    ❝The gunner's padded seat is mounted forward of the commander's on the left side of the main armament. It is roughly 1 foot 2 inches [36 cm] wide and 1 foot [30.5 cm] long and can be adjusted to heights of 1 foot 4 inches [41 cm] to 1 foot 8 inches [51 cm] in five positions. The seat has a backrest which is curved and padded and measures 1 foot 1 inch [33 cm] wide and 3 inches [8 cm] high.

OPPOSITE
The gunner's position is seen in this picture taken inside a Panther Ausf. A tank. The vertically oriented wheel on the left was for manually elevating or depressing the main gun. The horizontally oriented wheel was for traversing the main gun manually. The gunner's rubber brow pad is visible at the top of the picture. *(Michael Green)*

Conclusion: The gun arrangements in this vehicle are bad; the gun controls are badly positioned relative to the gunner's seat, the power traverse and elevating controls are unsatisfactory to use, and the vision range afforded is inadequate. "

The Panther tank gunner was the second most important man in the vehicle. His ability to work with the vehicle commander in acquiring and engaging enemy targets and accurately estimating the range to a target or targets often made the difference between success and failure on the battlefield for the tank and crew.

The vehicle commander typically was entrusted with the decision to open fire on a target or targets, since he usually saw them first from his higher position. He also made the initial range estimation. The gunner on German tanks had the authority to open fire on the enemy when he spotted a target or targets before the vehicle commander. On such occasions, the gunner estimated target range by using the range scale in his optical sight.

By rotating the range scale ring, located within the Panther gunner's sight, the gunner could lower or raise the aiming point in the sight and thus integrate the range-induced super-elevation with the target's terrain elevation.

Super-elevation refers to raising the main gun barrel of a tank to a firing angle higher than the direct line of sight to the target. Super-elevation compensates for the effects of gravity, which are ballistically predictable. The amount of super-elevation needed for a hit depends on the muzzle velocity and ballistic coefficient of the projectile, where the higher the muzzle velocity, the less need for super-elevation.

When the vehicle commander was not present, the gunner would take command of the tank. The gunner typically was considered a vehicle commander in training.

Lacking a stabilization system in either elevation or traverse meant the Panther tank had to come to a complete halt to accurately fire its main gun. However, the machine guns could be fired on the move for suppressing enemy infantry or antitank gun crews.

GUNNER'S OPTICS

In the original Ausf. D version of the Panther tank and the early production units of the Panther Ausf. A tank, the vehicle's gunner aimed the main gun with a telescopic articulated 2.5-power, two-lens binocular gun sight designated the *Turmzielfernrohr* 12 (T.Z.F. 12). Each lens featured a different sight reticle that contained seven small triangles that allowed the gunner to aim his weapon without obstructing the view of the chosen target. The height of the triangles in relationship to a target being viewed, and the distances between the triangles aided the Panther tank gunner in determining the range to a target. The triangles also could be used to determine the lead for a moving target. Around the circumference of each lens was a graduated range scale.

In late November 1943 and early December 1943, a new single-lens, articulated sighting telescopic sight with dual magnification, either 2.5-power with a 28-degree field of view or 5-power with a 14-degree field of view, began appearing on the Panther Ausf. A tank production line. The new single lens sight was designated the Turmzielfernrohr 12a (T.Z.F. 12a). It and the earlier two-lens binocular sight were produced by the German firm of Leitz.

The big advantage with articulated sighting telescopes was that the gunner did not have to move his head with the elevation or depression of the tank's main gun as his eyepiece would remain stationary.

The small external openings for the original two-lens Panther tank binocular sight were located on the left-hand side of the Panther tank gun shield. The single large external opening on the right-hand side of the Panther tank gun shield was for the coaxial machine gun. With the introduction of the new single-lens sight for the Panther tank gunner, an armored plug was welded into one of the two external openings on the left-hand side of the gun shield until such time as the foundries making the vehicle's gun shields could produce a new gun shield that did away with the now redundant second opening.

A U.S. Army report dated September 25, 1944, detailed the weight of the single lens sight as 47 lbs (21 kg) and the overall length as 45 inches (1.14 m). The same report described the mounting for the gunner's sight:

> The telescope is retained in a bracket that in turn is fastened to a shelf on the gun shield. The sight is immediately to the left of the weapon. A rod suspended from the top of the turret holds the main tube stationary in relation to the hull. The objective end of the telescope moves through vertical angles in unison with the weapon.

In *Armoured Firepower: The Development of Tank Armament 1939–1945*, Peter Gudgin described the merits of the German gunner's sights:

> The German telescopic sights are worthy of special attention, both for their greater convenience to the gunner, their reduction of vulnerability … and the sheer

This close-up picture shows the gunner's tilting foot pedals on a Panther Ausf. A tank used to hydraulically traverse the tank's turret. This was the same arrangement as found in the Tiger Ausf. E heavy tank. To the left of the two tilting foot pedals is a small red foot pedal used by the gunner to fire the tanks' coaxial machine gun. *(Michael Green)*

quality of their design and manufacture, as befitted a country with what was then the most advanced optical industry in the world. 🎝

The following description from a German prisoner of war in regard to the gunner's optical sight on the Panther tank appeared in a May 1944 Allied intelligence publication:

❝Panther personnel … are trained to engage a Sherman tank without hesitation at a range of from 2,000 to 2,200 yards [1.8 to 2 km]. They are taught that while the preferable range of 800 to 900 yards [731 to 823 m] will improve accuracy, it will not add greatly to the punch. The gun has an optical sight with three graduations: one for high-explosive shells, one for armor-piercing shells, and the third for the coaxially mounted machine gun. Each graduation has its own range subdivision. 🎝

A U.S. Army report dated September 25, 1944, provided a summary of the American military opinion on the gunner's sight in the Panther:

> "The telescope is well built but as in other models of German articulating telescopes, it appears to be over-complicated in design. Any damage to the front of the telescope would require the replacement and subsequent collimation of the entire sight to keep the dead time of the vehicle to a minimum."

In *T34 in Action*, authors Artem Drabkin and Oleg Sheremet described Russian tankers' opinion of German tank sights:

> "All the tank-men interviewed admired the gun-sights of German tanks. V. P. Bryukhov's recollections are typical: 'We always noted the high quality of the Zeiss gun-sight optics. They maintained that high quality till the end of the war. We had nothing like that. The gun-sights themselves were more convenient than ours. We had a triangle in the crosshairs and hairlines left and right. They had corrections for wind, distance, and so on."

Taken inside a Panther Ausf. G tank is this close-up photograph of the gunner's foot pedals employed for hydraulically traversing the tank's turret. This foot pedal arrangement is much simpler than the tilting foot pedal arrangement found in the Panther Ausf. A tank. *(Chun-Lun Hsu)*

A postwar French Army report on the various features of the Panther, translated in *Panther and Its Variants* by Walter J. Spielberger, had this to say about the gunner's target engagement time with his optical sight:

> " Once the commander has located a target, it takes between 20 to 30 seconds until the gunner can open fire. This data, which is significantly greater than the Sherman, stems from the absence of a periscope [sight] for the gunner. "

The Red Army T-34/76 tank had a 2.5-power straight tube sighting telescope, which had the advantage of being mounted rigidly alongside the main gun and thereby avoiding the linkage found with articulated sighting telescopes that might introduce a degree of error between the gun and the sight. The big disadvantage for straight tube sighting telescopes is the need for the tank's gunner to move his head up and down to match the elevation and depression of the vehicle's main gun. There also was a chance in battle that a fragment might enter through the exterior hole in the tank's gun-shield and pass down the sighting telescope into the gunner's eye.

In contrast to the German Panther tank with its articulated sighting telescope and the Russian T-34/76 tank with its straight tube sighting telescope, the earliest production units of the Sherman tanks had only a 1.44-power periscope gun sight. Dissatisfaction with the periscope gun sight led the U.S. Army to eventually mount 3-power straight tube sighting telescopes in their Sherman tanks by July 1943 providing the gunner with two options for acquiring targets. The Red Army adopted an articulated sighting telescope for the T-34-85 tank. In comparison to the relatively low power optical sights of World War II tanks, the U.S. Army's current M1A2 SEP Abrams main battle tank has a thermal imaging sight (TIS) that offers the vehicle's gunner and vehicle commander the option of a variety of power settings, which range from 3-power to 50-power.

An important factor to mention is that a tank without a well-trained crew does not function to its full potential. The late Colonel William Hamberg, of the U.S. Army 5th Armored Division, remembered on more than a few occasions during World War II that he became acutely aware of just how much the training of some German gunners had deteriorated as they were missing shots that should have been easy kills for more experienced personnel. Colonel Hamberg was witnessing just the tip of the iceberg as training standards in the German tank troops continued to deteriorate during the last year of the war in Europe.

WEAPON OF LAST RESORT

With all the other weapons in the Panther having failed, there was a weapon of last resort not often talked about in history books, but described by German tanker Bernhard Westerhoff to Edward Monroe-Jones during an interview. Westerhoff was a member of the 10th Waffen SS Panzer Division Frundsberg retreating from the Falaise pocket at the end of August 1944. His goal was to cross the Sein River about 12 miles to the south of the French city of Rouen:

"Wilfreid Ohse tugged at my sleeve as we were trudging along with the rest of the exhausted soldiers. He pointed to a wooded area on our left and said he saw a Panther tank behind some trees. I looked and confirmed that it was a Panther. Since we were both tankers it seemed strange to see a tank which from the distance looked undamaged. Ohse insisted we go look at the tank. I was not inclined to waste energy on a fruitless inspection of a Panther, but Ohse pulled me along.

We circled the tank and the tracks appeared to be intact. We climbed in with Ohse taking the driver's seat and I taking the loader's position. He shouted that the fuel was half full. It took us about 20 minutes to acquaint ourselves with the machine, since we were Panzer IV men. Soon I heard the Maybach roar to life and I realized that it would be much better to ride to freedom rather than walk. I shouted for Ohse to bring the tank into the column of marching men. He swung the tank into the line and many crowded onto its deck. With my chest about the hatch rim I encouraged the men clinging to the engine deck.

Hollering from those to the rear of the tank and from those on the engine deck alerted me to three Sherman tanks that were slowly advancing on the column from our right. The Shermans were between us and the river. That meant the Americans were trying to outflank our retreat. I waved for the riders to jump down. They obeyed and I yelled for Ohse to turn right and engage the enemy. I was performing the duties of the tank commander, gunner, and loader as I trained on the turret on the lead Sherman. The ammunition bin was empty. Now I knew why the Panther had been abandoned. I shouted for Ohse to gun the engine and push the Panther at top speed toward the Shermans. Actually, I hadn't an attack plan at all. I simply was furious at the Americans for having so much of everything while we had so little. In my jealous rage I determined to ram the Sherman. At least we could do some damage.

As our puny attack gained speed I kept the cannon barrel on the lead Sherman. Suddenly, the three American tanks reversed gears and retreated into the wood behind them. I was surprised that my bluff had produced panic in the Shermans, but was delighted at the outcome. We slowed, turned and again approached the column of marching men.

After two hours of slowly grinding northeast I could see ahead a bottleneck of men crossing a bridge. An officer yelled for me to drive the tank into the river, but a journalist with our division wanted a photo of the tank.

The officer said that the bridge could not hold the weight of a tank and that it was more important to save the men. I climbed down and Ohse set the tank in low gear, released the clutch and he too jumped to the ground. We watched our Panther bury itself in water and mud. We again joined the others in our march to Maastricht.

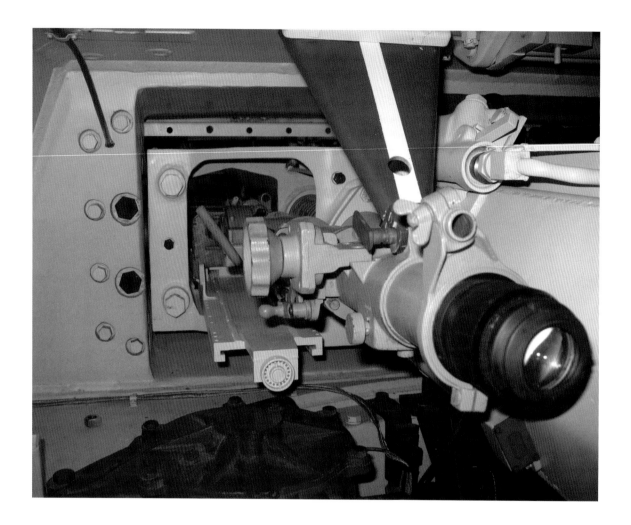

A *Turmzielfernrohr* 12a single lens, articulated telescopic sight is seen here mounted in a Panther Ausf. A tank. It had dual magnification: 2.5-power and 5-power. The low-power magnification provided a wide field of vision while searching for targets. The high-power magnification had a much narrower field of view and was used for engaging targets at longer ranges. The gunner's rubber brow pad is missing in this picture. *(Michael Green)*

PROPOSED PANTHER TANK OPTICS

To improve the accuracy of the 75-mm main gun that was to be mounted in the never-fielded Panther Ausf. F tank, the Germans planned on installing two new optical devices in the vehicle's redesigned turret. The first would have been a periscope gun sight with stabilized optics for the gunner that would have protruded through the roof of the Panther Ausf. F tank turret just in front of the shortened vehicle commander's cupola. Protection for the exterior optical head of the periscope sight would have been provided by an armored hood. This new periscope gun sight would have been installed as a backup system to a standard telescopic articulated gun sight on the vehicle.

The second optical device the Germans wanted to install in the turret of the Panther Ausf. F tank was a 15-power stereoscopic optical rangefinder with a four-degree field of view, for use by the gunner. With a baseline length of 4.3 feet (1.31 m) the stereoscopic rangefinder would fit across the width of the forward portion of the Panther Ausf. F tank turret with the protruding ends protected by rounded armored hoods.

The U.S. Army had installed stereoscopic optical rangefinders in its postwar M47 Patton medium tank and early versions of the M48 Patton medium tank series. However, the army found that too few crewmen possessed the ability to use such a device and instead went on to use coincidence rangefinders, beginning with a later model of the M48 medium tank series. This continued through the M60A1 main battle tank. The M60A3 main battle tank and the various versions of the M1 Abrams tank series use a laser rangefinder as their primary method of obtaining range to a target.

This close-up picture of the coaxial MG34T machine gun, mounted in the turret of a Panther Ausf. A tank, shows the overhead feed path for the 7.92-mm rounds from the canvas ammunition bag positioned on the right-hand side of the weapon. The spent cartridge cases dropped into a metal box directly below the machine gun. (David Marian)

FIRING THE MAIN GUN

To fire the Panther's main gun, the gunner pulled a steel lever pivoted to his manually operated elevation hand wheel (located to his left), which fired the weapon electrically. American, British, and Russian tanks employed a much cruder mechanical system. In both the Sherman tanks and the T-34 tank series, the main gun was fired with a foot switch.

Like all tanks, the Panther tank had an emergency firing device for the main gun. On the Panther tank, it was located on the floor below the front edge of the gunner's seat. A British Army report described it as the standard German push-button generator type, which was protected by a hinged strip of steel frame that prevented accidental operation.

In an article that appeared in the January–February 1993 issue of *Armor* magazine titled "Tank Gun Accuracy," Major Bruce J. Held and Master Sergeant Edward S. Sunoski described the powerful forces that impact a tank's main gun and a projectile upon firing:

> "Cannon systems are not completely rigid. Unleashing the energy that propels the projectile can also cause the cannon to move about its trunnions, recoil along its longitudinal axis, shake in its recoil mechanism, and bend and vibrate in all directions. This all starts to happen before the round exits the muzzle, so that by the time it does, the muzzle is not pointed in the same direction as when the trigger was pulled."

The authors of the article also examined the forces that affect a projectile once it leaves the muzzle end of a gun:

> "Finally, once a projectile enters free flight, it is subject to aerodynamic forces. These forces can alter the projectile's line of flight even further from the one originally intended. This is known as aerodynamic jump. A projectile's aerodynamic characteristics depend on its shape and its pitching/yawing motion. Pitching describes the up and down rotation of the projectile and yawing is the side rotation."

Because the Panther Ausf. D through Ausf. G tanks lacked any kind of stabilization system for the main gun, the vehicle had to come to a complete stop before the gunner could successfully engage a target. There was some thought by the Germans of developing a stabilized gun system for the Panther Ausf. F tank, but nothing ever came of it.

The only tanks with stabilized main guns during World War II were American. However, their main guns were stabilized in elevation only. Modern tanks like the American M1 Abrams series have two-axis gun and sight stabilization systems that dynamically compensate for elevation and traverse while the vehicle is moving.

TURNING THE PANTHER TANK TURRET

The 10-ton (9-mt) turret on all the various versions of the Panther tank was rotated on a circular ball bearing race either manually or with a power traversing system. A turret ring, located in the hull roof of a tank, is the circular opening in which the turret bearing fits. The size of the tank's main gun and its ammunition dictate the minimum diameter of a tank's turret ring since it must be of sufficient size to allow the gun to recoil and the crew to elevate and depress the main gun while still being able to load it.

The Panther Ausf. D tank came with a single-speed, power turret traverse system, which was operated by the gunner with a vertical lever to the right of his seat.

The Germans took the same two-speed hydraulic-power turret traverse system from the Tiger Ausf. E heavy tank and placed it in the Panther Ausf. A. A description of how the system worked comes from a passage describing various features of the Tiger Ausf. E heavy tank in a 1947 British Army document titled, *The Motion Studies of German Tanks*:

> " … The [gunner's] hydraulic power traverse system is controlled by a rocking footplate on the floor in front of the gunner's seat. The footplate is pivoted along the transverse axis. In the neutral position, the plate is tilted lower at the front than the back. On left traverse, the heel end of the plate is depressed until the plate is horizontal. On right traverse, the toe end of the plate is depressed to an angle of 24 degrees from the horizontal. "

The Ausf. G versions of the Panther came with a different two-speed hydraulic-power turret traverse system, as described in the same British military document:

> " The power traverse is hydraulically driven from the [engine] propeller shaft through the two-speed gearbox situated below the gun and on the right of the gunner's seat.

The opening for the coaxial MG34T machine gun can be seen here on the right side of this Panther Ausf. G tank's gun shield. Also visible in this picture is the sheet metal debris guard over the gap behind the gun shield. This feature began appearing on the Panther Ausf. G tank in August 1944. Arrayed around the top of the turret roof are three *Pilze* (sockets) for mounting a *Kran* (jib boom). *(Andreas Kirchhoff)*

Speed and direction of traverse are controlled by two foot pedals, each 3 inches by 4 inches [8 by 11 cm] on the turret floor in front of the gunner. … When the left or right pedal is depressed, the turret traverses left or right correspondingly. A linkage is fitted to ensure that the pedal plates remain horizontal, as they are depressed … In the vehicle inspected, the pedal movement [was] stiff to operate. Considerable foot pressure was required to overcome the inertia, and it was very difficult to start and check the traverse smoothly and at the right moment. "

In addition to the foot pedals for traverse, both the Panther Ausf. A and Ausf. G tanks featured a backup hand-operated lever to the right of the gunner's seat that he also could use to turn the vehicle turret if the need arose.

Due to the amount of inertia within the hydraulic turret traverse system, the Panther's tank gunner took final aim on his chosen target with the tank's manual turret traverse system, which consisted of a 10-inch (25-cm) diameter,

Seen in this picture is the *Kugelblende* (ball mount) on a Panther Ausf. A tank's glacis plate equipped with a 7.92-mm MG34T machine gun. It is surrounded by a spherical armored guard. This feature began appearing on production Panther Ausf. A tanks in late 1943. *(Michael Green)*

almost horizontal wheel directly in front of the gunner's seat. On the underside of the wheel was a 3-inch (76.2-mm) long handle that the gunner rotated to turn the turret. British Army tests on Panther tanks showed the manual turret traverse system required little effort but was very slow. There was also an auxiliary hand traverse lever by the loader's position in the Panther tank.

Unlike the German use of foot pedals for the power traverse of most of their tank turrets, the British and Americans used spade grips operated by the gunner's hands to power traverse their tank turrets. Although the British military test personnel felt the German design had the advantage of not hindering the gunner's body and of freeing the hands for other work, they believed the foot pedals had a number of disadvantages, which were listed in a 1947 British Army document titled *The Motion Studies of German Tanks*:

> ■ The locations of the turret traverse foot pedals in the Panther [Ausf. G] and Tiger tanks were badly positioned relative to the gunner's seats, and therefore were awkward to use.
>
> ■ The linkages from the pedals to the power traverse gearbox were too elaborate and needed regular lubrication. A lack of maintenance would make operation of the controls stiff and therefore inaccurate.

- The controls were likely to be inadvertently operated.
- The foot pedals were exposed to damage and mud.
- The gunner could take his feet off the pedals yet the turret still continued to rotate.
- The foot pedal mechanisms were incapable of 'fine' switches. "

On the Panther Ausf. D tank, the maximum turret traverse rate in power mode was 360 degrees in sixty seconds. On the Panther Ausf. A tank, the turret traverse rate was pushed up to 360 degrees in fifteen seconds — four times as fast. However, starting in November 1943, the factories began governing Panther engines at a lower maximum rpm, decreasing the maximum turret traverse rate to 360 degrees in eighteen seconds.

The power-operated turret traverse speed on all versions of the Sherman tank, except the 105-mm howitzer-equipped version (which lacked a power-operated turret traverse mechanism), was fifteen seconds to rotate the turret 360 degrees. The Red Army T-34 tank series could rotate their turrets 360 degrees in twelve seconds.

Although some American tankers assumed that the slower power traverse of the Panther tanks was a tactical disadvantage, a World War II document dated March 27, 1945, titled *U.S. Army Report on United States vs German Army* provided an opinion of an M36 tank destroyer (TD) crew, which gave a different perspective:

"Members of Company A state that, although the Mark V [Panther] tank has a much slower traverse than the M36 [which could rotate its turret 360 degrees in 15 seconds], it has never been their experience that it was not sufficiently fast enough to track any of our tanks, other than the M4 traveling at a very high speed. "

While the British and Russians generally preferred electrically powered turret traverse systems for their tanks, the Americans generally went for an electro-hydraulic turret traverse system on their tanks. When not enough electro-hydraulic turret traverse units were available, the American military used an electrical power traversing system.

An electro-hydraulic system energizes a hydraulic system by an electrically driven pump, rather than being shaft-driven. This meant that power traverse was available when the tank's engine was not running. When the Panther tank engine was not running, there was no power traverse on the vehicle, and the crew had to turn the turret manually.

Every Panther tank crewman was issued with a 9-mm semiautomatic pistol and holster to wear on his service belt. This picture shows the two types of semiautomatic pistols carried: the more common *Pistole, Modell* 38 (Walther) on the lower left and the well-known *Pistole, Parabellum, Modell* 1908 (P08), better known to most as the "Luger," on the upper right of the picture. *(Martin Morgan)*

SECONDARY WEAPONS

The Panther tank gun mount also provided a platform for setting the gunner's sighting telescope on the left side and a modified air-cooled 7.92-mm coaxial (or coax) machine gun, designated the MG34T, which had a different barrel sheath than the standard production model, on the right. The standard production model of the MG34 was introduced into German Army service in 1937 and had a rate of fire of between 800 to 900 rounds per minute.

The coaxial machine gun on all tanks is intended to be used against targets that do not warrant a main gun round, such as unarmored wheeled vehicles and unprotected infantry. The Panther loader was responsible for the loading and servicing of the coaxial MG34T.

At least one *Maschinenpistole* (MP) 38 or 40 was normally carried in the turret of every Panther tank. The weapon shown is an MP40 and like its earlier predecessor, the MP38, fired 9-mm rounds from a thirty-two-round box magazine. Weighing 8.82 lbs (4 kg), the weapon in theory could fire 550 rounds per minute. *(Martin Morgan)*

Taken inside a Panther Ausf. A tank is the radioman's view of his glacis plate mounted 7.92-mm MG34T machine gun. The sight is just to the left of the machine gun. The object that looks like a lamp shape was intended to fit over the radioman's head to help him steady the machine gun when fired. (Michael Green)

Beginning in late November and early December 1943, new production Panther Ausf. A tanks came off the assembly line with a *Kugelbende* (ball mount) for the fitting of a MG34T machine gun to be fired by the tank's radioman. The armored ball mount in the glacis plate of the Panther Ausf. A and the Panther Ausf. G tanks was surrounded by a spherical armored guard. Aiming of the machine gun by the Panther tank radioman was done with the coaxial mounting of a K.Z.F.2 telescopic sight on the left side of the weapon's breech. The Panther tank radioman was responsible for both the loading and servicing of the glacis plate mounted MG34T.

There also were provisions to mount a standard MG34 on top of the commander's cupola of the Panther, beginning with the Panther Ausf. D tank in August 1943. On the Ausf. A and G versions of the Panther tank, the mount to which the machine gun was affixed weighed 42 lbs (19.1 kg) and could be moved along a steel rail which encircled about three quarters of the vehicle commander's cupola. Some room was needed to open the

There was a slight change to the spherical armored guard that protected the *Kugelblende* (ball mount) on a Panther Ausf. G tank's glacis plate. There appeared to be a stepped embrasure intended to reduce the amount of bullet splash entering the ball mount. *(Martin Morgan)*

commander's overhead pivoting hatch. In March 1945, with the Panther Ausf. G tank, the steel ring around the cupola was replaced with a metal post to which the mount was attached.

Other weapons found inside the typical Panther tank would include a *Maschinenpistole* (machine pistol) 38 or 40. This 9-mm submachine gun was fed from a thirty-two-round box magazine and weighed 9 lbs (4 kg).

The *Nahverteidigungswaffe* (close defense weapon) projector was mounted in the roof of the Panther tank turret and operated by the loader. It was a breech-loaded device that traversed 360 degrees and could fire smoke grenades or an antipersonnel high-explosive (HE) grenade. Firing instruction would had to have come from the tank commander. *(Christopher Hughes)*

A bracket for this weapon was mounted inside the Panther tank turret. Hand grenades for protection from enemy infantry might also be found on a typical Panther tank.

Every crewman on the Panther tank was issued a pistol for self-defense, which he wore in a holster attached to his service belt. Two different types of semiautomatic pistols were issued to tank crews: the *Pistole, Parabellum*, Modell 1908, better known to most as the Luger, and the other more commonly issued pistol being the Pistole, Modell 38, generally referred to as the Walther P38. Both pistols came with eight-round detachable box magazines.

Beginning in December 1943, the pistol ports in all new Panther Ausf. A tank turrets coming off the productions line were done away with in anticipation of the mounting of a device known as the *Nahverteidigungswaffe* (close defense weapon). This breech-loaded projector was mounted in the turret roof of the Panther tank, over the loader's position. The projector's launch tube was fixed in elevation at 50 degrees and could be rotated 360 degrees in its mount. There was no aiming system for the device; the loader instead relied on directions from the tank commander to point the device in the general direction of the threat. The projector was able to fire either a 92-mm high-explosive antipersonnel grenade or various smoke grenades.

Production shortfalls caused a delay in the shipments of the close defense weapon to the factories building the Panther Ausf. A tank. This delay lasted until March 1944. As a result, the opening in the roof of the Panther Ausf. A turrets not fitted with the close defense weapon was covered by a steel plate secured by four bolts.

CHAPTER THREE

PROTECTION

Placing a well-armed tank into combat is all for naught if it does not have a sufficient amount of armor protection to operate on the battlefield without some measure of immunity from its expected threats. The Panther tank represented a radical departure from previous German tank protection design practices by incorporating sloped armor into its basic shape, rather than plates hung vertically. As a result, the Panther tank achieved protection levels superior in many ways to the legendary Tiger Ausf. E heavy tank, yet weighed nearly 10 tons (9 mt) less.

War, however, dramatically speeds up the gun/armor race. Hitler sensed this, and twice during the Panther tank design phase in 1942 interceded to demand that the frontal armor of the vehicle be increased. This culminated in the heavily up-armored Panther II tank design in which nearly every front and side armor plate was increased in thickness. The resultant weight increase would have overtaxed the engine (which remained the same) and dramatically cut the vehicle's mobility to less than that of the Tiger Ausf. E heavy tank. As a result of this issue and others, the Panther II tank was cancelled and elements of its design incorporated into the Panther Ausf. G tank.

SLOPED ARMOR

The most important feature in the Panther tank's design regarding protection was its use of sloped armor, which the Germans copied from the T-34/76 tank that had so impressed them. Sloped armor provides two advantages in protecting a tank. First, highly sloped armor aids in deflecting incoming AP projectiles so that they do not penetrate the vehicle. In addition, the geometry of a sloped plate is such that its thickness when measured in the horizontal plane is greater than the perpendicular thickness of the plate itself.

Postwar British military studies of sloped armor led them to conclude that the optimum slope for the glacis plate of a tank to resist penetration by APC projectiles was between 50 and 70 degrees. Against attacks by projectiles containing a subcaliber tungsten core, they found that a glacis slope of 60 degrees or more would provide optimum protection. A vertical plate defines a 0-degree slope for armor design purposes.

A British Army wartime report from the Department of Tank Design Materials Division Armour Branch dated February 11, 1944, and based on examining captured Panther Ausf. D tanks in Russian hands, clearly made the connection between the Panther's sloping armor arrangement and that found on the T-34/76 tank and even that of the Sherman tank:

> " ... the design of the nose is perhaps the most marked innovation. Instead of the usual construction of driver's front plate at nearly vertical, glacis plate at nearly horizontal and upper and lower nose plates [Panzer III and IV medium tanks and the Tiger Ausf. E heavy tank] the first three plates are replaced by one long sloping plate of 85-mm thickness at an angle of 57 degrees, making a V-shaped front with the lower nose plate, which is 75-mm thickness at 53 degrees. The appearance is very that of the nose of the T-34, and may also show the influence of the American Sherman. The sloping front plate is also mortised to the superstructure side plates.
>
> This new design of the nose prohibits the usual German method of construction whereby hull and superstructure are fabricated as separate subunits, and accordingly in the Panther the superstructure is integral with the lower hull. "

The first generation of Sherman tanks had a 50-mm-thick glacis plate with a slope of 56 degrees. The superstructure sides were only 38 mm thick and vertical. The second-generation Sherman tanks had a 63-mm glacis plate sloped at 47 degrees, while the superstructure sides remained 38 mm thick and vertical. The glacis plate on the T-34 tank series tanks was 45 mm thick and

The rolled homogenous armor (RHA) sloping side plates of the Panther tank's superstructure and turret can be seen on this Panther Ausf. G tank belonging to the U.S. Army Ordnance Museum in Maryland. In the interest of simplifying the construction of the Panther Ausf. G tank, its superstructure side plates were placed at a less oblique angle than its predecessors. *(Christophe Vallier)*

sloped at 60 degrees, while the superstructure side plates were 40 mm thick and sloped at 40 degrees.

The same February 11, 1944, British military report also highlighted another Panther Ausf. D tank similarity to the Red Army's T-34/76 tank:

> "Another feature of the T34 which appears in the Panther is the use of sloping side plates for the superstructure. These are 45-mm thick and at an angle of 42 degrees. They overhang the track, thus giving pannier space for ammunition stowage and a wide base upon which to mount the turret ring."

The upper portion of the Panther tank hull projected outward over the suspension systems, as it did on the Sherman tank and the T-34 tank series.

In March 1943, the Germans discontinued the use of face-hardened armor (FHA) glacis plates on the Panther Ausf. D tank and switched to the use of rolled homogenous armor (RHA) glacis plates. Due to a backlog of parts, Panther Ausf. D tanks built as late as August 1943 might still have had a FHA glacis plate. The vehicle pictured is a Panther Ausf. D tank. *(Virginia Museum of Military Vehicles)*

In tank designs such as this, the upper hull is the superstructure, and the portions that overhang the road wheels and tracks are known as "sponsons" to the American military and "panniers" to the British military. The German word for superstructure is *Panzerkastenoberteil*.

TYPES OF ARMOR

During its service life, the Panther tank featured three different types of armor protection. The earliest built Panther Ausf. D tanks employed face-hardened armor (FHA) on their glacis plate as well as all armor surfaces on the front, rear, and sides. However, the practice of face-hardening the glacis plate was discontinued in March 1943. Researcher Thomas L. Jentz deduced that, based on the backlog of premanufactured FHA, the first completed Panther Ausf. D tanks without FHA glacis plates would have rolled off the assembly

A Panther Ausf. A tank, caught on a narrow French country road in Normandy, has been struck at close range by a number of projectile strikes to its glacis plate. The forward portion of the superstructure side plate, which could be either face-hardened armor (FHA) or rolled homogenous armor (RHA) after July 1944, has shattered on the vehicle here. *(Patton Museum)*

The inspiration for the sloped armor on the Panther tank came from the Red Army's T-34/76 medium tank. The Red Army was pushed to develop the T-34 series by the lessons they learned during the Spanish Civil War (1936–39) when the tanks they supplied to the Republican side proved inadequately armored. (Michael Green)

lines in August 1943. The Germans continued to employ FHA for the sides of the Panther tank until July 1944.

FHA is normal steel armor plate put through an extra heating process to harden its outer surface while retaining the toughness of the original armor plate. Although standard, blunt-nose steel AP projectiles often would shatter on impact with FHA plate, the widespread introduction of APC projectiles by the various combatants during World War II made it obsolete. A U.S. Army report issued in March 1950 and titled *The Vulnerability of Armored Vehicles to Ballistic Attack* described some of the problems when employing FHA:

> "Face-hardened armor has very limited shock resistance, due to its brittleness which is a result of high hardness. It is more difficult to manufacture face-hardened armor than [rolled] homogenous armor, since carburizing necessitates heating in a furnace for a considerable period of time. In addition, distortion often occurs during heat-treatment, and straightening of distorted plates leads to the development of cracks; other cracks may even occur for some time after finish of manufacture, due to stresses set up within the plate."

"Homogeneous" means that the material has the same characteristics throughout its thickness.

A description of the term "shock" in context of tank armor comes from the same report:

> **"** The term 'shock' refers, in general, to a sudden change in motion of a mechanical system and is concerned with the magnitude and the duration of the forces developed. A sharp blow on a steel plate will cause the plate to act like an extremely flexible membrane, and to vibrate back and forth like a drumhead. The vibration is generally composed of superimposed vibrations of several frequencies. The high frequency vibrations will generally have small displacements and high accelerations, while the lower frequencies are generally associated with the large displacements and lower accelerations. **"**

To protect the internal components and crew of the Panther tank from the effects of shock, most of the vehicle's internal fittings and small stowage items were mounted on frames made from steel strips with a 16-mm gap between the frame and hull and turret plates. The 1950 American report *The Vulnerability of Armored Vehicles to Ballistic Attack* explained that equipment mounted inside tanks subject to attack should be shock mounted to withstand tank turret/hull shock displacement as great as 1 inch and hull accelerations as high as 10,000 times the acceleration of gravity. To withstand this type of stress, the report recommended that the shock mounts should be designed to bring the attached internal equipment up to the velocity of the supporting structure slowly enough so that the acceleration would not render the equipment inoperative.

CHANGES ARE IMPLEMENTED

In place of the FHA glacis plate on Panther Ausf. D tanks built up until July 1943, the Germans eventually switched to rolled homogeneous armor (RHA) for the glacis plate of the Panther Ausf. D tank, which was built until September 1943. In July 1944, they switched to using RHA on the sides of the hull, superstructure, and turret on later models of the Panther tank. The British Army picked up on the switch from FHA to RHA on the Panther tank, as seen in this extract from a British War Office Technical Intelligence Summary No. 147 dated October 11, 1944:

Throughout the Panther tank's production run, its gun shield and commander's cupola were made of cast homogenous armor (CHA), despite the fact that CHA does not offer the same ballistic protection levels as rolled homogenous armor (RHA) plates of similar thickness. The big advantage of CHA is the ability to mold it into almost any shape. Pictured is a knocked-out Panther Ausf. A tank. *(Patton Museum)*

❝A model D tank [Panther] examined in Russia had flame hardened armour on the superstructure sides, hull sides and lower nose plate. All of the main plates of the model D, A and G tanks examined in this country were, however, machineable quality [RHA].❞

Another big advantage of RHA is that it provided superior protection when struck by AP projectiles due to its ductility, which is the property of a material that allows it to withstand large amounts of deformation before fracturing, a feature lacking in face-hardened armor. RHA also did well in protecting against the shock waves generated by large-caliber AP projectiles striking the exterior of a tank's armor, as well as the blast from HE projectiles. The big disadvantage of RHA is its inability to form easily in other than a flat state.

Throughout its service life, the Panther tank series employed cast homogenous armor (CHA) for the gun-shield and cupola. CHA was given its shape by casting and provided optimum ballistic protection properties by subsequent heat treatment. The biggest advantage of CHA was that it can be molded into almost any shape, furnishing curved surfaces of any desired thickness, hence its use in making gun shields and cupolas on the Panther tank. A disadvantage of CHA is the fact that its ballistic performance is poorer than that of RHA.

Despite the fact that CHA has poorer ballistic performance than RHA, it was extensively employed on Sherman tanks. Although all versions of the Sherman tank featured CHA turrets and were intended to have CHA hulls, a lack of foundries meant that not all hulls were constructed of CHA. Many were constructed of RHA. The Red Army T-34 tanks had CHA and RHA turrets, with hulls constructed solely of RHA.

ARMOR HARDNESS

An important factor in determining the ability of steel armor plate to resist penetration by AP projectiles is not just its thickness or its ductility, but its hardness. Steel armor plate is heat treated to make it harder. As hardness increases, there is a proportional increase in its resistance to penetration.

Pictured is an early model Panther Ausf. D tank, captured by the Red Army during the Battle of Kursk, which has a complete penetration through the left side superstructure plate. Once inside an armored vehicle, the AP projectile will ricochet within it and become a casualty producer or detonate onboard ammunition. *(Patton Museum)*

However, there is a tradeoff, because as armor hardness increases, there is a decrease in its ductility, which means that it becomes more brittle. This decrease in ductility weakens armor's resistance to penetration. To restore the ductility of steel armor plate, it is placed through an additional heating process referred to as tempering, which reduces brittleness and restores ductility. The difficult part for the armor designers is to determine the armor hardness level that provides the optimum resistance to penetration.

The hardness of tank armor typically is described by its Brinell Hardness Number (BHN). A Brinell hardness test determines the BHN and is described in a March 1950 U.S. Army report titled *Vulnerability of Armored Vehicles to Ballistic Attack* as taking a hardened steel ball of specific physical dimensions and forcing it into a sample of armor steel for thirty seconds under a 3,000-kg (6,600-lb) load. BHN is the quotient obtained by dividing the applied load, measured in kilograms, by the area of the impression, measured in square millimeters.

In his book *Technology of Tanks*, author Richard M. Ogorkiewicz described the evolution of the BHN in tanks:

The damage that can be done to armor plate can vary for numerous reasons, including the size and composition of the AP projectile compared to the armor plate struck and the striking angle and velocity of the AP projectile. Projectile strikes have gouged out the armor on the glacis plate of a Panther Ausf. A tank. (Patton Museum)

Sometimes an AP projectile will not penetrate an armor plate, but will push, or dish, the plate inward, a condition called "bulging." While cracking or cleaving of the armor plate may occur, there is no projectile penetration as is seen in this picture of a Panther tank turret struck at least three times by large-caliber rounds. *(Patton Museum)*

❝The relatively thin, 8 to 14-mm plates of steel armor used in the tanks of the First World War were heat treated to a Brinell Hardness Number (BHN) ranging from 420 to as much as 650. But, as plates became thicker and were joined by welding instead of being riveted on to an angle iron framework, armor had to be less hard. Thus, from the 1930s onwards, armor plate became generally of machineable quality steel with a hardness ranging from about 390 BHN for thin plates to 280, or even 220 BHN for very thick plates.❞

In *Panzer Tracts No. 5-1 Panzerkampfwagen "Panther" Ausfuehrung D* by authors Thomas L. Jentz and Hilary Louis Doyle, the German ordnance BHN specifications for standardized RHA and CHA are broken down by what was required for certain armor thickness categories:

❝ ▪ Armor 16-mm to 30-mm thick was to have a BHN between 309 to 353.

▪ Armor 35-mm to 50-mm thick was to have a BHN between 278 and 324.

▪ Armor 55-mm to 80-mm thick was to have a BHN between 265 and 309.

▪ Face-hardened armor was to have a BHN of 555 to a depth of 4-mm to 6-mm for armor plate 80-mm thick.❞

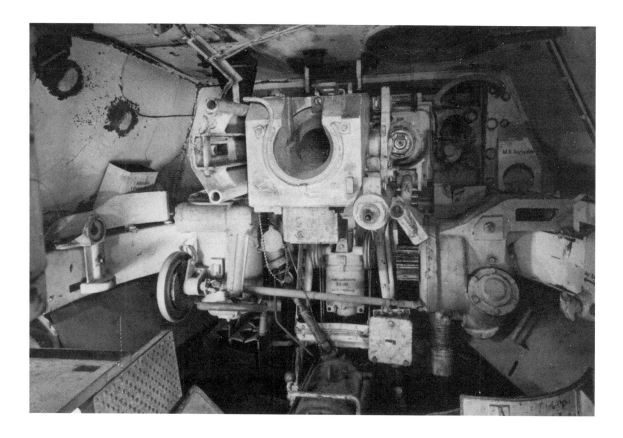

Damage from the impact of an AP projectile can cause fragments or splinters from the rear of an armor plate to break off into the interior of an armored vehicle. This is referred to as "spalling" and is particularly hazardous to personnel inside armored vehicles. Visible in this interior picture of a Panther tank turret are two large caliber projectile strikes that have caused the left side turret wall on a Panther tank to crack and also could have caused spalling to occur. *(Patton Museum)*

QUALITY CONTROL ISSUES

Some authors have concluded that as the German military-industrial complex came under increased pressure from Allied bomber raids, and in conjunction with the loss of access to certain key alloys needed to continue to manufacture armor of sufficient hardness, the quality of some of the armor plate for tanks like the Panther tank would be substandard and lack ductility.

According to the Combined Intelligence Objective Sub Committee G-2 Division, SHAEF (Rear) report discussing German armor plate dated July 17, 1945, German alloy content varied with the thickness of the steel armor plates being made. The thicker the plate, the more alloys were used. Alloys were intended to stop quench cracking (splitting of steel) during the heat treatment of thicker armor plates. Right up to the end of the war, steel armor plates 55 mm or thicker had very high alloy content. However, the Germans did reduce the alloy content in thinner steel armor plates.

The alleged loss of ductility in German steel armor plate supposedly showed up in captured Panther tanks subjected to ballistic tests conducted by the U.S. 12th Army in France, beginning on August 19, 1944, at the small French town of Isigny.

The purpose of the ballistic tests conducted at Isigny was to determine the comparative effectiveness of the main gun ammunition fired by both the second-generation Sherman tank armed with a 76-mm main gun and the British 17-pounder (76.2-mm) against the glacis plate of the Panther tank.

The trial subjects chosen for the 12th Army Group ballistic tests were three captured Panther Ausf. A tanks. After firing a variety of AP rounds against these vehicles, two reports were issued, a preliminary report on August 21, 1944, and the final report on August 30, 1944. From the final report comes this extract describing the glacis plates on the three trial Panther tanks and the effects of the projectile strikes:

> "The general characteristics of the frontal armor are: glacis plate 85-mm (3.35 inches) at 55 degrees and nose plate 65-mm (2.56 inches) at 55 degrees. Using an armor basis curve, the vertical equivalent of the glacis plate is 187-mm (7.36 inches) and of the nose plate 139-mm (5.47 inches) …. Wide variation was found in the quality plate on the three tanks. Tank No. 2 (hereafter referred to as the 'best plate') sustained 30 hits at ranges from 600 to 200 yards without cracking. Tanks No. 1 and 3 (hereafter referred to as average plate) cracked after relatively few hits. "

Armor basis is the protection afforded by a given thickness of armor at a slope, expressed in terms of the thickness of armor required to give the same protection at a zero slope.

Researcher Carey Erickson performed a detailed analysis on the original test photographs supplied with the Isigny report. He concluded that the Panther Ausf. A tank labeled as No. 1 and listed as having only average plate had in fact a face-hardened glacis plate. This can be observed by the characteristic flaking that occurs only when face-hardened armor is penetrated by an AP projectile. Erickson explains that encountering a face-hardened glacis plate on a Panther Ausf. A tank was not impossible because it could have come from leftover stocks to meet production quotas as German tank production was under greater and greater pressure to put weapons into the hands of the Panzer divisions by 1944.

Erickson also notes that it took nine hits into the hard outer surface of the face-hardened armored Panther tank labeled No. 1 to make it susceptible to penetration. Pictorial evidence also shows that the Panther tank labeled No. 3

OVERLEAF
Partial penetration is when an AP projectile does not have enough energy to penetrate through an armor plate or cause spalling to break off from the rear of the armor plate. Tankers who have survived partial penetrations comment on the shock/pressure wave that reverberates through their vehicles when struck. American military personnel look over a destroyed Panther Ausf. A tank. *(Patton Museum)*

and described as having an average plate had significant prior battle damage with extensive cracking across its glacis plate. This damage should have excluded tank No. 3 from even being part of the testing process. Erickson makes the valid point that the Panther tank labeled No. 2 with the best plate reflected the true quality of Panther glacis plates for most of World War II and not the face-hardened armored Panther tank or the battle damaged example used at Isigny.

Erickson is not the only one who believes that Panther armor remained free of serious defects for the duration of the war in Europe. Jentz and Doyle stated in their book *Germany's Tiger Tanks VK45.02 to Tiger II: Design, Production and Modifications* that "There is no proof that substandard German armor plate was used during the last years of the war. All original documents confirm compliance with standard specifications throughout the war."

Evidence for the quality of late-war German armor plate can be found in a postwar U.S. Army Aberdeen Proving Ground firing test (Project number 5044: July 16, 1945), which consisted of American 90-mm M82 AP projectiles fired at an early production Panther Ausf. D tank and at a late-war produced Panther Ausf. G tank. (late-war being the time period of supposed inferior steel). The 90-mm M82 AP rounds punched two holes through the Panther Ausf. D tank's glacis plate with significant break out due to FHA brittleness in the face of overmatching projectiles. The 90-mm M82 AP projectiles did not penetrate the glacis plate of the Panther Ausf. G tank but did achieve a penetration through the glacis plate machine gun mount. The end result being only "scoops" upon the late-war glacis plate, not an indicator of substandard late-war armored steel against an overmatching projectile.

ARMOR PLACEMENT

A good tank design is a compromise of armor protection, firepower, mobility, and reliability. However, because no single tank can ever carry enough armor to completely protect itself from all battlefield threats from all directions, a tank's armor is always heaviest on areas most likely to be hit.

World War II tank designers used common sense in deciding where to place the thickest armor, reasoning that, whenever possible, a tank would be faced toward an enemy and its turret would be pointed toward incoming fire (this minimized its cross-sectional silhouette area and also protected the suspension). A British Army report dated May 5, 1944, titled *Armour Branch Report on Armour Quality & Vulnerability of Pz.Kw.V (Panther)* summarized their opinion on the vulnerability of the Panther tank:

> **"**In the first place, it will be appreciated that a tank having the weight, firepower and speed characteristics of Panther cannot (with the existing state of the art and science of armor quality and disposition) profess all round immunity to up-to-date anti-tank weapons. Facing with this problem the German designers have followed a course which we ourselves would recommend for a tank of this description, namely, make the hull and turret front immune as far as possible against the most common anti-tank gun, and having decided from considerations of mine blast, HE attack, and structural strength, the thickness of the belly roof and rear plates, allot the remainder to the hull and turret sides. **"**

Postwar studies based on historical experience confirmed that the World War II intuitive design approach was correct, and the heaviest armor should go on a 60-degree frontal arc. This frontal arc encompasses the front of both the hull and turret of a tank. A British Army postwar study titled *A Survey of Tank Casualties* summarized information based on approximately 1,600 tank

The shock waves generated by an AP projectile or the blast from an HE projectile striking an armored vehicle can be considerable depending on the weight of the striking projectile or explosive charge as well their velocity. Shock displacement can be as great as 1 inch (25 mm). A burned out Panther Ausf. G tank sits at the side of a road. *(Patton Museum)*

141

casualties, most being from northwest Europe. It stated that 65 percent of recorded projectile strikes were on tank hulls and about 35 percent on tank turrets. Approximately 40 percent of all projectile strikes on turrets and hulls in all theaters impacted the front of the vehicle, and 40 percent of those tank casualties were the result of a single penetration.

The postwar study concluded that although tank hulls take twice as many projectile strikes as do tank turrets, the proportion of projectile strikes on tank turrets was about twice as great as would be expected for the size of area exposed. As mentioned, this can be accounted for by the fact that a tank's turret must be exposed so that fire can be brought to bear on the enemy, whereas the hull of a tank can be kept behind cover when firing or hidden by grass or brush on the battlefield.

From the Office of the Ordnance Officer Headquarters Third United States Army in a report dated March 19, 1945, and titled *Examination of Causes of Rendering Tanks Inoperative* comes this passage offering some interesting battlefield observations:

> " … The recognizable groups of hits … show that the German and American gunner is shooting for the driver and assistant driver on his front shots. The American aims more for the final drive than the German. On the side shots, the German is still shooting at the spot on the forward sponson in which [main gun] ammunition was stored in early M4 tanks. It is evident from this study that neither the American 75-mm or the 76-mm gun is capable of destroying any German [late-war] tank. "

PANTHER TANK TURRET

The sides of the Panther tank turret were 45 mm thick and sloped at 25 degrees. Each side of the Panther tank turret consisted of one large plate, bent inward toward the rear end to meet the comparatively narrow straight back plate. Like the turret side plates, the turret rear plate was 45 mm thick and sloped at 25 degrees.

The roof of the Panther tank turret was 17 mm thick and slightly bent so that it sloped down toward the gun shield. The British military felt that a 4.2-inch mortar bomb or larger artillery projectile detonating on the roof of the Panther tank turret would no doubt result in serious plate rupture and the entry of blast and fragments into the interior of the vehicle's turret.

Due to the size of the Panther tank turret, the vehicle did not feature any deflector strips or guards on the top of the tank's superstructure, as did the Sherman tank. Deflector strips or guards are intended to protect a tank's turret ring from bullet splash or splatter, which is defined as the fragments resulting from the impact of ball or AP projectiles. According to a British military document dated May 5, 1944, titled *Armour Branch Report on Armour Quality & Vulnerability of Pz.Kw.V (Panther)*, it was thought possible that very accurate shooting at close range with a 7.92-mm Besa machine gun might jam the turret ring of the Panther tank. The same report also suggested that firing at the turret ring of the Panther tank with various antitank guns might jam it and render the vehicle inoperable.

The CHA turret front plate on the Panther tank series was 100 mm thick and sloped at 12 degrees, while the cylindrical CHA gun shield ("mantlet" to the British military), which extended over nearly the entire width of the turret front, was 100 mm to110 mm thick. This combination made the front of the Panther turret proof against the majority of tank and antitank weapons fielded by its opponents in 1943. However, by 1944, with the Allies

Blast is a high- pressure wave front that results from the detonation of high explosives. The extent of any blast is dependent on the amount and type of explosive. Damage to tanks from blast is caused for the most part by HE projectiles, land mines, and grenades. Pictured is a Panther Ausf. A tank that has either been overturned by a large aerial bomb or tipped over by an U.S. Army bulldozer. *(Patton Museum)*

introducing new and improved tank and antitank weapons, as well as more potent ammunition, the front of the Panther's turret would prove to be a weak spot.

User input no doubt alerted the Wa Pruef 6 to the problem of the now-vulnerable turret frontal armor on the Panthers Ausf. D through Ausf. G tanks. The solution was to appear on the follow-on version of the Panther Ausf. G tank, designated the Panther Ausf. F tank. This version of the Panther tank initially was to be fielded by June 1945. However, the German surrender in May 1945 brought the program to an untimely end.

The Panther Ausf. F tank would have consisted of a modified Panther Ausf. G tank chassis with a new, narrower profile and more heavily armored turret, referred to in German as the *Schmalturm* (narrow turret). The RHA turret front plate on the Panther Ausf. F tank was sloped at 20 degrees and 120 mm thick, while the CHA gun shield was 150 mm thick. The RHA turret roof on the never-fielded Panther Ausf. F tank was 40 mm thick and flat. The side and rear of the new Panther version were 60 mm thick and sloped at an angle of 25 degrees.

The never-fielded Panther Ausf. F tank turret would mount a modified version of 75-mm L/70 main gun designated the 7.5 cm Kw.K. 44/1 L/70.

An August 27, 1945, British Army report described the advantages of the new narrow turret for the Panther Ausf. F tank:

The internal components of tanks (such as radios or instrument panels) that might be subject to displacement by the shock of a striking projectile often are mounted on shock-absorbing brackets that allow for sufficient clearance between the shock mount and an armor wall to prevent damage. Shown are two destroyed Panther Ausf. A tanks on a French road in Normandy. (Patton Museum)

“ ▪ Elimination of the possibility of shots being deflected off the curved gun mantlet [gun shield] into the driving compartment

▪ Increase in armor protection without a corresponding increase in weight of the turret

▪ Reduction of the frontal area exposed to attack without restricting the space within the turret required for servicing the gun

▪ Installation of a stereoscopic rangefinder

▪ Substitution of a coaxial MG42 [machine gun] instead of a MG34 [machine gun]

▪ Reduction in production costs of the turret

▪ Installation of the necessary accessories to enable the complete tank to be quickly converted by personnel into either a command tank (Pz Bef Wg) Panther or a night fighting Panther with infrared sighting gear ”

The same report went into more detail on comparing the original Panther tank turret with the new narrow turret:

“ By using the new type of gun mantlet [gun shield], it is possible to have a much narrow turret front plate about 3’ 1” [94 cm] at top and 5’ [1.5 m] at bottom and so reduce the area exposed to attack.

The only means of defeating blast by tanks is the use of sufficient armor thickness. However, weight restrictions mean this is not always possible. The most vulnerable areas on tanks to blast include tank commander cupolas, hatches, engine deck, and optics. Ambushed at the side of a French field is this Panther Ausf. A tank, which has suffered numerous penetrations through its right-side flank. (Patton Museum)

The turret front consists of a homogeneous plate not calling for expensive machining as did the old Panther turret. It was possible to increase the armor thickness without increasing the overall weight of the turret, owing to the smaller front plate, the new type of gun mantlet [gun shield] and simplification of certain installations in the turret. "

Postwar U.S. Army testing showed that grenades are capable of developing considerable blast and can be effective in causing extensive damage if detonated on the armored grille cover of a tank's engine compartment. The grille opening affords openings through which blast can pass and damage an engine or cooling system. Pictured is a destroyed Panther Ausf. G tank. (Patton Museum)

SHOT TRAP

There was another flaw in the design of the Panther tank's frontal turret protection. Because the thick CHA gun shield was cylindrical, it sometimes caused AP projectiles that struck below its transverse center line to deflect down through the relatively thin armor over the driver's and radioman's positions, causing serious damage and casualties. This is commonly referred to as a "shot trap." In U.S. Army technical terms, a shot trap is a reentrant angle. A description appears in the March 1950 U.S. Army report titled *The Vulnerability of Armored Vehicles to Ballistic Attack*:

"A reentrant angle is an angle formed by surfaces of a vehicle such that attack striking either surface may be ricocheted against the other surface. Such angles incorporated into the design of armored structures are undesirable from a protection standpoint. Projectiles ricocheting from, or traveling along the surface of, reentrant angles may cause hits (by the projectile or fragments there from) on surfaces affording less protection, and which otherwise would be unexposed to attack. Sloping surfaces should be arranged so that impacting projectiles are not deflected into other areas of an armored vehicle."

A British Army report dated May 5, 1944, titled *Armour Branch Report on Armour Quality & Vulnerability of Pz.Kw.V(Panther)* highlighted the fact that the reentrant angle on the Panther tank gun shield was vulnerable to not only AP projectiles, but also conventional HE artillery rounds:

"If 25-pounder [88-mm] or 105-mm HE shell are fired so as to detonate on the lower half of turret mantlet [gun-shield], it is considered that the weak roof structure over the driver's and co-driver's [radioman's] compartment would collapse to the

The original cast homogenous armor (CHA) cylindrical gun shield, seen here being attached to a restored Panther Ausf. A tank and covering almost the entire width of the turret front, was somewhere from 100 to 110 mm thick. While proof against the majority of battlefield threats in 1943, the Panther tank gun shield was sometimes overmatched by 1944 and 1945.
(Michael Green)

147

extent of allowing dangerous blast to enter, and severely injure or kill the driver and co-driver. It would seem, therefore, that from the point of view of direct frontal attack, whether by AP or HE, the 'Achilles Heel' of the Panther is the relatively weak hull roof structure in combination with the peculiar design of the external mantlet. **"**

Many American soldiers who had some time on their hands at the conclusion of the war in Europe went sightseeing. The remains of German military equipment that often littered the countryside were of keen interest. Here we have American soldiers looking over a Panther tank that had suffered a catastrophic explosion. *(Andy Wood)*

The German answer to the problem of the reentrant angle on the Panther tank's cylindrical gun shield was a new gun shield with a much thicker lower portion, often referred to as a "chin," which presented a nearly vertical surface to incoming projectiles. The new chin gun shield began appearing on some Panther Ausf. G tanks in September 1944. However, not all Panther Ausf. G tanks coming off the production lines featured the new chin armor gun shield as some retained the original cylindrical gun shield.

PANTHER TANK HULL

A strongpoint of the Panther tank protection was no doubt its 80-mm thick glacis plate sloped at 55 degrees. A key element in the ability of the Panther glacis plate to resist penetration was the use of interlocking box joints also known as "finger joints." A March 1950 U.S. Army report titled *Vulnerability of Armored Vehicles to Ballistic Attack* was most impressed by this German practice and describes how 90-mm AP projectile strikes on the glacis plate of a Panther Ausf. G tank resulted in weld cracking as long as 62 inches (1.57 m) from single rounds. However, the interlocked box/finger joint design prevented the displacement of the armor.

The Panther Ausf. A tank originally was built with the roof plate (not the engine deck) interlocked with the side superstructure plates by box joints, as was done with the Panther Ausf. D tank. To speed up production, the box joints were ordered dispensed with on new production Panther Ausf. A tanks, and straight-sided roof plates were employed in their place. Due to the lag in this policy being implemented by the various factories building the Panther Ausf. A tank, interlocking roof plates could be found on that version of the Panther tank until it was replaced by the follow-on Panther Ausf. G tank.

The builders of the Sherman tank never employed interlocking box/finger joints in its construction. Depending on the factory, some Red Army T-34 series tanks rolled off the factory with interlocking box/finger joints.

The Panther tank's glacis plate was just one portion of the tank's armor skin. The remainder of the vehicle's armor protection levels were much more modest. The belly armor on the bottom of the majority of Panther Ausf. D hulls and some Panther Ausf. A tanks was, like that of the roof plate, a mere 16 mm thick. Sometime in mid- to late 1943, Panther Ausf. As tanks began leaving the factories with 30-mm-thick front belly plates, intended to minimize damage from antitank mines. The addition of the 30-mm-thick front belly plate was continued into the Panther Ausf. G tank.

A British Army report titled *Armour Branch Report on Armour Quality & Vulnerability of Pz.Kw.V (Panther)* indicated that they didn't believe a

To correct all the vulnerabilities discovered in combat by the German tank troops with the existing design of the Panther tank series, a new improved turret referred to by the Germans as the *Schmalturm* (narrow turret) was devised that was intended for the never-to-be-fielded Panther Ausf. F tank. Pictured is one of the experimental narrow turrets brought back to England after World War II for technical evaluation. *(Patton Museum)*

single antitank mine bursting under a track would immobilize a Panther tank. However, the report concluded that two antitank mines going off simultaneously and bursting on the inner edge of a track would almost certainly immobilize a Panther tank and would probably rupture the belly plate of the vehicle.

The Panther Ausf. D and Ausf. A tanks featured superstructure side plates that were 40 mm thick and sloped at 40 degrees. The vertical hull plates were also 40 mm thick, although they were offered a measure of protection by the tank's road wheels.

In lieu of the two-piece superstructure plates on either side of the Panther Ausf. D and Ausf. A tanks, the Panther Ausf. G tank rolled out of the factory with a single-piece superstructure on either side of the vehicle. To maintain the same level of flank protection offered on the earlier models of the Panther tank, the superstructure side plates on the Panther Ausf. G tank were made 50 mm thick as they now only had 29 degrees of slope, which offered less resistance to projectile strikes.

The relatively thin side superstructure armor was of major concern to the German tank troops throughout the Panther tank's time in service. From a translated German document via a British Army report appears this extract reminding those in charge of the vulnerabilities of the vehicle:

> It is particularly important to ensure flank protection for the sensitive sides of the Panther tanks. The Panzer Regimental commander must always keep a reserve of tanks up his sleeve, which he can use at a moment's notice to block any threat from the flank … This reserve should normally be about 1,100 yards in the rear. It has been found advisable to let the available Mark IV tanks in the Panzer Regiment take over the task of protection from the flanks, while the Panthers quickly press on and drive a wedge into the enemy position …

The British also quickly figured out just how susceptible the Panther tank's flanks were to penetration as can be seen in this extract from a report dated May 24, 1944, and titled *Armour Branch Report on Armour Quality & Vulnerability of Pz.Kw.V (Panther)*:

> The hull and turret sides of Panther, even having regard to the up-armoring of the front at their expense appears weaker than would have been expected in a tank of its weight. The reasons for this are not readily forth-coming without a detailed weight distribution investigation, but the fact remains that the hull and turret sides

are weak to 6-pounder [57-mm], 75-mm and 17-pounder [76.2-mm] attack …. In addition to the vulnerability of the hull sides, the danger of cordite [propellant] fires arising from penetration is high, since the ammunition is stowed un-protected in the panniers [a portion of the tank's superstructure overhanging the tracks]. **"**

Field reports by Panther tank units fighting in Russia confirmed that the flanks of the Panther tank were penetrated by 76.2-mm projectile strikes at range above 1,093 yards (1,000 m). Such hits often would result in ammunition or fuel fires, which meant the tank could not be returned to service.

During an interview with the authors, Dr. Wolfgang Sterner, a former Panther tank commander, described what it is like when a tank is penetrated by an AP projectile:

"Being hit in a tank while in battle, I would compare it to a big car crash. It's a tremendous shock and noise inside the tank. The tank becomes dark or you see flames [and] the engine stops. Then you hear the crying of the wounded people if

There was an unforeseen design flaw with the original cylindrical gun shield on the Panther tank series. It was discovered in combat that an enemy projectile striking below the transverse centerline of the cylindrical gun shield could be deflected downward into the vehicle's hull as seen in this picture. *(Patton Museum)*

To correct the reentrant angle created by the original cylindrical gun shield on the Panther tank series, many Panther Ausf. G tanks featured a new chin gun shield, an example of which is pictured here, that had its lower portion thickened as well as flattened to prevent projectiles from being deflected downward into the vehicle's hull. (Patton Museum)

they are still able to cry. The smell of course, and the fumes, first impels you to open your hatch, because the tank will blow up in seconds. As a tank commander, however, you shouldn't do that without checking on your crew. You must always try to save the wounded inside your tank if possible at all. If you don't do that, you will lose the leadership of your crew very soon. Sometimes you have no choice, if the tank starts to burn all over right away you must get out quickly. Losing your crew or part of it in such manner is really hard to take. "

Corporal Clarence E. Land stated in a March 27, 1945, document titled *U.S. Army Report on United States vs German Armor*: "I haven't seen a German tank knocked out, that was hit in the front; you always have to hit them in the side or rear compartment."

Not everyone found a flank shot on a Panther tank a sure thing, as evident from this quote from a U.S. Army tanker named Francis W. Baker of the 2nd Armored Division in the same report:

"I was a tank commander of a Sherman medium tank mounting a 75-mm gun. The Germans staged a counterattack with infantry supported by a least three Mark V [Panther] tanks. Ordering my gunner to fire at the closest tank, which was approximately 800 yards [731m] away, he placed one right in the side, which was completely visible to me. To my amazement and disgust, I watched the shell bounce off the side. My gunner fired at least six more rounds at the turret and track. I was completely surprised to see it moving after receiving seven hits from my gun. "

SPACED ARMOR

To help compensate for the weak flank armor of the Panther tank, the Germans mounted spaced armor, consisting of thin, 5-mm soft steel armor plates, on either side of the Panther Ausf. D tank's superstructure, beginning in April 1943. These spaced armor plates were referred to as *Schuerzen* by the Germans, and on the Panther Ausf. D and Ausf. A tanks they were hung on brackets attached to the bottom of the superstructure panniers/sponsons.

On the Panther Ausf. G tank, the spaced armor plates were attached to narrow, horizontally oriented metal fenders that extended along the length of the superstructure plates on either side of the tank. The long, narrow fenders were themselves supported by five steel brackets welded to the superstructure plates.

The thin spaced armor plates applied to the Panther tank also were mounted (in a variety of sizes) on the Panzer III and IV medium tanks as well

A side view of the new chin gun shield fitted to some production Panther Ausf. G tanks. As with so many other changes to the Panther tank series, the implementation of changes to the tank was not immediate, but occurred gradually beginning in September 1944. *(Patton Museum)*

153

From a British Army wartime report comes this line illustration of the various dimensions of the new chin gun shield for the Panther Ausf. G tank. Technical evaluation of opponent's equipment was done by all sides in World War II to learn how to better deal with the enemy when encountered on the battlefield. *(Patton Museum)*

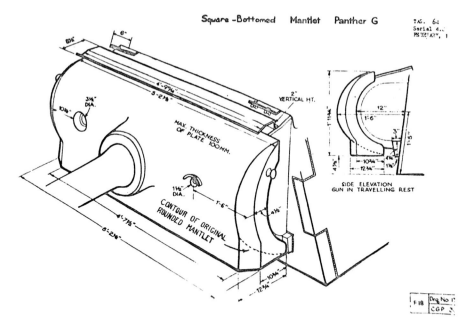

as a number of other German AFVs. A June 1944 British military report assigned the spaced armor plates found on a Panther a BHN of 105.

The spaced armor plates mounted on the sides of the Panther tanks and other German AFVs were intended to protect their thin vertical side hull plates from being penetrated at close range by Red Army 14.5-mm antitank rifles, such as the single shot PRTD-41 or the gas-operated semiautomatic PTRS-41, which had a five-round magazine. The 14.5-mm antitank rifles fired either steel or tungsten-cored projectiles, which had a muzzle velocity of 3,314 ft/sec (1010 m/s) and could penetrate about 40 mm of armor at 109 yards (100 m).

Spaced armor works against small-caliber AP projectiles, like the Red Army's 14.5-mm rounds, because the outer plate either breaks up the incoming projectile or turns the projectile upon impact so that it strikes against the main armor plate of a vehicle at an angle instead of straight on, thereby decreasing its ability to penetrate.

The spaced armor plates fitted to the Panther tank were never intended to defeat shaped charge warheads because development of the shaped armor plates was started after exposure on the Eastern Front to the Red Army 14.5-mm antitank rifles. This was before the Germans encountered shaped charge weapons such as the U.S. Army 2.36-inch Bazooka or the Red Army

RPG-43 hand grenade. A shaped charge warhead is an explosive charge with a lined hollow cone at the nose end, which develops a high-velocity jet upon detonation and burns through the armor plate.

German tests also showed that the spaced armored plates on the Panther tank were effective in resisting HE projectiles. The British concluded the same thing about the Panther's spaced armor as seen in this extract from a report dated May 24, 1944, and titled *Armour Branch Report on Armour Quality & Vulnerability of Pz.Kw.V (Panther)*:

> **"**Provision is made for the attachment of external skirting plates at each side. With these in place, HE against the hull sides will be ineffective. Without these however, HE detonating against the side below the pannier [a portion of the tank's superstructure overhanging the tracks] will burst a length of side weld admitting blast. Resultant damage to the track is not likely to be so serious as to immobilize the vehicle.**"**

In *Germany's Panther Tank; The Quest for Combat Supremacy*, editor Thomas L. Jentz states that it was the successful application of the thin spaced armor steel plates to the sides of Panther Ausf. D tank that saved the vehicle from being cancelled in favor in the more heavily armored Panther II tank.

ENGINE DECK ISSUES

The engine deck on the Panther tank was only 16 mm thick. This in combination with the layout on the engine deck made the Panther prey to HE air bursts, according to a British military report dated May 24, 1944, and titled *Armour Branch Report on Armour Quality & Vulnerability of Pz.Kw.V (Panther)*:

> **"**It would appear that the only areas of the roof of the vehicle vulnerable to this form of attack are the air inlet and outlet louvers set in the engine compartment roof, and occupying 35 percent of its total area .... It is thus apparent that fragments from HE air bursts (25-pounder and 105-mm) occurring at heights between 10 and 30 feet, or possibly higher, may enter the grilles and cause damage to radiators or fuel tanks. Fragments from bursts occurring below 10 feet are unlikely to enter the grilles unless the point of detonation is on or immediately above the hull roof.**"**

The U.S. Army conducted a series of ballistic tests on captured Panther tanks at the end of World War II and confirmed that the RHA glacis plate on the tanks was of extremely high quality. This close-up picture shows the gouges that 90-mm AP projectiles made on the glacis plate of a Panther Ausf. A tank. *(Patton Museum)*

No doubt, Wa Pruef 6 also figured out from user input that the Panther's engine deck was a weak spot, not just from artillery air bursts, but from aerial attack by Allied aircraft. To address this issue, Wa Pruef 6 had in December 1944, authorized Panther units to take some of the spaced armor plates, typically mounted on the sides of the vehicle, and modify them to serve as horizontal covers over the air inlets and outlet louvers located on the engine deck.

Photographic evidence shows that at least one Panther regiment not only added spaced armor plates over the engine decks of their vehicles, but also mounted spaced armor plates over the roof of their tank's turrets for additional protection from overhead attack.

In an interview with the authors, former Panther tank commander Dr. Wolfgang Sterner compared the threat from artillery versus attack by ground attack aircraft:

"With artillery fire, you took your chances. Heavy artillery fire shakes you up. But it does not harm your tank so much. It is a strain on the nerves because it makes an entire tank shake, but you could maneuver and move to a different position.

But if a fighter-bomber spotted you, you were usually finished. Not all the time; sometimes they ran out of ammunition, or sometimes they had to turn back because their fuel was gone or the weather became worse. If they had lots of fuel

and lots of ammunition and the skies stayed clear, they come after you, over and over again until the bitter end. "

SMOKE LAUNCHERS

The terminal effect of a hit on the left superstructure plate of a Panther Ausf. A tank in Normandy, France, can be clearly seen with a complete penetration by an AP projectile. The consequences to the crew of a tank struck and penetrated by a large AP projectile strike are gruesome in the extreme as attested to by those who witnessed such destruction. *(Patton Museum)*

Early series production Panther Ausf. D tanks rolled off the factory floor with *Nebelwurfgeraet* (smoke launcher equipment) mounted on either side of their turrets. The smoke launcher equipment consisted of three launcher tubes grouped together in a pod. Each launcher tube was set at a slightly different angle and was preloaded with a smoke grenade. The smoke grenades were intended to be fired when the need arose to shield a Panther tank from enemy observation.

In practice, the smoke grenade on the Panther Ausf. D tank could be involuntarily set off in their launchers by small-arms fire, with the resulting smoke temporary incapacitating the vehicle's crew. This caused the smoke launcher equipment to be discontinued on the Panther Ausf. D tank in June 1943.

CAMOUFLAGE PAINT

Many might discount the true value of elaborate camouflage paint schemes on tanks as it is the last thing that tank crews typically worry about. Whatever the merits might be, the German military devised a variety of paint schemes for their tanks, much to the delight of legions of tank modelers who live and die by the supposed accuracy of their painted models.

For the first month of production, the Panther Ausf. D tank left the factory in a base coat of dark gray (Dunkelgrau RAL 46). In February 1943, the Germans switched to using a base coat of dark yellow (Dunkelgelb nach Muster) on the Panther Ausf. D tank. This was in turn replaced by a variation designated as Dunkelgelb RAL 7028, a somewhat tan color. It then fell to the units in the field to apply a camouflage scheme using two complementary colors, dark olive green (Olivgruen RAL 6003) and red brown (Rotbraun RAL 8017), that best matched the terrain in which they found themselves operating. This same selection of camouflage paints also was applied in turn to the Panther Ausf. A and Ausf. G tanks. In wintertime, a whitewash was applied over the existing camouflage paint schemes.

From *Wehrmacht Heer: Camouflage Colors 1939–1945* by Tomas Chory appears this description of what led to such a wide variety of camouflage patterns appearing on German tanks like the Panther:

With the introduction of the Panther Ausf. G tank, the thin-spaced armor plates were attached to a narrow horizontal metal fender that ran almost the entire length of the superstructure side plates. A partial example of that metal fender can be seen in this picture of a late-model Panther Ausf. G tank hull being restored at the French Army Tank Museum. *(Michael Green)*

"If we consider the various means used for applying the paint (spray guns, brushes, brooms, rags, and sometimes even hands), different ways of diluting the color pastes and the varying 'painting' ability of the various crews, there is no wonder that the result was an almost infinite number of camouflage variants, as clearly shown in the contemporary photographs. Naturally, there existed deviations from the official regulations caused by supply shortages, technical problems, and time constraints."

Red Army soldiers pose with their single-shot 14.5-mm PTRD-41 antitank rifle. This 79-inch (201-cm) long weapon weighed 38 lbs (17.3 kg) and took a two-man team to manhandle around the battlefield. At close range this weapon posed a threat to the sides of the Panther tank and resulted in the fielding of the spaced armor applied to the vehicle beginning in April 1943. *(Patton Museum)*

In August 1944, a general order mandated that all new Panther tanks leave the factory with a new standardized camouflage paint scheme referred to as *Licht und Schatten-Tarnung* (light and shadow) or *Hinterhalt-Tarnung* (ambush). This ambush pattern consisted of the standard tan (Dunkelgelb RAL 7028) base with patches of dark olive green (Olivgruen RAL 6003) and red brown (Rotbraun RAL 8017) painted over it. All the various colors then had contrasting colors applied in spots either using stencils or by masking the tank's exterior surfaces and then painting the spots on. As allied air superiority in 1944 forced German tanks crews to seek overhead cover whenever possible, the new paint scheme was intended to simulate the effect of light filtering through trees.

The Germans decided to drop the standard tan (Dunkelgelb RAL 7028) base for the Panther tank in September 1944, with new tanks leaving the

factories painted only with a red oxide (Rot RAL 8012) primer upon which tan (Dunkelgelb RAL 7028), dark olive green (Olivgruen RAL 6003), and red brown (Rotbraum RAL 8017) could be applied in various patterns. Contrasting spots were then added to all the painted-on colors to maintain the ambush paint scheme begun the previous month.

During the last few weeks of the war in Europe, as the German logistical system collapsed, supplies of every sort, including paint, were in short supply. Those tank factories still in operation painted their vehicles in whatever paint was available.

The official U.S. Army view on the effectiveness of camouflage painting of vehicles appears in this extract from an April 1944 manual titled *Camouflage of Vehicles*:

> **"**Camouflage painting is not a cure-all. Alone, it cannot be relied on to do more than render a vehicle obscure, making it hard for an enemy gunner to locate the vehicle and confusing him as to the location of vulnerable areas. Nor can it conceal a moving vehicle, because other sight factors, such as dust, reflections, and motion itself, will betray its presence. **"**

NONMAGNETIC COATING

The factories building the Panther tank began applying a nonmagnetic coating, referred to by the Germans as *Zimmerit*, to all new production vehicles, beginning in September 1943. The nonmagnetic coating also was applied in the field. The Germans feared that Red Army infantrymen might attach magnetic mines to the Panther tank. The purpose of nonmagnetic coating is described in a July 1945 British military report written by Major J.W. Thompson and Mr. C.E. Hollis and titled *"Zimmerit" Anti-magnetic Plaster for AFVs*:

> **"**The function of Zimmerit was simply to provide a non-ferro-magnetic gap between the steel armor of the tank and the magnets of the mine. In other words, a non-magnetic standoff, not a mysterious repelling force. The gap created was sufficient enough to reduce the attracting force of the magnets. **"**

The same British report explained how the material was applied to German tanks, like the Panther, and other armored fighting vehicles (AFVs):

To counter the threat posed by the large number of Red Army antitank rifles encountered on the Eastern Front, the Germans attached thin soft steel plates to either side of the superstructure of their Panther tanks. An example of this spaced armor concept, as seen on this beautifully restored Panther Ausf. A tank belonging to the Military Vehicle Technology Foundation. *(Christopher Hughes)*

" The Zimmerit was applied to the surface in two coats, using a sheet metal trowel. The first coat was 5-mm thick and was marked out in squares using the edge of the trowel. This coat was allowed to dry at ordinary temperatures for 24 hours. The second coat was applied thinner and marked with wavy lines with a metal comb. The criss-cross squares increased the adhesion of the second coat, while the comb markings gave camouflage finish, plus poor contact for mines. After the application of both coats, the surface was treated by a gas blow-lamp to harden it. This took about an hour per tank and no difficulty was experienced in getting satisfactory hardness without the Zimmerit becoming brittle. "

Researchers who have studied the nonmagnetic coating applied to the Panther tank have uncovered the fact that at one factory, the material was applied with a roller instead of trowel. There also seems to have been a variety of different patterns of the nonmagnetic coating applied to Panther tanks by different factories.

The practice of applying the nonmagnetic coating to the Panther and other German tanks and armored fighting vehicles was discontinued in September

1944 based on the unfounded belief that the material caught fire when struck by a projectile. The material itself was composed of 40 percent barium sulphate, 25 percent polyvinyl acetate (white carpenter's glue), 15 percent ochre pigment, 10 percent zinc sulphide ZnS, and 10 percent sawdust, with the consistency of soft putty.

RUSSIAN RESPONSE TO THE PANTHER TANK

The first to deal with the Panther's glacis plate in combat was the Red Army, which encountered the then-untested vehicle in combat in July 1943, during Operation Zitadelle. When German military forces withdrew from the battlefield, Red Army technical evaluation teams collected seven fully functioning Panther Ausf. D tanks and twenty-three knocked-out examples. The knocked-out vehicles were inspected in great detail by Red Army technicians in order to understand the nature of the damage inflicted on the tanks by Red Army personnel and weapons.

This Panther Ausf. A belongs to the collection of the French Army Tank Museum. It is painted in a late-war camouflage scheme referred to as *Licht und Schatten-Tarnung* (light and shadow) or *Hinterhalt-Tarnung* (ambush). *(Martin K. Morgan)*

The spaced armor plates, referred to as *Schuerzen* by the Germans, on the Panther
Ausf. D and Ausf. A tanks were attached to six metal hangers, seen here on a
Panther Ausf. D tank, welded to the bottom of the vehicle's panniers/sponsons.
These metal attachments could not be welded to the superstructure side plates
of the Panther Ausf. D tank without destroying the ballistic strength of the
face-hardened armor (FHA) employed until July 1944. *(Virginia Museum of
Military Vehicles)*

On almost all of the knocked-out Panther Ausf. D tanks inspected by the Red Army following Operation Zitadelle, the glacis plate was intact. Even Red Army 122-mm AP projectiles had ricocheted off the Panther tank glacis plate, leaving only 40-mm deep gashes. However, it was noted that a projectile strike near the glacis plate welds caused them to crack. A 76.2-mm projectile strike could penetrate the lower front hull armor plate on the Panther tank and the vehicle's gun shield. Both 76-mm and 85-mm projectile strikes could knock off the vehicle commander's cupola on the Panther tank.

In December 1943, to acquire more detailed statistics on what would kill a Panther tank, the Red Army conducted ballistic tests at the NII GBTU (Main Armor Test Command Research Institute) test center in Kubinka, near Moscow. The full spectrum of antitank weapons used by the Red Army was employed in the ballistic tests, including American and British lend-lease guns. The goal of the trial was to find the armor strength of the Panther tank and detail the optimal distances and the strategies needed to combat it on the battlefield.

The following guns were used: Soviet 45 mm, British 6-pounder (57 mm,) American 75 mm, Soviet 76.2 mm, 85 mm, 122 mm, and 152 mm. The final test subject was the NII-6 HEAT antitank grenade. The weapons were fired from various distances to determine the penetration. All the guns except for the 76.2-mm and 85-mm guns were fired at 90 degrees to the Panther's

Belonging to the German Army Technical Evaluation Center is this restored Panther Ausf. G tank. The camouflage paint scheme applied to the vehicle shows one of the many variations possible within existing parameters of the of the standard tan, dark olive green, and red brown paints in use from February 1943 until August 1944. *(Andreas Kirchhoff)*

superstructure/hull, while the 76-mm and 85-mm guns were fired at 30 degrees, 60 degrees, and 90 degrees to the superstructure/hull of the panther tank.

The results of the tests are summarized in Table 1.

TABLE 1

Weapon	80-mm glacis plate	45-mm side armor
NII-6 antitank grenade	15–20 m	15–20 m
45-mm tank gun	No penetration from any distance	300–500 m
57-mm tank gun	No penetration from any distance	700–900 m
76.2-mm tank gun	No penetration from any distance	1,000–1,300 m
85-mm tank gun	No penetration from any distance	1,000–1,500 m
122-mm D-25 tank gun	1,500 m	2,000–2,500 m
152-mm gun-howitzer	1,500 m	2,000–2,500 m

This postwar-built Panther Ausf. G tank belonging to the Tank Museum at Bovington, England, has sported a variety of paint schemes over the decades. In this photograph, it has a tan base coat with an overlay of dark olive green and red brown that was in use from February 1943 to August 1944 on Panther tanks. *(Tank Museum, Bovington)*

The distance in the table is the maximum distance from which the penetration happened at 90 degrees to the Panther superstructure/hull.

The conclusion of the firing tests confirmed that the Red Army's 122-mm and 152-mm main guns were able to deal with the Panther tank at typical combat distances.

The reasons for the poor performance by the Red Army's 76.2-mm and 85-mm guns were determined to be the poor metallurgical quality of their ammunition and their relatively low muzzle velocity. At the same time, the British 57-mm gun (the 6-pounder) was judged to be equivalent to the Soviet 76.2-mm gun due to the superior quality of its ammunition and its higher muzzle velocity. Yet, despite the better quality, it, too, was useless against the glacis plate of the Panther tank.

Visible on the reversed turret of this Panther Ausf. D tank is one of two sets of smoke launcher pods mounted on either side of the vehicle's turret. Visionary in concept, the implementation proved faulty when user experience showed that the equipment's location proved overly vulnerable to enemy fire. (Patton Museum)

The tests allowed the Red Army to determine the best tactics to fight the Panther tank and revealed its weak spots. This told the local commanders that they needed to concentrate heavy artillery in the places where likely attacks by the German armor was going to occur, while the lighter guns were to be set up in ambush positions off to the flank. It also led to the appearance of the bigger self-propelled guns like the Su-100 and JSU-122/152 later in the war. The tests were very useful and paved the way to improvements in fighting the Panther tank and other German late-war tanks and armored fighting vehicles.

BRITISH RESPONSE TO THE PANTHER

Having been dealing with German tanks since the invasion of France in the summer of 1940, the British Army had attempted to anticipate what the Germans would field next and have a weapon on hand that could destroy it when the time came. One of the results of this preoccupation was the fielding of the 17-pounder (76.2-mm) gun, which was accepted into service in May 1942. First deployed as a towed antitank gun, the 17-pounder eventually was mounted on variety of tracked and armored vehicles, the best known being the Sherman Firefly. As a tank main gun, the weapon was designated the 17-pounder, quick-firing Mark IV.

The Firefly began appearing in British Army service in early 1944. By the time D-Day rolled around and the British and American armies had landed in Normandy, France, almost 350 Fireflies were in service. It was this tank and gun that the British Army anticipated could deal with any German tank encountered in Western Europe. Unfortunately, its main tank killing rounds, the ABCBC Mk VIII T Shot, did not prove equal to the task assigned.

The British Army 4th Royal Tank Regiment wrote in its unit history that their 17-pounder "only nicked" Panther tanks. From the postwar unit history of the British Army 23rd Hussars appears this observation about the effectiveness of the 17-pounder mounted in the Sherman Firefly on a number of Panther tanks knocked out in battle by another unit:

    " … The 17-pounder was more encouraging (as related earlier we were equipped with one 17-pounder tank for every three 75-mm) for it penetrated the front of the Panther's turret at 300 yards [274m], though it did not always go through the sloped front plate of the hull [glacis]. On the whole, we decided that head-on Panthers should be treated with circumspection. In point of fact we found ourselves in just that position a few days later, and the results were just as unhappy as our trial shoot indicated. "

Late in 1944, the Sherman Firefly received small numbers of the new armor-piercing discarding sabot (APDS) round that boasted improved penetrative powers. The new round was designated the Super-Velocity Discarding Sabot (SVDS) and weighed 28.4 lbs. The projectile portion had a muzzle velocity of 3,950 ft/sec. The downside of the new APDS round was a certain inaccuracy in early production lots, which frustrated all concerned.

Despite the Sherman Firefly not being the optimum solution for dealing with the Panther tank, the British Army continued to build them until the war in Europe was coming to a close, with a final production number of some 2,200 units completed upon the conclusion of the conflict in May 1945.

The planned replacement for the Sherman Firefly was the well-known Centurion Universal tank. Six prototypes of the tank, then designated the A41, were rushed to Western Europe to see combat with Panther or Tiger tanks. Unfortunately, the A41 prototypes arrived just after the German surrender in May 1945.

OVERLEAF
In the workshop of the Tank Museum, Bovington, is their Panther Ausf. G tank, in its current paint scheme. The new paint scheme for this tank attempts to capture the look of the vehicle after September 1944 when the base color of Panther tank was switched from tan to a red oxide primer upon which other colors were applied, in this case the former tan base color. (David Marian)

AMERICAN RESPONSE TO THE PANTHER TANK

The U.S. Army first encountered small numbers of Panther tanks (Ausf. D and Ausf. A) while engaged in Italy in early 1944, almost a year after the Panther's combat debut on the Eastern Front. However, the vehicles did not make much of an impression upon the American frontline forces fighting there because they were used in small numbers and restricted by poor terrain.

The small number of Panther tanks encountered in Italy had fostered the false belief among the U.S. Army senior leadership that the Panther tank, like the Tiger Ausf. E heavy tank, was only going to be fielded in small numbers, and there was no need to spend the time and effort in developing and fielding tanks or tank destroyers able to destroy it in combat.

The U.S. Army senior leadership was so unconcerned about meeting the Panther tank on the European battlefield that they turned down the offer of up-armed second-generation Sherman tanks, armed with 76-mm main guns, even though there were already 102 of the 76-mm gun-armed Sherman tanks in England prior to the invasion of France on June 6, 1944: D-Day.

The British Army did not make the same mistake the U.S. Army did regarding the fielding of the Panther tank. They had grasped right away that the Panther tank was not going to be formed into a small number of independent battalions like the Tiger Ausf. E heavy tank, but was intended as a replacement for the much more numerous Panzer III and IV medium tanks in the Panzer divisions.

Following the U.S. Army landings on Omaha and Utah Beach on D-Day, there was a quick push inland. It was shortly thereafter that the American military had a shock when they discovered what an incredible terrain obstacle the Normandy hedgerows created. The thick and tall century-old hedgerows began right behind the American landing beaches, and extended up to 50 miles inland in some areas. They provided excellent defensive positions to the German defenders. To make matter worse, the U.S. Army started to encounter many more Panther tanks than they had expected and they proved much harder to kill than anticipated. In reaction, all 102 of the 76-mm gun-armed Sherman tanks in England were transported to Normandy by July 25, 1944.

In *Faint Praise: American Tanks and Tank Destroyers during World War II*, author Charles M. Baily described how the U.S. Army in Normandy tried to find out which weapons could actually kill a Panther tank on July 28, 1944:

OPPOSITE
Hampered by Allied air superiority, especially during the last two years of the war, the German tank troops turned to using foliage whenever possible to hide their tanks from aerial observation. This photograph shows a Panther Ausf. A tank, which is being covered by foliage to hide it from marauding ground attack aircraft. The German tanker on the rear of the tank is to there to alert the crew on the approach of enemy aircraft so evasive action can be taken. *(Patton Museum)*

❝Aggravated by the tough hide of the Panther tanks during the first weeks of the Normandy campaign, the First Army set about finding exactly what weapon could destroy that tank. A board of officers moved a Panther to a suitable location and fired at it with virtually every weapon available, including rifle grenades, 40-mm antiaircraft guns, and 105-mm howitzers. The results were disheartening. Three-inch guns had a chance against the turret mantle [gun shield] at very short range, 200 yards [183m]. Only the 90-mm gun and the 105-mm howitzer proved capable of penetrating the Panther glacis plate.❞

A trio of parked Panther Ausf. D tanks are shown camouflaged with varying levels of foliage. To mask their tell-tale outline from aerial observation, the turrets have been turned with their long main gun tubes pointed over the rear hull of the vehicles. Notice the tanker taking a nap on the commander's cupola of the middle vehicle. *(Patton Museum)*

The comparative firing tests against Panther tanks conducted the following month at Isigny, France, only confirmed that the 76-mm main gun mounted on the second-generation Sherman tanks (in which the U.S. Army had placed so much faith to deal not only with the Panther tank, but with the Tiger heavy tanks) was a failure when firing its standard ammunition. This appears in the extract from the conclusion section of the Isigny report: "[The] 76-mm APC, M62 is considered an unsatisfactory ammunition for use against heavy armor because of its inferior penetration."

An example of the problem second-generation Sherman tanks armed with the 76-mm main gun and firing the standard APC round had in dealing with late-war German tanks, like the Panther, comes from this quote by 2nd Lt.

Frank Seydel, Jr. of the 2nd Armored Division in a March 1945 U.S. Army document titled *U.S. Army Report on United States vs German Armor*:

> "On March 3 [1945] at Bosinghoven, Germany, I took under fire two German Mark V Panther tanks at a range of 600 yards [549m]. At this time, I was using a 76-mm gun, using APC for my first round. I saw this round make a direct hit on a vehicle and ricochet into the air. I fired again at a range of 500 yards [457m] and again observed a direct hit, after which I threw about 10 rounds of mixed AP and HE, leaving the German tank burning. This experience proved to me that German armor plate is superior to ours ... "

Eventually, the U.S. Army managed to field a more powerful HVAP round for the 76-mm main gun on second-generation Sherman tanks, designated the T4. The first of the T4 HVAP rounds showed up in Europe in August 1944. Sadly, like the standard M62 APC round, it could not penetrate the glacis plate on the Panther tank. It could punch a hole in the Panther tank gun shield at 1,000 yards (914 m). The standard M62 APC could only do the same at 200 yards (183 m). However, due to the continuing shortage of

This close-up picture of a restored Panther Ausf. G tank shows the texture of the nonmagnetic coating, referred to as *Zimmerit* by the Germans, applied in various patterns to all new Panther tanks built between September 1943 and September 1944. The variety of texture patterns seen with Zimmerit had a lot to do with the manner of application. *(Andreas Kirchoff)*

A serious threat to the sides of the Panther tank throughout the war on the Eastern Front was the Red Army's 76-mm divisional field gun M1942 (ZiS-3), seen here being towed into combat. This weapon doubled as a fairly effective antitank gun as did all Red Army artillery pieces. *(Patton Museum)*

tungsten, there were never enough T4 HVAP rounds around, as seen in this wartime quote by U.S. Army Major Paul A. Banes, Jr. in the March 1945 document *U.S. Army Report on United States vs German Armor*:

> "Our tank crews have had some success with the HVAP 76-mm ammunition. However, at no time have we been able to secure more than five rounds per tank, and in recent actions this has been reduced to a maximum of two rounds. In many tanks all this type has been expended without being replaced."

A STOP GAP APPEARS

The 1st Army's firing tests on a captured Panther tank, conducted on July 28, 1944, had showed that the towed M2 90-mm antiaircraft gun was the only weapon in the U.S. Army inventory that could penetrate the glacis plate of the Panther tank at a reasonable range. As could be guessed, a hue and cry quickly arose in the U.S. Army for a 90-mm main gun equipped tank destroyer to be fielded. That vehicle turned out to be the M36 tank destroyer.

The U.S. Army Ordnance Department had actually began experimenting with a 90-mm main gun-equipped tracked vehicle back in early 1942. However, lack of interest by the U.S. Army Tank Destroyer Command and even General Dwight D. Eisenhower, who discounted any need for the M36 tank destroyer for the upcoming invasion of France, meant that the first vehicles didn't make it to Europe until autumn 1944. A great deal of hope was placed on the M36 tank destroyer being able to handle the Panther and Tiger tanks.

The M3 90-mm main gun on the M36 fired the original version of the M82 APC projectile at a muzzle velocity of 2,650 ft/sec (807.72 m/s). An improved version of the M82 APC projectile would leave the barrel of the M3 90-mm main gun at 2,800 ft/sec (853.44 m/s). This meant the penetrative powers of the APC rounds were sometimes sufficient, at short ranges, to kill a Panther tank, as seen from this quote from the March 1945 document titled *U.S. Army Report on United States vs German Armor*:

> " Technical 4 Brill, gunner, First Platoon of Company B, fired two rounds of 90-mm APC on December 25, 1944, near Calles, Belgium, into the front of the Mark V [Panther] tank at a range of 200 yards [183m]. Both rounds penetrated the front slope and set the German afire. "

At increased ranges, the situation for the crews of the M36 was a bit different, as shown in the following extract from the same U.S. Army report:

> " Lt. Clinton Brooks stated that at Gereonsweiler, Germany, on November 23, 1944, a Mark V [Panther] tank fired at the side of an M36, the No. 2 gun of his platoon, sending a round completely through the side. Lt. Brooks opened fire with the 90-mm at 3,000 yards [2,743m] firing a total of 20 rounds of which approximately half were APC. The German tank was hit many times without damage. The M36 was forced to withdraw from the fire of the same tank. "

The commander of the U.S. Army 703rd Tank Destroyer Battalion wrote a letter dated December 15, 1944, to the commanding general of the First Army about the poor performance of the 90-mm main guns on his M36 tank destroyers. In that letter, he stated that the 90-mm main guns on his M36 tank destroyers could only make penetrations on the glacis plate of the

Panther tank about half the time at ranges between 150 and 300 yards (137 to 274 m).

The introduction of the M304 (T30E16) HVAP round for the M36 in January 1945 improved the odds of killing a Panther tank as it had a muzzle velocity of 3,350 ft/sec (1022 m/s) and could penetrate the glacis plate of a Panther tank at 450 yards (411 m). However, the M304 round was always in short supply.

The most common opponent of the Panther tank from 1944 until the end of World War II was the Red Army's T-34-85 medium tank armed with an 85-mm main gun. The Panther's gun shield and glacis plate generally were immune to the standard BR-365 AP main gun round fired by the Red Army tank; the sides of the Panther tank were vulnerable, however. (Michael Green)

COMBAT IMPRESSIONS

The growing amount of frustration many U.S. Army tankers had in dealing with the late-war German tanks is clearly seen in this quote from Lieutenant Colonel Wilson M. Hawkins, commanding officer of the 3rd Battalion, 67th Armored Regiment, who stated his opinion in a document titled *U.S. Army Report on United States vs German Armor*:

"If it was possible to trade tanks with the Germans, I would prefer to fight in the present German Mark V [Panther] or VI [Tiger] against the present U.S. medium tank [M4 Sherman] and tank destroyer [M36] with the 90-mm gun."

At the other end of the U.S. Army rank structure appears this quote from the same U.S. Army World War II document from Corporal Thomas G. McLane regarding his impression of the Panther tank:

"In my estimation the German Mark V [Panther] tank is superior to our medium tank M4, in both armor and armament. Our success in Europe is a result of superiority in numbers and superiority in good old guts, not a result of superior tanks."

Not every American tanker fighting in Western Europe during World War II had a face-to-face encounter with a Panther tank. Tom Sator, a loader on an M4 Sherman medium tank belonging to the elite 4th Armored Division, does

Heading toward Berlin is a column of Red Army T-34-85 medium tanks. The tank became more of a threat to the Panther tank when it started to be supplied in the summer of 1944 with a small number of the more potent BR-365P hyper-velocity armor-piercing (HVAP) rounds for its 85-mm main gun. Having a tungsten-carbide core, the BR-365P could penetrate the glacis plate on the Panther tank at less than 500 yards (457m). *(Patton Museum)*

PANTHER TANK KILLER

Dean and Nancy Kleffman conducted an interview with Clarence Smoyer of the 3rd Armored Division during the division's annual reunion held in 1985. The interview was conducted on behalf of the Patton Museum of Armor and Cavalry oral history collection.

" I was a gunner in Company E, 32nd Regiment, 3rd Armored Division, and we were one of the first crews to get the M26 Pershing tank. After we got the new tank, they took us out to a valley to test fire the gun before we went into combat. They started us off by having us shoot at houses that were about 1,200 yards away.

Once we began hitting the houses with our 90-mm gun, they made it even harder for us by telling us to shoot at the chimneys on the distant houses. The chimneys soon began disappearing in a series of explosions. They kept increasing the target distance on us to test our skill, and for the final one they chose a house 1,500 yards away with two chimneys. I remember announcing that I was going to attempt to get the first chimney on the right side of the house. I fired, and the chimney went up in pieces. The one on the other side of the house was a red brick chimney, and just the top of it stuck out over the roof. We set up and fired, and the red brick flew all over the place. I then heard people cheering, saying what a great gunner I was.

From there we went on to the German city of Cologne. As we approached the city, there was a great deal of artillery fire. Our battalion leader got on the radio and said, 'Gentlemen, I give you Cologne; knock the hell out of them.'

As we approached the city, we found that the Germans had jammed streetcars underneath the overpasses to slow us down. They weren't much of a problem to deal with, and we pulled them out with cables. As we continued into the city, they stopped us at an intersection. I don't know why. Being in the tank half the time, I didn't know which direction I was facing, but I could see the Cologne Cathedral to my left. We sat there quite awhile, and as the German

not even remember seeing a Panther tank during his time in combat. What he remembers is using a lot of HE against antitank guns and his tank's machine guns on German soldiers armed with hand-held *Panzerfausts* (a one-shot throw-away recoilless antitank weapon). This impression is backed up by U.S. Army statistics that show the majority of main gun rounds fired by American tanks during World War II were HE and not AP.

James Francis was a gunner on a Sherman tank with the 12th Armored Division from December 1944 until the German surrender in May 1945. He never saw any German tanks until after the war. His major battlefield encounters involved finding himself in the gun-sights of three German antitank guns, two of them towed 88s and one a 75-mm towed antitank gun. All three encounters cost him a tank but, thankfully, not his life.

soldiers came into the intersection, we fired on them.

Eventually, a German tank (Panther) came around the side of a building; by the time we got an armor-piercing shell into the cannon, he realized that there was a bunch of us over there and he backed up. We fired armor-piercing shells through the building that he backed up behind, thinking we might get a lucky hit and knock him out, which we didn't.

After awhile we went down one street, and Company F went down the street beside us, which was the street that the German tank had backed down to the cathedral on. It now sat in front of the cathedral and everybody thought it was knocked out. A Signal Corps cameraman had gone ahead of us and was up in a building shooting pictures of our tanks when the German tank suddenly opened fire on our column and knocked out a tank, the lead tank. One man climbed out of the top of that tank, with a leg missing, and then rolled onto the ground and died. That same man had just heard from the battalion commander three weeks before about receiving his battlefield commission. I heard that two other men in that tank also died.

When the lead tank was hit, they radioed us to go down another street, to take out the German tank. Somehow or another, the German tank crew knew what we were doing; they came up to the intersection approaching and were waiting for us. Our plan had been to come up to the intersection corner and slowly pull around just far enough to see where the German tank was, and then let me turn the turret and get a shot off. After that, we would quickly back up.

As soon as our driver saw the gun on the German tank, less than one hundred yards away, instead of stopping the tank to give me a chance at a shot, he floored the throttle as fast as he could through the intersection, and I fired on the move and hit him right below the gun shield. Because we weren't sure if we killed everybody in the tank, we fired two more shots into it, and that was the end of the German tank and crew. "

A SOLUTION FINALLY APPEARS

It wasn't until the closing months of the war in Europe that the U.S. Army received small numbers of a new tank that was the near equal of the Panther tank. That vehicle was the M26 Pershing heavy tank (redesignated a medium tank in 1946). Armed with the same M3 90-mm main gun as mounted in the M36 tank destroyer, it was still outclassed by the 75-mm main gun on the Panther tank, except at range over 1,000 yards (914 m) where the heavier AP 90-mm projectile would lose less velocity than the lighter AP projectiles that the Panther tank's main gun fired.

The five-man Pershing tank weighed roughly 46 tons (42 mt). Although lighter than the Panther tank, the Pershing tank had a lower power to weight

The turret-less SU-85 was introduced into Red Army service in 1943 to deal with the German Panther medium tank and the Tiger Ausf. E heavy tank. Based on a T-34 chassis, the tank destroyer mounted an 85-mm main gun. With the introduction of the T34-85 medium tank into Red Army service in 1944, the SU-85 was up-armed with a 100-mm main gun and designated the SU-100 tank destroyer as seen here. (*Christophe Vallier*)

ratio than the Panther. The ground pressure on both tanks was about the same with the Pershing tank coming in a bit wider than the Panther tank. Armor protection levels on the front of the Pershing and Panther were about the same with the American tank being slightly shorter than the German tank. The Panther tank carried more main gun rounds than the Pershing tank because they were smaller and lighter.

Like the Panther tank, the Pershing tank had been rushed into service and had a host of teething problems. Despite its problems, U.S. Army tankers were more than happy to see it. From R. P. Hunnicutt's *Pershing: A History of the Medium Tank T20 Series* comes this apt summary of the entire Pershing tank time in World War II:

"The Pershing story might well be summarized by the words of U.S. Army Captain Elmer Gray replying to the tank crews at Aachan [Germany] when they asked if the Pershing was equal to the German King Tiger and Panther. His answer was, 'Hell no, but it is the best tank we have yet developed and we should have had it a year earlier.'"

CHAPTER FOUR

MOBILITY

Maximum speed of the Panther tank with a gasoline-powered engine was officially listed as 34 miles per hour (55 km/h) on a level road. This was dropped down to 28 mph (45 km/h) in November 1943. This fact was later picked up by the British Army after they translated captured Panther manuals in late 1944. The typical cruising speed for a Panther on a level road was normally restricted to about 20 mph (32 km/h), while the operational speed off-road was about 15 mph (24 km/h) or less.

The official maximum speed of the first-generation gasoline engine-powered Sherman tanks on a level road was about 25 mph (40 km/h) for a short distance, while the sustained speed on a level road was about 20 mph (32 km/h). However, some Sherman tank veterans state that it was possible to push the vehicle up to 30 mph (48 km/h) for short distances. First-generation diesel engine-powered Sherman tanks were credited with a top speed of 32 mph (51 km/h). The T-34/76 medium tank could reach a maximum road speed of 34 mph (52 km/h) on a level road and a maximum off-road speed of 25mph (40 km/h).

The five interconnected fuel tanks in the rear hull of the Panther tank held 190 gallons (720 liters) of fuel, which supposedly gave the vehicle a maximum radius of action on roads of approximately 124 miles (200 km)

Today's tanks can reach a maximum speed of 60 mph (96 km/h) on level ground. Panther tank crews were restricted to about half that on favorable terrain. More important to a tank crew than the top speed their vehicle can reach on level ground is their vehicle's ability to quickly maneuver from one firing position to another on the battlefield. *(Ground Power Magazine)*

and off road about 62 miles (100 km). One fuel tank was located behind the engine, with two each on either side of the engine. All the fuel tanks were filled from the top of the rear engine deck through a single opening, with an armored cap, which connected to the fuel tank located behind the engine.

From the Panther handbook, oriented toward the enlisted men, comes the warning about refueling the tank:

"It is clear that the Panther burns quickly when knucklehead Paul sleeps during refueling! Don't spill any fuel, if you want to live longer. Take a look at something about, so take note: With caution you go to work! The fuel is mixed with lead it damages eyes, skin, and wounds!

Re-fueling by yourself is an art! Check before if your canister contains gasoline and no diesel .... Then first clean the funnel. Cap off, leave the sieve in. Pour always carefully, when the exhaust pipe is hot! If it is windy, stand into the wind. Whether it rains or snows, bend over the fuel tank filling hole to protect it. But even proper refueling is useless with leaky fuel lines, connectors and fuel pumps. So double-check all these! Clean out fuel and dirt that accumulates outside the fuel tanks. Never start the engine, if there is oil or fuel in the hull."

By way of comparison, a typical gasoline-powered Sherman tank had a maximum radius of action on roads of approximately 130 miles (209 km), while a diesel-powered version had a maximum radius of action on roads of approximately 150 miles (241 km). The diesel-powered T-34 tank series had a maximum radius of action on roads of approximately 190 miles (300 km). As with the Panther tank, off-road travel by either the American or Russian tanks would cut their radius of action by half.

The reason for the difference in operational range between the gasoline-powered tanks and diesel-powered tanks is the much greater thermal efficiency of diesel engines and therefore lower fuel consumption.

From *The Tank* by A. S. Antonov, published in 1954, appears this passage explaining the Russian decision to favor diesel engines in most of their World War II era tanks:

“The petrol engines normally used for motor and aircraft were relatively uneconomical when adopted for tanks. The increased power of such engines

The Panther tank's rear hull was divided into three large compartments, seen here on an unrestored Panther Ausf. G tank. at the French Army Tank Museum. The compact gasoline engine sat in the center watertight compartment, with the radiators and associated fans located in the adjacent compartments. *(David T. Lin)*

entailed a corresponding increase in fuel consumption; thus, in order to provide the vehicle with sufficient fuel, it was necessary to install enlarged fuel tanks, thereby increasing the size and weight of the vehicle. Moreover, the use of petrol in a fighting tank constituted a serious fire hazard. Finally, automobile and aircraft engines were not considered suitable for the more arduous operating conditions of a tank. After a brief period of service, therefore, these engines came to be little used in tanks. **"**

This picture shows the upper rear hull plate of a Panther Ausf. G tank with the engine access panel in the raised position. Visible is the sheet metal housing for the two oil-bath air cleaners that sat on top of the engine. It is obvious from this picture that access to the Panther engine was extremely difficult for both the crew and maintenance personnel. *(Andreas Kirchhoff)*

PANTHER ENGINE

Because the Panther tank engine was rushed into service, it suffered the same teething and reliability problems that bedeviled so many other automotive components that made up the vehicle. This would prove to be a serious Achilles heel for the Panther tank throughout most of its relatively short service life. General Heinz Guderian summed up the importance of the engine in a tank's design by stating: "The engine of the panzer is a weapon just as the main gun."

The original liquid-cooled 12-cylinder V-type gasoline-powered engine fitted into the Panther tank generated 650 horsepower at 3,000 rpm. Designated the Maybach HL210 P30, it descended from aero origins. Gasoline-powered engines were popular with many nations during World War II because of their relatively low production costs. In addition, the installed weight of gasoline-powered engines relative to their power output typically was lower than those of diesel-powered engines.

OPPOSITE
Pictured is the rebuilt and operational Maybach HL230 P30 engine that went into the Panther Ausf. A tank restored by the Military Vehicle Technology Foundation. The Panther engine was a compact, gasoline-powered, water-cooled V-12. Being gasoline-powered, the Panther engine had a very high fuel consumption level. *(David Marian)*

With the sheet metal housing for the two oil-bath air cleaners that sat on top of the Panther tank engine removed for this photograph, the engine's four carburetors can be seen. Late-war German reports mention the improved reliability of Panther engine and attribute the majority of motor failures to bearing damage and broken connecting rods. *(David Marian)*

The Sherman tanks used a combination of air-cooled and liquid-cooled gasoline and diesel engines. The 9-cylinder air-cooled gasoline-powered radial engines for its first-generation Sherman tanks (the M4 and M4A1) generated 400 horsepower at 2,400 rpm. A liquid-cooled diesel-powered version of the Sherman tank (M4A2) generated 410 horsepower at 2,900 rpm. A shortage of air-cooled radial engines would push the U.S. Army to take into service a Ford-designed and -built liquid-cooled V-8 gasoline-powered engine Sherman tank (M4A3) that produced 500 horsepower at 2,600 rpm. The T-34 tank series depended on liquid-cooled diesel engines throughout its service life that produced 500 horsepower at 1,800 rpm.

Unlike its American and Russian tank counterparts, the Panther tank engine sat in a watertight compartment at the center rear of the tank's hull. This came about due to a German Army high command requirement for the Panther tank to be able to ford relatively deep water obstacles. Their fear was that their existing inventory of portable bridges was not equal to carrying the weight of the vehicle. To address this requirement, the early production units of the Panther Ausf. D tank came with a hole on the upper rear engine deck, covered by a flap, for the fitting of a telescoping air intake pipe that would allow a fording depth of 13 feet (4 m).

Tests with the Panther tank fording system in July 1943 proved unsuccessful, and the requirement was dropped in August 1943 as other tests showed that the German Army's existing portable bridges could support the weight of a Panther tank. The Panther tank series would retain the ability to wade up to about 5 feet (1.524 m) of water throughout its service life.

The original hole for the telescoping air intake pipe on the rear engine deck of the Panther tank was retained on the vehicle as an air intake vent for the engine and covered with a wire mesh screen to keep out debris. To prevent battlefield fragments from entering the small air intake vent, an armored cowling appeared on the last version of the Panther tank to cover the vent.

The original fording requirement set by the German Army high command, which resulted in the Panther tank's engine being installed into a watertight compartment, meant that it was inadequately ventilated throughout its service life and no doubt led to its very short lifespan.

Visible in this picture are the radiators and their associated overhead fans, which occupied the compartments on either side of the centrally mounted liquid-cooled Panther tank gasoline engine. At the rear of the engine compartment are the fuel receptacle (on the left) and the water receptacle (on the right). *(Patton Museum)*

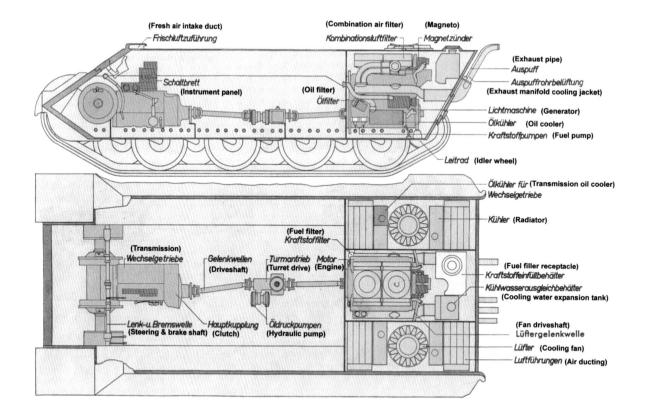

(Fresh air intake duct)
Frischluftzuführung

(Combination air filter)
Kombinationsluftfilter

(Magneto)
Magnetzünder

(Exhaust pipe)
Auspuff

Auspuffrohrbelüftung
(Exhaust manifold cooling jacket)

Schaltbrett
(Instrument panel)

(Oil filter)
Ölfilter

Lichtmaschine (Generator)
Ölkühler (Oil cooler)
Kraftstoffpumpen (Fuel pump)

Leitrad (Idler wheel)

Ölkühler für (Transmission oil cooler)
Wechselgetriebe

Kühler (Radiator)

(Fuel filter)
Kraftstofffilter

(Transmission)
Wechselgetriebe

Gelenkwellen
(Driveshaft)

Turmantrieb
(Turret drive)

Motor
(Engine)

(Fuel filler receptacle)
Kraftstoffeinfüllbehälter

Kühlwasserausgleichbehälter
(Cooling water expansion tank)

Lenk-u. Bremswelle
(Steering & brake shaft)

Hauptkupplung
(Clutch)

Öldruckpumpen
(Hydraulic pump)

(Fan driveshaft)
Lüftergelenkwelle

Lüfter (Cooling fan)

Luftführungen (Air ducting)

A wonderful color illustration from a German World War II manual on the Panther tank shows the various internal components located in the vehicle's hull and their location from both an overhead and side view. The need for the floor of the turret basket to clear the drive train dictated the height of the Panther tank. *(Military Vehicle Technology Foundation)*

DEVELOPMENTAL HISTORY

Development of the Maybach HL210 P30 engine was ordered in June 1941, and the first production example came off the factory floor in February 1942. It was the same engine as fitted into the early series production units of the Tiger Ausf. E heavy tank fielded in August 1942. The maximum speed the German Tiger Ausf. E heavy tank could attain on level roads was about 24 mph (39 km/h) with the Maybach HL210 P30 engine.

A quick consensus arose among those concerned with the development and fielding of the first batch of Panther tanks that the initial production vehicles powered by the Maybach HL210 P30 engine were underpowered. This was the same conclusion being reached on the early series production units of the Tiger Ausf. E heavy tank equipped with the same engine.

In order to correct the problem with the underpowered Maybach engine model in both the Panther and Tiger tanks, a decision was made to redesign the engine by substituting a heavier cast iron engine block in place of the original light alloy engine block and boring out the cylinder diameter.

This in turn pushed up the engine output from 650 to 700 horsepower at 3,000 rpm.

A caveat to the listed gross horsepower of tanks appears in this extract from *Technology of Tanks* by Richard M. Ogorkiewicz:

> "The power available for propelling tanks is not however that normally quoted, which is the maximum gross engine power. It is considerably lower than the latter, first of all because of the power absorbed by the fans required to circulate air for cooling the engine and the transmission …. Additional power losses occur in the final drives, the efficiency of which is typically about 97 percent. As a result, the power available at the sprockets to drive a tank amounts to only 70, or at most 74 percent of the gross engine power. However, even at full load, it can be only 61 percent of the gross power."

Reflecting the changes to the existing Maybach HL210 P30 engine design, it was redesignated the Maybach HL230 P30 and began appearing in the Panther Ausf. D tank in May 1943. Although the increase in horsepower

All the upper rear overhead hull plates are mounted in this picture of a Panther Ausf. A tank. The wire mesh debris guards that fit over the fan housings as well as the cast steel armored grilles are missing from this vehicle. The uncompleted turret for the tank shown sits on a metal bench behind the vehicle's hull. *(Michael Green)*

failed to raise the maximum operational speed of the Panther Ausf. D tank, it did relieve some of the strain on the engine when the vehicle went off-road.

A wartime U.S. Army report, dated December 4, 1944, described features of the Maybach HL210 P30 engine:

> "The engine is of the overhead valve, overhead camshaft type and uses two very large valves per cylinder .... This engine utilizes twin Bosch magnetos, one for each bank of six cylinders and except for the use of impulse couplings are almost identical to those manufactured by American Bosch for use in the Ford tank engine. The spark plugs used in this engine are manufactured by Bosch and are very similar to the American Bosch spark plugs. They are of the conventional type automotive design with a single electrode and side wire and appear to be a hot type plug. There is only one spark plug per cylinder."

From the U.S. Army document titled *U.S. Army Report on United States vs German Armor* comes this quote by Major Philip C. Calhoun comparing the Panther engine to the M4A3 Sherman tank equipped with a Ford V-8 liquid-cooled engine:

The air sucked in by the Panther tank's two large rear hull fans came in through air-intake louvers protected by large cast steel armored grilles on the Panther Ausf. D and A tanks. An unrestored armored grille is being removed from a Panther Ausf. A tank with the aid of an overhead crane.
(Michael Green)

A close-up picture of one of the adjustable shutter arrangements employed to regulate the amount of air entering the radiators on the Panther Ausf. D and Ausf. A tanks. This feature was dispensed with on the Panther Ausf. G tank. Allied tankers used tarps to control the amount of air that entered their tank's radiators. *(Michael Green)*

❝The Ford motor is evidently a better motor for our tank than the Maybach or Mercedes is for their tanks, though the German motors have plenty of ready power and Mark V [Panther] tank can get away from a stationary position, but it doesn't stand up under the beating that ours does. ❞

A crew chief of a U.S. Army maintenance section shared somewhat similar sentiments in the same wartime document: "In observing the engine of a Mark V [Panther] in operation I think that it is far superior to our radial engines but not superior to our Ford engines in respect to long life and fuel consumption."

The belief that the Panther was equipped with a Mercedes engine might have been inspired by a British wartime report dated January 9, 1945, which quotes a German prisoner of war:

❝PW states that there has been a lot of talk that the Panther was to receive a new engine, i.e. Mercedes Benz 1,400 horsepower, based on an aero engine which had the advantage of being smaller and more powerful than the present Maybach engine. PW has however, never seen a Panther with the Mercedes Benz engine. ❞

tank featured smaller
cast steel armored
grilles on the top of a
redesigned rear engine
upper deck. This was
done to minimize
damage to the very
vulnerable radiators
from overhead fire or
artillery fragments.
The wire mesh debris
guards that fit over the
fan housings as well
as the cast steel
armored grilles on this
particular vehicle are
incorrect. (Andreas
Kirchhoff)

STARTING THE PANTHER ENGINE

The engine on the Panther tank could be started by a number of different methods. The normal method was by means of a conventional type rotary electric starter motor that used the sliding armature principle found in many other German vehicles. The electric starter was operated through relays actuated by a button on the driver's instrument panel. It was the only 24-volt electric unit in the tank as all others were 12 volt. The change from 12 to 24 volts for starting was performed automatically after the starter switch was depressed.

Located above the electric starter in the Panther tank's rear hull compartment was an inertia starter, which was energized by means of a crank that was inserted in an opening in the rear hull plate of the vehicle. The inertia starter had the ability to start the engine even when cold and operated very satisfactorily. Late-model production Panther tanks did away with the inertia starter and depended on a portable shaft connected to a small vehicle known as the *Kubelwagen* to start the engine if the need arose.

The Panther tank also could be started by towing it. The last method available for starting the Panther tank engine encompassed an auxiliary gasoline power plant that was not part of the vehicle, but that powered a shaft that was projected through an opening in the rear hull plate of the tank and engaged the rear end of the crankshaft.

To permit quick starting of the Panther tank engine during extreme cold weather operations, there was a heat exchanger located at the rear of the vehicle's engine. The crew took an onboard blowtorch and projected a hot flame into the heat exchanger from outside of the tank through an opening in the rear hull plate normally covered by an armored flap. The warmed water from the heat exchanger would then flow through a long pipe into the engine. The heated water then passed out through the engine by way of a main water inlet pipe and into an intercooler, where it went through the heat exchanger again, creating a space heating effect.

A close-up picture of the shutter arrangement found on late production Panther Ausf. G tanks. According to noted researcher Thomas L. Jentz, these were intended to be mounted only on the right side of the rear engine upper deck armored plate, in place of the cast steel armored grilles. *(Chun-Lun Hsu)*

ENGINE ACCESSORIES

Dust was kept out of the Panther Maybach HL230 P30 engine with two oil-bath air cleaners that required cleaning every 400 miles (644 km) under normal conditions or every 80 miles (129 km) under very dusty conditions. Dissatisfaction with this arrangement led to the installation of two combined centrifugal and oil-bath-type air cleaners in the Panther tank, which required cleaning under normal conditions at 1,600 miles (2,575 km) and every 400 miles (644 km) in dusty conditions.

Cooling for the Panther Ausf. D tank engine and accessories was provided by four vertically oriented radiators, in their own separate watertight compartments, with two on either side of the engine compartment surmounted by a single large 24-inch (61-cm) horizontally oriented engine-driven cooling fan. The radiator on the forward right-hand side of the engine was divided into two sections. One section was used for the cooling of the transmission oil and the other for the engine coolant, while the other three radiators were used to cool the engine. There was a cap on the upper rear hull plate of the Panther tank to add more water to the vehicle's four radiators, covered by an armored flap.

The liquid cooling system of the Panther tank was of the pressure type with a pressure relief valve built into the cap of the mixing tank. In addition to drawing air through the cooling radiators, the suction of the large horizontally oriented engine-driven cooling fans was employed for three other jobs on the Panther, according to a U.S. Army report from December 4, 1944:

> "The exhaust manifolds of the engine are completely shrouded with sheet metal covering [Panther Ausf. G tank], which is ducted into the fan compartment below the fan. This causes air to be drawn over the heated exhaust manifold and discharged into the fan compartment. The air that is drawn into the exhaust shrouds serves to scavenge the engine compartment to a slight extent.

Starting in May 1944, the two rounded cast steel armored guards seen on the Panther Ausf. D and Ausf. A tank, which protected the exhaust pipe penetrations in the lower rear armor hull plate, were replaced on all new production Panther Ausf. G tanks with square welded armored guards as shown here. (David T. Lin)

Another air duct leads from this fan compartment to the front of the tank where secondary ducts go to the clutch, transmission, and steering brakes. Heated air from these parts is drawn rearward through this duct into the fan compartment.

The last opening into the fan compartment is utilized to scavenge heated air from the engine compartment and in some vehicles includes a duct for removing dirt from the air cleaner pre-cleaners. "

Belonging to the collection of the U.S. Army Ordnance Museum is this Panther Ausf. G tank, which features the sheet metal covers applied to the engine exhaust pipes of all Panther Ausf. G tanks coming off the production lines beginning in June 1944. Its purpose was to shield the heat-induced glow of the engine exhaust pipes. *(Christophe Vallier)*

Four armored air-intake louvers were on the Panther top rear hull plate, one for each radiator, covered by wire mesh to keep out debris. The degree of cooling for the Panther Ausf. D and A tank engines was regulated by a complex arrangement of shutters operated by a member of the crew, which controlled the amount of air-flow entering the radiators to expedite engine warm-up during cold weather and to maintain operating temperatures during cold weather. There was no thermostat in the coolant flow.

With the production of the Panther Ausf. G tank, the shutters used to regulate the cooling of the Panther Ausf. D and Ausf. A tank engine were eliminated. The Panther Ausf. G tank also came with smaller air-intake louvers on the roof of the rear hull plate than those found on the Panther Ausf. D and A tanks.

CREW COMFORT

There was no crew heater in the Panther Ausf. D tank or in early versions of the Panther Ausf. A tank. To rectify this situation a crew compartment heater (*Kampfraumheizung*) was eventually developed and fitted to later production units of the Panther Ausf. A tank beginning in January 1944. It used the engine cooling system in the tank's rear hull to suck in air from the left-hand side engine-driven cooling fan and then run it through the radiators, thereby warming it and then running some of that warmed air (via ductwork) into the vehicle's fighting compartment, with the rest of the warmed air expelled through the two air-intake louvers on the left-side cooling system. The crew could regulate the amount of warm air coming into the fighting compartment with an adjustable vent in the firewall, which separated the fighting compartment from the engine compartment.

When the reverse flow installed on the Panther Ausf. A to put warm air into the crew compartment, the air flow path no longer led past the left-side manifold, meaning it was not being cooled. Left in that condition, the manifold would soon get hot enough to glow. Therefore, a second flow path was installed parallel to the left manifold to dump heat back outside the tank. This resulted in the two smaller pipes installed on either side of the Panther Ausf. A tank's left-hand side exhaust pipe.

The Panther Ausf. G tank received a new crew compartment heater arrangement in October 1944. The protruding armored device fitted over the left-hand side engine-driven cooling fan cowling. Some of the heated air generated by the radiators and blown out by the fan could then be diverted by ducting into the tank's crew compartment. This did away with the need to have the extra cooling pipes on either side of the left engine exhaust pipe as was fitted to many of the Panther Ausf. A tanks.

In May 1944, the rounded cast armor guards that protected the exhaust pipe penetrations through the rear hull plate on the Panther Ausf. G tank were replaced by square welded armored guards.

Sheet metal covers were added to the engine exhaust manifold pipes (except for the curved cowls) on Panther Ausf. G tanks, built after June 1944, in order to hide the hot glowing pipes from enemy observation at night. A more elaborate flame suppression muffler system, known in German as the *Flammenvernichter*, went onto the engine exhaust manifold pipes on Panther Ausf. G tanks, beginning in October 1944. It prevented

OVERLEAF
This picture shows the original two exhaust pipe arrangement on the rear hull plate of the Panther Ausf. D tank. With the introduction of the Panther Ausf. G tank, the builders returned to the two exhaust pipe arrangement on the rear hull plate of the tank. (*Virginia Museum of Military Vehicles*)

flaming backfires from the engine exhaust manifold pipes alerting the enemy to the battlefield presence of Panther tanks.

Beginning in December 1944, thin elevated armored covers were added on the Panther Ausf. G tank over the intake and exhaust air access points on the top of the rear hull roof to prevent artillery fragments and bullets from strafing aircraft entering the tank's hull and damaging the vehicle's cooling system.

ENGINE SHORTCOMINGS

The adoption of the HL230 P30 in the Panther Ausf. D tank did not automatically solve all the problems inherent with the engine design. Issues with blown head gaskets had to be solved, and several other modifications were introduced to the engine design.

In September 1943, an order appeared that all Maybach HL230 P30 engines delivered for the Panther tank before August 1, 1943, were to be exchanged with newly built engines due to design flaws in the earlier production units of the engine.

New production Panther Ausf. G tanks began appearing with a *Kampfraumheizung* (fighting compartment heater) beginning in October 1944.
An easily identified external feature of that device was the raised fan tower seen here on the left side of the vehicle rear engine upper hull plate.
(Chun-Lun Hsu)

The factories building the Maybach HL230 P30 engine began a program of derating the engine to 2,500 rpm at maximum load in November 1943 in order to prolong its life span. The derating of the Panther tank engine dropped the maximum listed speed of the vehicle from 34 mph (52 km/h) to 28 mph (45 km/h). It also lowered the maximum engine output from 700 to about 580 horsepower on the Panther. The success of this effort was mixed; a British Army report in June 1944 reported that a German POW had stated that the engines in one Panther battalion had an average life span of only 450 miles (724 km).

From a translated German Army report dated April 22, 1944, which appears in *Germany's Panther Tank: The Quest for Combat Supremacy* by Thomas L. Jentz, comes these observations from a Panther unit:

> “Maybach HL230 P30 Motors: In general, the newer motors have a significantly longer lifespan than the first series. The longest distance achieved by a motor is

Beginning in October 1944, the stop-gap measure of hiding the glow of the hot exhaust pipes from enemy observation by the fitting of sheet metal covers was discontinued and replaced with the *Flammenvernichter* (flame suppressor) seen on this Panther Ausf. G belonging to the collection of the Tank Museum, Bovington. *(David Marian)*

1,700 [1,056 miles] to 1,800 kilometers [1,118 miles] in three of seven Panthers that are still available. The motor failures that did occur were all of the same nature, bearing damage and broken connecting rods. **"**

This same report also mentioned that gasoline was overflowing from the engine's carburetors and was being ignited and causing engine fires.

The problem with the Panther tank engine catching fire also appeared in a British military test carried out in 1948 under the auspices of the Fighting Vehicle Design Department (FVDD) on a small group of Panther Ausf. G tanks and variants:

"Engine compartment fires occurred in each of the four vehicles involved in the trial, in the majority of cases more than once. The fires generally started in the vicinity of the carburetors and had been attributed to a tendency for carburetor flooding, the actual conflagration breaking out as a result of a backfire. **"**

In case of an engine fire on the Panther tank, there was an automatic fire extinguisher system installed in the engine compartment. As such systems were then in their infancy it proved far from perfect and engine heat often triggered the fire extinguisher system sensors, leaving less of the extinguishing agent for when there was a real engine fire. A British Army report dated May 5, 1944, titled *Armour Branch Report on Armour Quality & Vulnerability of Pz.Kw.V (Panther)* concluded that the vehicle was well designed against the outbreak of fire and that should a fire

ENGINE RATING DEFINITIONS

There are three power ratings for a vehicle engine: rated, installed, and sustained.

Rated power is the product of the highest torque at rated speed that a bare engine can deliver on a test stand and is typically used when describing a vehicle's maximum horsepower.

Installed power is the power remaining after cooling fans, water/oil pumps, and other engine support loads are subtracted from rated horsepower.

Sustained power is the maximum continuous power that can be delivered without overheating. Modern combat vehicle cooling systems are designed to cool the engine enough so that it can deliver its maximum power continuously in very hot environments. However, dirt buildup, coolant condition, fan speed controller adjustment, and other factors can reduce the sustained power available to the driver.

breakout, it was probable that the on-board fire extinguisher would be relatively effective. It went on to conclude that due to the engine compartment layout that with the vehicle's engine stopped, there would be insufficient air to support combustion.

Sometime in September 1944, two dozen Panther Ausf. G tanks built by MAN drove off the production line fitted with all steel tired road wheels with internal rubber cushioning, one of which is seen here. It was no doubt an experiment to test their durability. *(Patton Museum)*

POWER-TO-WEIGHT RATIO

One of the key mobility performance indicators for any tank is the ratio of engine horsepower divided by gross vehicle weight. This measure is called the power-to-weight ratio. It governs the acceleration of a tank, which is of crucial importance when changing firing positions or climbing a slope or traveling off-road and since it governs the acceleration of a tank, the changing of firing positions.

The roughly 50-ton (45-mt) series production Panther had a power-to-weight ratio of about 14 horsepower per ton with the 700 horsepower version of the HL 230 P30, which was lower than the original Panther prototype.

The power-to-weight ratio of the original first-generation 33-ton (30-mt) Sherman tanks was about the same as the Panther tank with the 700 horsepower HL 230 P30 engine. The 37-ton (33-mt) second-generation Sherman tanks, with the same engines as the first-generation versions, had their power-to-weight ratio drop to 13.5 horsepower per ton.

The 30-ton (28-mt) T-34/76 tank had a power-to-weight ratio of between 17 and 19 horsepower per ton, while the heavier 35-ton (32-mt) T-34-85 tank had only 14.2 horsepower per ton with the same engine. By way of comparison, the most modern version of the U.S. Army's M1 Abrams tank series, weighing in at about 70 tons (63 mt), boasts a power-to-weight ratio of 21.4 horsepower per ton.

The drop in the power-to-weight ratio for the series production Panther tank was directly attributable to the up-armoring of the tank to meet the threat of ever more deadly enemy antitank weapons, a not uncommon problem to all the tank designers of World War II. In turn, the extra weight imposed on a chassis and automotive components designed for a tank

This picture shows the horizontal storage arrangement for the 16-ton (15-mt) *Winde* (jack) on the rear hull plate of a Panther Ausf. A tank. This arrangement had a drawback as it meant that the jack had to be removed before the crew could open the rear hull plate armored engine access panel, located behind the jack, in order to check on the engine. *(Christopher Hughes)*

originally envisioned to be 15 tons (13.6 mt) less in weight led to the mechanical unreliability that robbed the Panther tank of its rightful place as the best medium tank of World War II. Most of the blame for this state of affairs has to be placed on the designers of the Panther, who by now had enough empirical data to know that any design will grow by a certain percentage from drawing board to in the field.

To overcome the problem of having the *Winde* (jack) blocking the rear hull plate armored engine access panel on the Panther tank, a larger 22-ton (20-mt) jack was eventually moved to a vertically oriented position between the twin exhaust pipes on later production units of the Panther Ausf. A as seen here. *(David T. Lin)*

ROAD WHEELS

In theory, the large, interleaved road-wheel configuration of the Panther offered a more even distribution of loads along a track's length, thus contributing to a lower ground pressure. In practice, the advantages were small relative to the disadvantages. One of the little-known disadvantages with interleaved suspensions is that they work (flex) the track in torsion and lower track life. Several of the better-known disadvantages of interleaved track are discussed in an extract from *Panther & Its Variants* by Walter J. Spielberger:

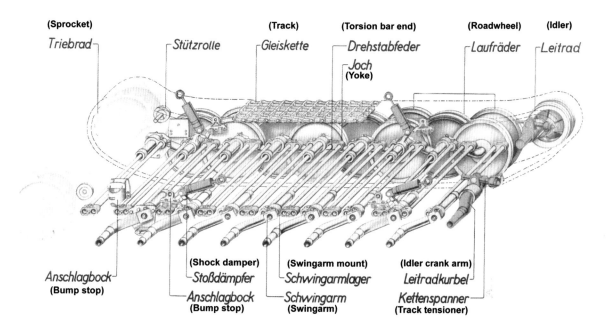

(Sprocket)		(Track)	(Torsion bar end)		(Roadwheel)	(Idler)
Triebrad	Stützrolle	Gleiskette	Drehstabfeder		Laufräder	Leitrad
			Joch (Yoke)			

Anschlagbock (Bump stop)

(Shock damper) Stoßdämpfer
Anschlagbock (Bump stop)

(Swingarm mount) Schwingarmlager
Schwingarm (Swingarm)

(Idler crank arm) Leitradkurbel
Kettenspanner (Track tensioner)

"The disadvantages of this type of running gear became readily apparent during the muddy periods in Russia; during sudden frost the heavily clogged overlapping road wheels would become frozen together if the mud had not been cleaned off beforehand. Shell damage would cause the bogie wheels [road wheels] to jam together; separating them could only be accomplished with difficulty. In addition, a single damaged wheel often necessitated the removal of several. For these reasons this technologically advanced running gear design was never built again following World War II."

The Panther tank rode on thirty-two large 34-inch (86-cm) diameter interleaved rubber-rimmed road wheels (eight dual sets on either side of the hull). Road wheels were assembled from two formed steel halves that bolted together originally with sixteen bolts and later with twenty-four bolts. They had a replaceable one-piece molded rubber tire in between them.

As an experiment, two dozen Panther Ausf. G tanks were equipped with steel-rimmed road wheels, with internal rubber cushioning, in place of the original rubber-rimmed road wheels. Historical pictorial evidence shows that these Panther Ausf. G tanks saw employment during the German Ardennes Offensive, better known to Americans as the Battle of the Bulge.

This beautiful color illustration comes from a World War II German manual on the Panther tank. It shows all the various features that made up the tank's unique suspension system. The off-road mobility of the Panther tank's suspension system was not matched on other tanks until the 1970s. (James D. Brown)

OPPOSITE
The 16-ton (15-mt) or 22-ton (20-mt) Winde (jack) mounted on the rear hull plate of the Panther tank series was intended to assist the crew in removing or attaching their tank's road wheels to their road arms, as seen in this wartime photograph. (Patton Museum)

A British Army report dated January 11, 1945, provided a description of the steel-rimmed road wheels, referred to by the British as bogie wheels:

"Some Panthers of recent production are equipped with steel tyred [tire] bogie wheels instead of the previous types of rubber tyred wheels. The steel wheels are insulated from the hub by two rubber rings clamped by means of 12 equally spaced bolts between the disc pressings. The new bogie wheels are similar to the steel rimmed wheels which have already appeared on the Tiger models E & B. The rim has an overall diameter of two feet 7½ inches and 3 inches wide [20 cm to 76.2 mm]."

The drive sprocket of a Panther Ausf. A tank is seen here. The vehicle's two drive sprockets were mounted on the tank's two final drive units. It was the drive sprockets that took the engine torque and turned the vehicle's tracks. Being located at the front of the tank meant the Panther tank's drive sprockets were more vulnerable to enemy weapons such as antitank mines. *(Michael Green)*

A downside that came with the addition of steel-rimmed road wheels on the Panther Ausf. G tank was an increase in the weight of the tank of 2.2 tons (2 mt). In German, the steel-rimmed road wheels were known as *Gummisparende Laufrollen*. A handful of Panther Ausf. G tanks, built in early 1945, featured steel-rimmed road wheels mixed in with their rubber-rimmed road wheels.

The Sherman tanks never sported steel-rimmed road wheels. It was the Russians who originally came up with the concept of steel-rimmed road wheels for their KV series of heavy tanks. Due to rubber shortages, some T-34/76 tanks coming off Soviet assembly lines began sporting steel road wheels, with internal rubber cushioning, as early as August 1941. Other T-34/76 tanks began appearing with a mixture of both rubber-rimmed and steel-rimmed road wheels. Some of the steel-rimmed road wheels built for the T-34/76 tank lacked internal rubber cushioning.

Located directly behind the front drive sprockets on the Panther tank was a small rubber-tired roller that prevented the vehicle's tracks from bunching up on the drive sprocket when in reverse. This feature was eventually replaced on the final production units of the Panther Ausf. G tank with a *Gleitschuh* (skid shoe). *(Michael Green)*

This factory picture of an uncompleted Panther Ausf. A tank shows the final drive (minus the drive sprocket) at the front of the hull. The final drive was one of the most serious weak spots in the Panther tank design and plagued the vehicle throughout its service life. Also visible are the vehicle's spindles and road wheel hubs. *(Patton Museum)*

SPINDLES AND TORSION BARS

The Panther tank road wheels were mounted on spindles with bearings at the ends of forged steel road arms, sprung by thirty-two high-strength transversely mounted steel torsion bars arranged in sets of two that spanned the bottom of the vehicle's hull. According to a British military report from the Department of Tank Design dated September 1944, the twin torsion bar arrangement on the Panther tank is referred to as *Haarnadelfederung* due to its resemblance to a ladies' hairpin.

The two torsion bars springing each road wheel were connected in series, i.e., the first bar was connected to the road arm and spanned the width of the hull, where it was linked to a second identical bar running parallel to the first. The second bar was then anchored to the hull adjacent to the first bar's road arm bearing. The net effect was to greatly soften the spring rate and permit increased road wheel vertical travel, reducing the incidents of "suspension bottoming," significantly improving cross-country performance.

Each Panther's track consisted of eighty-six individual interlocking steel track links connected by steel pins. The Germans referred to it as *Trockenbolzen-Scharnierkette* (dry single-pin track). Total weight of the Panther tank tracks on either side of the hull was 4,501 lbs (2050 kg). *(Patton Museum)*

As the Panther tank went over uneven ground, the mass of the vehicle acting against the motion of the road arms caused the twin torsion bars to rotate. The twisting action of the twin torsion bars pushed the road wheels down to keep them on the ground. Because the pure springing action of the twin torsion bars alone would cause the Panther tank to pitch uncontrollably, even on relatively smooth ground, the tank had shock absorbers fitted to its suspension system road arms to prevent the vehicle from oscillating. The reduction of oscillation is known as damping, which is important to reduce tank crew fatigue and motion sickness when traversing rough terrain at higher speeds.

The torsion bar arrangement on the Panther tank provided it with a suspension travel of 20 inches (51 cm). By way of comparison, the German Tiger Ausf. E and B heavy tanks had a bit less than 9 inches (23 cm) of suspension travel, while the T-34 tank series had roughly 9.5 inches (24 cm) of suspension travel. The first-generation Sherman tank had only about 4 inches (10.2 cm) of suspension travel. The postwar German Army Leopard I main battle tank introduced in 1965 had 15 inches (38 cm) of suspension travel, while the Leopard II main battle tank, which entered German Army service in 1979, had 21 inches (53 cm) of suspension travel.

A close-up picture of the original adjustable idler wheel design that appeared on the Panther Ausf. D tank and remained in use until October 1944 when it was replaced by a larger idler wheel design on the Panther Ausf. G tank. Idler wheels maintain track tension as they run around a tank's drive sprocket. *(Christopher Hughes)*

Torsion bars became the suspension system of choice for both German and American tanks during and after World War II because of their light weight and simplicity combined with their ability to store more energy in relation to their weight than any other types of suspension spring mechanism. Torsion bar suspension systems also appeared on the wartime Russian KV series of heavy tanks as well as its successors, the IS-II and IS-III heavy tanks.

The first-generation Sherman tanks rode on a vertical volute spring suspension system (VVSS), while the second-generation Sherman tanks would ride on the horizontal volute spring suspension system (HVSS). The VVSS consisted of vertically mounted volute (coil) springs that were helically wound steel strips whose inner turns were displaced along a central

The last design version of the idler found on the Panther tank series appears here on a Panther Ausf. G tank. In addition to being larger than the original version, it was self-cleaning. The original design was not self-cleaning, which led to problems with a buildup of debris. *(David Marian)*

axis to give the finished spring a conical shape. As the name indicates, the volute springs in the HVSS were mounted horizontally on the bogie unit of the Sherman tank rather than vertically. Neither of these systems would appear on American tanks designed and built after World War II.

The T-34 tank series rode on an independent suspension system, referred to as the Christie suspension system, which consisted of large road wheels connected to long vertical coil springs located within the tank's hull. There were no return rollers on the Christie suspension system, which did not appear on any tanks designed and built after World War II.

There are disadvantages with torsion bar suspension systems, as detailed by Richard M. Ogorkiewicz in *Technology of Tanks*:

> The advantages of torsion bar suspensions are however accompanied by a number of disadvantages. Thus, while the installation of the torsion bars across the bottom of a tank hull is simple and well-protected, it also increases their height. This is undesirable in itself and can also significantly increase the weight of tanks when they are heavily armored.

An independent suspension system with torsion bars appeared on both the Ausf. D version of the German Army Panzer II light tank with large road wheels and the Ausf. E model of the Panzer III in 1938 with small dual road wheels. The Panzer IV tank rode on a leaf spring suspension system with small dual road wheels. The advantage of small road wheels was that more of them could be used and in turn more evenly spread the weight of a tank over the length of its tracks.

TRACKS

Like many tank tracks, those on the Panther tank were made up of interlocking steel track links connected by steel pins, which did not have bushings. Tank tracks connected by steel pins without bushings are referred to as "dead track." Tank tracks held together with steel pins covered by rubber bushings are called live track. The Sherman tank employed live tracks and the Russian T-34 tank series used dead tracks.

The big advantage of dead track is that it is easier to repair. Torsional stiffness of the cast steel track with steel track pins was also a plus when it came to track retention in comparison to more resilient rubber bushed tracks that were often used by the Sherman tank. Sherman tanks also used all steel tracks.

Live track requires special tools to get the track back at the angle at which there is neutral torsional stress in the bushings. The big advantage of live track, with bushings, is that it keeps out dirt that acts as a grinding compound in dead track every time the track links flex.

The tracks on each side of the Panther tank were made up of 86 individual track links weighing 46 lbs (21 kg) each and were 26 inches (66 cm) wide. The tracks on the Panzer IV medium tank were 16 inches (41 cm) wide while the combat tracks on the Tiger Ausf. E heavy tank were 28.5 inches (72 cm) wide and 32 inches (81 cm) wide on the Tiger Ausf. B heavy tank. The tracks on the first-generation Sherman tank were only 17 inches (43 cm) wide. The second-generation Sherman tank had tracks that were 23 inches (58 cm) wide. The tracks on the T-34 tank series were 20 inches (51 cm) wide.

The importance of width for tank tracks is described by Richard M. Ogorkiewicz in *Design and Development of Fighting Vehicles*:

> "Whichever the type, tracks need to be as wide as possible to keep to a minimum the pressure exerted by the vehicle on the ground. The higher this pressure the greater is the depth to which the tracks sink into soft ground and the greater, therefore, is the amount of work done in propelling the vehicle or, in other words, the higher is the resistance to its motion."

The advantage of wider tank tracks on the Panther tank appears in a quote by Captain Henry Johnson in the wartime document titled *U.S. Army Report on United States vs German Armor*:

> "The wider tracks on the Mark V [Panther] and the Mark VI [Tiger] enables it to move much better cross-country and in muddy or snow-covered terrain, than do the narrow tracks of the Sherman tank. The field expedient of duck bills added to widen the Sherman tread, aids but does not affect the advantage the Mark V and Mark VI tanks have. It is my opinion that the Mark V and Mark VI enemy tank is far superior in maneuverability to our own Sherman tanks."

To improve their off-road traction, the Panther tank steel track links, like those of the Sherman medium tank and the T-34 series tank, had grousers cast onto the side in contact with the ground. Ice cleats could be attached to the center of every fifth or seventh track link on the Panther tank for

A restored example of a Panther tank transmission awaits its installation in a vehicle. As with the Panther tank's final drives, the vehicle's transmission was a source of serious problems throughout its short career. This lack of reliability meant the German Army would transport its Panther tanks by rail whenever possible to save wear and tear on the vehicle's transmission and extend its limited service life.
(David Marian)

operating on ice and snow. When the ice cleats were fitted to a Panther tank's tracks, the vehicle could not be driven at speeds greater than 9 mph (15 kph). Panther tanks were supposed to be equipped with forty individual ice cleats each weighing about 9 lbs (4kg).

GROUND PRESSURE

Related to track width and one of the key factors affecting the mobility of a tank's design is the ground pressure of the vehicle's tracks on soft soils. The lower the ground pressure, the easier it is for a tank to cross poor terrain. This pressure is generally described in pounds per square inch (psi), with a standing man having a psi of 7 and the average automobile having a psi of 35. The Panther tank featured a psi of 11.6 while the 56-ton Tiger Ausf. E heavy tank had a psi of 14.7. The 70-ton (63-mt) Tiger Ausf. B heavy tank,

the heaviest turreted tank of World War II, had a psi of 15. The first-generation Sherman tanks sported a psi of 12.9 and the heavier and wider second-generation Sherman tanks had a psi of 13.9. The T-34/76 tank featured a psi of 8.5 and the heavier T-34-85 tank had a psi of 11.6. The KV-1 heavy tank came in with a psi of 11.

The fact that the roughly 50-ton (45-mt) Panther had a lower psi than the much lighter first- and second-generation Sherman tanks is not that strange. Ground pressure decreases for any given weight as more track surface comes in contact with the ground, which reinforces the importance of track width. This is also seen in a quote from a March 1945 U.S. Army document titled: *U.S. Army Report on United States vs German Armor*:

> ❝ I have compared the depth to which our tanks sink alongside of German Mark V [Panther] tanks in soft ground. Before the addition of track extensions, our medium tanks sank six to eight inches (15 to 20 cm) while the Mark V tracks were not over four inches (10 cm). ❞

Staff members of the Military Vehicle Technology Foundation are pictured lowering the transmission unit into the front hull compartment of a Panther Ausf. A tank. Although the transmissions in the U.S. Army M4 Sherman tank and the Red Army T-34 tank series were much simpler in design than that found in the Panther tank, their outstanding value was their ruggedness. *(Michael Green)*

One lesson learned by the Germans early in World War II was that the highest loaded road wheel on a track determined how deep that track would sink in soft soil. The application of this lesson was applied to the Panther tank suspension design with its interleaved or overlapping road wheels, which provided more road wheels to support the load hence lower unit ground pressure with less sinkage. This benefit can become an important factor with a column of tanks crossing a soft soil field that might have planted land mines. In this case tanks would often stay in a column playing "follow the leader" for the sake of safety. Ruts would be formed by the tracks and excessive sinkage into the soil was very undesirable because at some point hull bottom contact occurs and the mired down vehicle(s) may have to be towed free.

DRIVE SPROCKETS AND IDLERS

Tank tracks are under the control of the vehicle's drive sprockets, which deliver the "tractive effort" between the tank and the ground. Drive sprockets receive their power from a tank's engine by way of the transmission. A large gear ratio is used in the tank's final drives to reduce the transmission speed and increase the torque at the sprockets.

The Panther tank's drive sprockets were located at the front of the vehicle's hull, as were those on all German tanks from the Panzer I light tank through the Tiger Ausf. B heavy tank. The reason for this had to do with the location of the vehicle's front-mounted transmission. The tank's designers wanted the driver's controls to be where they could easily connect to the transmission for shifting, clutching, steering, and braking.

The transmission and drive sprockets for the Sherman tank, like that on the Panther tank, also were located in the front hull. In contrast, the drive sprockets and transmission on the T-34 tank series were located at the rear of the hull. This was a tradeoff the Russians made for the steep slope on the tank's glacis plate and having the vehicle's turret mounted so far forward. Although there are exceptions, almost all post-World War II tanks tend to have their drive sprockets located at the rear of their hulls along with their engines and transmissions.

Located just behind the drive sprockets on the Panther tank were very small rollers. These were intended to make sure the tank's tracks disengaged from the drive sprockets during reverse travel when low track tension caused

by suspension compression at one or more road wheel stations might otherwise allow the tracks to wrap around the drive sprockets.

At the opposite end of every tank drive sprocket is the idler wheel, one for each track, which reverses the direction of the tracks at the unpowered end of the vehicle. Those on the Panther tank were mounted on a cranked axle that rested in bushings, located inside the Panther tank hull. The idlers were adjustable so they could be employed to increase or decrease track tension. The access points for adjusting the two idlers for the Panther tank were found on the rear hull plate, both covered by armored flaps. The original idler wheel design on the Panther tank had problems due to a

To assist in the removal of components like the transmission from the Panther tank, German field repair units were provided with portable overhead cranes such as the one pictured, which could be erected in the field whenever needed. It took about a day to remove the transmission from a Panther tank. *(Patton Museum)*

buildup of ice or mud and was replaced in October 1944, on the Panther Ausf. G tank, with larger self-cleaning idler wheels.

The Panther tank's interleaved road wheels were arranged so that the last set, just ahead of the rear located idler wheels, were spread wide apart, stabilizing the track strand in torsion as it rose up to the idler wheel.

TRANSMISSION

The transmission on the Panther tank was located in the front hull, between the driver and radioman, and connected by the drive train to the engine in the rear of the tank's hull.

When the need arose to remove the transmission from the vehicle's front hull, the large overhead armored roof panel that contained the driver and radioman's overhead hatches was unbolted and pulled aside by using an overhead crane or a temporary jib crane in the case of the Panther Ausf. G tank. That same crane could then be employed to remove the transmission unit in question and place a repaired or new transmission back into the vehicle.

An April 1946 British military document titled *The Transmission of the German Panther Tank* described the vehicle's synchromesh transmission (gearbox to the British), which had seven forward gears and one in reverse. The Sherman tanks had six gears, five forward and one in reverse. The T-34 series tank also had six gears, five forward and one in reverse:

> " Judged from a performance point of view we would consider the Panther tank to be over-geared by British standards. There is little possibility of gears six and seven being employed on cross-country terrain. It is, however, common German practice to provide one or more gears which are for road use only and in this respect the vehicle is comparable with other German AFVs [armored fighting vehicles]. "

The same report goes on to describe the British view on why the Panther was over-geared:

A close-up picture of the overhead armored housing portion of the electrically operated vent located in between the Panther driver and radioman on a Panther Ausf. A tank. The one on the Panther Ausf. G tank differed in shape. *(Michael Green)*

> Where one has a gearbox giving six or more speeds the luxury of a gear for road use only can be enjoyed. It is likely that the gear ratios were based on the original design weight of 35 tons, and when the weight of the machine increased to 44 tons some adjustment should have been made to the final drive ratio.

In a series of postwar interviews with Heinrich Ernst Kniepkamp, the senior engineer at Wa Pruef 6 told his interviewers that the high speed gearing of German tanks, like the Panther, was a requirement set by the German Army high command and could be employed only in a set of very favorable conditions seldom present since German tanks were normally transported by rail as close to the battlefield as possible.

The April 1946 British military document titled *The Transmission of the German Panther Tank* also touched on a serious design issue that cropped up with the gear arrangement in the Panther transmission:

> The synchromesh mechanism while reasonably satisfactory for most of the gears is quite inadequate as regards the changes from 2nd to 3rd speed. The theoretical analysis shows that a synchronous 2-3 change is improbable and this is confirmed by the statements of prisoners of war, and by the damaged condition of the 3rd speed dogs on all gearboxes examined. On one machine at FVPE [Fighting Vehicle Proving Establishment] the dogs were so worn that they would not remain in engagement in 3rd gear .... Judged from evidence obtained on the battlefield, and statements from prisoners of war, the transmission does not appear to have had a very good reputation for reliability .... It may be that the transmission was put into production without adequate time having been spent on development.

From the Panther handbook, which was aimed at the enlisted men, comes this translated warning about shifting the transmission:

> Always pay attention to the road in front of you and never think about girls, vacation, or pork chops! Then you also recognize the pitfalls quickly in the terrain, rises and ditches and therefore shift into the appropriate gear beforehand. When driving downhill use the same gear that you would have used to go up. That way you use your motor for braking, but once in a while tap your foot brake gently or you will rev your engine too high.
>
> One knows that all the racing champions don't spare themselves, but spare their cars. Remember the three most important consideration about shifting; how, why,

and when. Don't hesitate to shift. If you shift, shift quickly. Timely shifts will make for a soft ride. If you spend time fearing to shift, then you have wasted too much time. The transmission is there to be used. "

Located on the underside of the overhead front hull plate, just above the Panther tank transmission, is a vent that protrudes out over the top of the upper hull plate. The upper portion is an armored casting and is located directly below the front hull mounted main gun travel lock. It could be opened and closed with a threaded adjuster that moves a steel plate. The design of the exterior armored vent covering on the Panther Ausf. G differed from those found on the earlier Panther Ausf. D and Ausf. A tanks.

STEERING SYSTEM

With modern tanks, such as the American M1 Abrams main battle tank series, steering is smooth, infinitely variable, and regenerative so that there is virtually no transmission power loss in a turn. The Panther *Fahrer* (driver) had no such luxury. He was confronted with a single fixed-radius controlled differential steering system that offered him only seven fixed-radius turn possibilities, with the turning radius depending on what transmission gear he selected prior to making his turn. If the Panther driver anticipated a turn that did not fit within the seven fixed radii, he would be forced to skid steer using the vehicle's disc brakes. (Skid steering slows down one track by brute force so that the tank turns in the direction of the slower track.)

As Table 2 shows, the Panther turning radius was directly proportional to the selected forward gear range.

TABLE 2

Gear	Turning Radius
First Gear	16 feet (5 m)
Second Gear	36 feet (11 m)
Third Gear	59 feet (18 m)
Fourth Gear	98 feet (30 m)
Fifth Gear	150 feet (46 m)
Sixth Gear	200 feet (61 m)
Seventh Gear	265 feet (81 m)

From a U.S. Army report dated January 12, 1945, appears this description of the Panther steering system:

"Except for the ability of the tank [Panther] to make a pivot turn about its own axis, its steering system does not contribute to satisfactory maneuverability and this tank [Panther], even though it has a higher top speed that a medium tank M4A1, could not keep up with the medium tank on a course where curves were frequent. It is readily realized that practice in operating these vehicles [Panthers] would contribute greatly to driver skill and, therefore, increased mobility; but it should be pointed out that in any event it is necessary for the [Panther] driver to gauge any approaching turn and select the proper transmission ratio to negotiate that turn. It has been pointed out that the [Panther] driver can always select a low enough gear ratio so that the tank can turn any curve it may reach, but this has a definite disadvantage in that it means anticipation of the turn sufficiently far in advance to permit the vehicle's [Panther's] speed to drop low enough so that the desired low gear can be engaged, and has the further disadvantage that the vehicle's forward

Visible is the left-hand disc braking unit on a Panther Ausf. D tank without its sheet metal covering. It was located in the front hull alongside the driver's position. *(David Marian)*

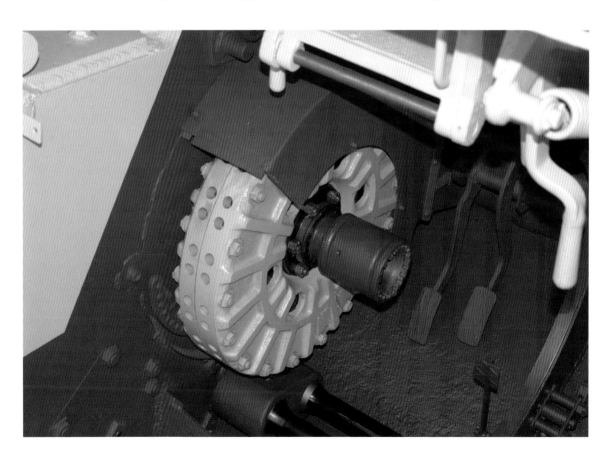

The driver's direct vision port is seen here on a Panther Ausf. A tank with its hinged armored flap in the open position. The ballistic glass visor in the driver's direct port, like all the periscopes in the Panther tank, was replaceable when damaged. *(Michael Green)*

speed may be slower than is necessary or desirable. The skid turn feature of the steering system, which is utilized by pulling the steering lever all the way and locking one track, cannot be employed at speeds in excess of approximately 8 to 10 mph [13 to 16 km/h], and can only be used when the vehicle is in second gear, as the engine will be stalled if such a turn is made in a higher gear. "

Staff Sergeant Alvin G. Olson was impressed by the Panther tank's ability to make a pivot turn around its own axis, as is seen in this quote from a March 1945 U.S. Army document titled *U.S. Army Report on United States vs German Armor*:

"I saw a Mark V [Panther] tank turn in place and move off in a new direction without having to use the back up and move forward system that our tankers are compelled to use. "

Like the Panther tank, the T-34 tank series could also make a pivot turn around its own axis.

An explanation of how the steering system on the Panther tank worked appears in an April 1946 British military document titled *The Transmission of the German Panther Tank*:

"In order to steer it [the Panther tank] it is necessary to cause one track to run slower than the other. This is achieved by removing the brake from the sun-wheel of the epicyclic which is required to run slower and engaging a clutch. This clutch connects the sun-wheel, by means of gearing, to the input shaft of the gearbox [transmission] in such a way that it is driven in a direction opposite to that of the annulus when the forward gears are engaged. Speed is thus subtracted from the

The early production units of the Panther Ausf. D tank sported two Bosch *Tarnlampe* (headlights), one on either side of the glacis plate above the track guards. Beginning in July 1943, Panther tanks reverted to having just one headlight on the left side of the glacis plate, just above the track guard, as seen here on a Panther Ausf. A tank. With the Panther Ausf. G tank, the single headlight was mounted above the left fender. *(Michael Green)*

planetary assembly and the output shaft on that side runs slower than when the sun-wheel is held stationary. The planetary assembly on the other side is not affected and runs at the same speed as formerly. The mean speed of the of the vehicle is thus slightly reduced when executing a turn in a forward gear ... The radius turn provided by the steering mechanism is supplemented by a skid turn obtained by independent operation of the main brakes. "

The Sherman tanks had a controlled differential steering system, while the T-34 tank series came with a passive clutch and brake steering system.

The first twenty-three Panther Ausf. D tanks built came with a passive clutch and brake steering system because the single fixed-radius controlled differential steering system for the vehicle was not ready for installation until March 1943. Those Panther tanks fitted with the passive clutch and steering system were later updated with the single fixed-radius controlled differential steering system.

Unlike older power-wasting clutch and brake steering systems, controlled differential steering systems as found in the Sherman tank and more modern tracked vehicles let the left and right sprockets turn at different speeds without significant loss of power. The difference in track speeds is controlled by steering levers that hold back or release gear elements inside the steer unit. The simpler clutch and brake steering system fitted in the T-34 tank series required that the driver disengage the inside track from engine power in order to apply the brake. This resulted in imprecise steering and added the possibility of stalling the engine as the track was reengaged. With the controlled differential arrangement, both tracks on a tank remained connected to the engine and were driven at different speeds during a turn.

In a July 1943 German industry report translated in *Panther & Its Variants* by Walter J. Spielberger, there is a summary comparison between the single-radius Panther steering system and the dual-radius Tiger Ausf. E steering system. A modified version of the dual-radius steering system that went into the Tiger Ausf. E also went into the larger and heavier Tiger Ausf. B:

" Compared to the dual-radius steering of the Tiger, the single-radius steering as used in the Panther is a compromise solution fraught with serious drawbacks. The fixed radius in the production version is too small in quite a few cases, and in some too large. "

Spielberger explained in the same book that the designers of the Panther tank did not install the more successful dual radius steering system that went into the Tiger Ausf. E tank because the German manufacturing industry informed them that they did not have the resources to make enough of the internal teeth gearing necessary for the number of Panther tanks envisioned as being built.

German engineers who helped design the Panther tank told British interviewers after the war that they themselves believed the single-radius steering system was not regarded as satisfactory from a general point of view. This belief appears in a passage from April 1946 British military document titled *The Transmission of the German Panther Tank* quoting a German engineer:

> For a vehicle with a maximum speed of 45 km/hr [28 mph] this type of steering control was not at all suitable. However, in a more general view from the vehicle's standpoint it was somewhat satisfactory in that either the change speed box [transmission] or the final drive or both would fail first.

The driver's position on a Panther Ausf. A tank with some main gun ammunition storage on the left and the driver's instrument array on the right. Clearly visible are the driver's steering levers and the gear shift handle on the right. *(Michael Green)*

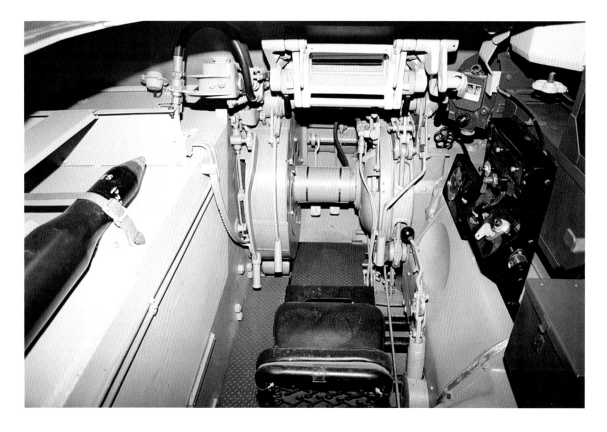

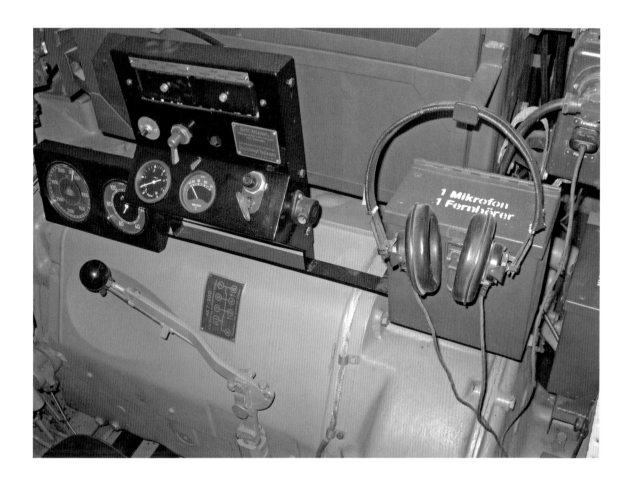

FINAL DRIVES

The Panther's final drives, which were connected to the tank's exterior drive sprockets and turned the vehicle's tracks, also tended to suffer frequent service failures, according to what German tankers told British interviewers. British personnel who had a chance to inspect Panther drive units attributed these failures to inadequate bearings together with low core strength and lack of case hardening of critical sections of the compound idler gear.

A postwar French Army report on the various features of the Panther, translated in *Panther and Its Variants* by Walter J. Spielberger, described the problem with the Panther tank's final drive:

> " The truly weak spot of the Panther is its final drive, which is of too weak a design and has an average fatigue life of only 150 km [93 miles]. Half the abandoned Panthers found in Normandy in 1944 showed evidence of breaks in the final drive. "

Shown in this picture taken inside a Panther Ausf. A tank is the driver's instrument array, which is seen on the left and is mounted on the transmission housing. Also visible is the driver's gear shift lever, mounted below his instrument array. To the right of the instrument panel is the driver's headset. *(Michael Green)*

U.S. ARMY OBSERVATIONS ON THE PANTHER

The characteristics of a captured Panther Ausf. G tank are described in a March 27, 1945, document titled *U.S. Army Report on United States vs German Armor*. The Panther also is compared in some sections to the second-generation Sherman tank then in service with the division, which is referred to in the report as the M4A3E8. The correct designation would be the M4A376(W).

Speed The Mark V [Panther] had a maximum speed of 18 miles per hour over terrain where tracks sank approximately one inch. The M4A3E8's speed was approximately the same. Some individual M4A3E8s were found that could outrun the Mark V in a speed test, while others fell slightly behind. The maximum speed of the Mark V on hard-surfaced highway was 38 miles per hour. No comparison was made with the M4A3E8 on the road.

Turret Speed When power driven, the turret traversing speed was one-half that of the M4A3E8. Manual traversing speed depending on the operator, but the Mark V was in all cases slower than any American tank, and very difficult except when the tank was level.

Trafficability Operating across typical ground, the Mark V left a track imprint ½-inch deep. It did not break through the ground surface. Similar results were obtained with the M4A3E8. Other tanks of the M4 series with narrow track and no track extension broke through the ground surface, leaving a track imprint two inches deep.

Gasoline Consumption Tank capacity of the Mark V is 135 gallons; consumption cross- country: approximately three gallons per mile; consumption on highway: approximately two gallons per mile. American gasoline was satisfactory without any readjustments of time or carburetor.

Tracks Track blocks are removed by knocking out two drift pins. Track tension is adjusted by turning one large nut. Crews agreed that track adjustment and maintenance were easier on the Mark V than American tanks. During approximately 75 miles of operation, both on roads and cross-country, tracks have given no trouble except for track guides. These were broken when the tank was recovered.

Lubrication A master grease fitting inside the turret lubricates all bearings in the tank. This is a desirable feature.

Radiators There are four radiators under the rear deck with total capacity of 35 gallons. These are vulnerable to shell fragments and strafing through openings on back deck.

Engine The power plant has required no maintenance other than first echelon. The repair or replacement of any part would require complete removal of the engine from the housing. Continual operation at high speed across difficult terrain causes overheating within one-half hour.

Ammunition Place is provided for 73 rounds of 75-mm ammunition. Ammunition is accessible. The capacity for the two machine guns could not be determined.

Equipment Personal equipment, blankets, field bags, etc., was found stowed in a box on the outside. The turret has more space inside than the American M4 series. The space in the driver's seat and assistant driver's compartment is approximately the same in the two tanks. Driver's seats not readily adjustable as in our tanks.

Visibility When buttoned up, the assistant driver and loader see through periscopes fixed to the right obliquc. The driver has a flexible periscope. The gunner has vision only through the telescope sight. The tank commander has all-around vision. The M4A3E8 has greater visibility than the Mark V, which is comparatively blind when buttoned up.

Fordability The Mark V tank forded water to a depth of 59 inches. Although it would take greater depth for a short time (up to 70 inches), there was a tendency for water to splash through the fan openings in the top deck. The M4A3E8 forded water safely up to 30 inches. It could ford up to 36 inches, but water tended to splash into the exhaust.

Guns and Sights The telescopic sight on the 75-mm gun of the Mark V tank is adjustable. By pushing a lever on the right side, the magnifying power is controlled, there being two settings, two and six power. There is also an adjustable reticle in the sight (used in setting off range) and a simple, effective antiglare device.

Panther Tank Strengths:
- Heavy armor on the front slope plate
- High-velocity weapon (75-mm) with excellent sights
- Good cross-country mobility, but no better than the M4A3E8
- Easy track adjustment and track maintenance
- High fordability and ease of preparation for amphibious operations

Panther Tank Weaknesses:
- Because of no periscope sight for the gunner and lack of gyrostabilizer on the Mark V, firing with any accuracy during movement would be impossible
- Limited visibility of crew members
- Slow traversing speed of turret
- Overheating of engine during difficult operation
- Bright glow of exhaust stacks at night after engine runs for a short period
- Difficulty in performing maintenance on engine
- Thin armor plate (5/8-inch) over driver and engine compartment
- Large openings on top of rear deck for cooling fans vulnerable to shellfire and strafing
- Lack of gyrostabilizer
- Lack of escape hatch
- Heavy gasoline consumption
- No control of turret traverse by tank commander, only by the gunner
- No AA (antiaircraft) gun provided.

In an April 1946 British military document titled *The Transmission of the German Panther Tank* it was reported that the directors of the French firm of LATIT were approached by the Germans during the war years to see if they could build a final drive for the Panther. They had therefore been given the assembly drawings of the vehicle's final drives. Although nothing ever came of it, it does show how unhappy and desperate the Germans were in trying to fix some of the tank's design flaws.

The same British military postwar report on Panther tank transmissions has a translation of a German document by Dr. Puschel of the firm of MAN covering the final drive failures examined at an ordnance depot:

> " The main cause of these failures was fatigue of the compound intermediate gear due to the low-core strength of the material used and the absence of case

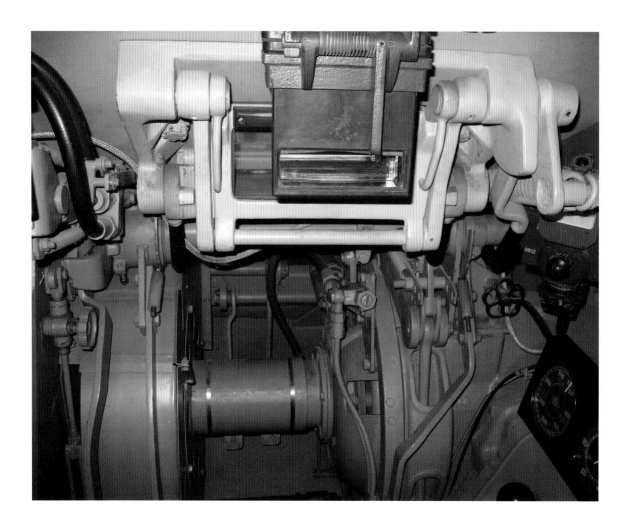

When the driver of a Panther Ausf. D or Panther Ausf. A tank felt that it was no longer safe to view the outside world through his glacis-mounted direct vision port, he would close the hinged armored flap that covered the opening for the vision port and then flip down the overhead periscope, seen here at the top of this picture. *(David Marian)*

hardening at the critical sections. Lack of case rigidity was thought to have contributed to the intermediate gear failures and was the apparent cause of the roller bearing failures. Inadequate lubrication due to badly cast in oil-ways also caused some trouble. The use of split ring dowels (Hettmann sleeves) with only a few bolts to retain the main drive gear to its flange proved unsatisfactory. This difficulty was subsequently overcome by the obvious solution, namely, fitting bolts. "

According to researcher Thomas L. Jentz, German industry made a number of modifications to the final drive units on the Panther Ausf. G in September and October 1944 to increase the durability of the unit.

Jacques Littlefield, the late president and founder of the Military Vehicle Technology Foundation, which restored a Panther Ausf. A tank, talked about

This picture shows an overhead view of the 360-degree rotating and tilting periscope fitted on a Panther Ausf. G tank. In the background is the exterior bracket for supporting the tank's main gun when not in combat. U.S. Army postwar testing showed that rotating and tilting periscopes were very vulnerable to the effects of blast from high-explosive (HE) rounds. *(Andreas Kirchhoff)*

his impression of why the final drives on the Panther proved to be such a problem in an interview with the authors:

> We had the final drives on our Panther tested and found that the alloy and gears used in their construction were as good as we could make them today. I suspect the main problem with the final drive was that they were designed for a much lighter version of the Panther than eventually rolled out of the factories. Once they started to up-armor the Panther, there was no room to beef up the final drives to handle the extra weight.

TEST CONCLUSIONS ON THE PANTHER TANK

Shortly after World War II, the British military attempted to conduct their standard cross-country mobility test with a small number of Panther Ausf. G tanks and variants. However, the vehicle's design flaws cut the tests short. An extract from that 1948 report done under the auspices of the Fighting Vehicle Design Department (FVDD) explains what happened:

> On commencement of the trials it soon became apparent that, owing to the inherent unreliability of the steering mechanism and the proclivity of the engine to catch fire, it would be impractical, if not impossible, to cover the full trials program.

A captured German tanker told his British captors in an interview written up in a British military report from the Department of Tank Design and dated September 1944 that the automotive problems with the Panther were not nearly as serious as perceived by them. The British summary of that interview is listed here:

> PW denied the statement that the Panther, from the point of view of engine, was a poor tank. He said that like all tanks it had teething problems but once these had been overcome it was much superior to the Pz.Kpfw IV. The following are a few of the defects and there [sic] improvements:
>
> 1) The steering clutch had given trouble but this was due to the inexperience of the drivers.
>
> 2) The inability on the part of the driver to engage third gear had been due to his

With the introduction of the Panther Ausf. G tank, the glacis mounted direct vision port and the driver's two fixed overhead periscopes disappeared. In their place appeared the single 360-degree rotating and tilting periscope seen here. This particular example is missing the periscope. *(Chun-Lsu Hsu)*

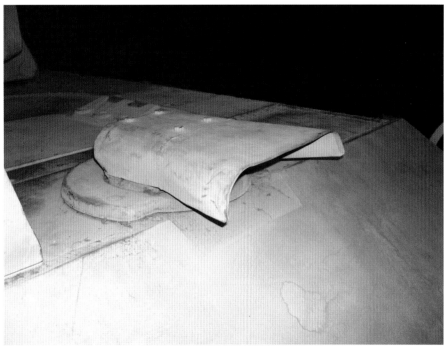

Beginning in July 1944, a rain guard was fitted over the driver's periscope on the Panther Ausf. G tank. This particular example of a rain guard is mounted on the driver's periscope of the only remaining Panther II chassis. *(Chun-Lsu Hsu)*

lack of experience in synchronizing engine speed with gear box speed. There was no difficulty once the driver had gotten used to his tank.

3) The final drive had given trouble but now had been improved.

4) The faults in the pressure lubrication system had been due partly to the oil pump. This had been improved and an eight main bearing had been fitted."

The German prisoner of war in the report went on to discuss the Panther engine and his opinion of it:

"The 231 (23.1) Liter HL 230 was the most powerful tank engine that PW knew about. He agreed that it was too weak for the Tiger II [Tiger B]. He stated that it was originally built too compact and that it got too hot. Hence the trouble with the cylinder head gasket. An experienced driver was essential. It has now been greatly improved. The centrifugal governor on the carburetor was excellent idea."

In a March 1945 U.S. Army document titled *U.S. Army Report on United States vs German Armor*, Lieutenant Colonel Wilson M. Hawkins listed some observations about the Panther mobility in comparison with different types of American tanks:

"It has been claimed that our tank [Sherman] is the more maneuverable. In recent tests we put a captured German Mark V [Panther] against all models of our own. The German tank was the faster, both across country and on the highway and it could make sharper turns. It was also the better hill climber."

In a January 4, 1945, U.S. Army report appears this passage describing a hill-climbing contest between a Panther tank, a Sherman tank, and a prototype M26 Pershing heavy tank:

"The first operation was on a 28% dirt slope that was frozen solid and partially covered with ice. The Panther tank negotiated this slope in both directions with ease and there was virtually no track slippage, even during steering. Medium tank M4 equipped with the chevron steel grouser tracks T54E1, and with the rubber block track T51 equipped with a standard grouser on every block were unable to climb the slope. A heavy tank T26E3 equipped with a modified T81 track was also unable to climb the slope. This modified T81 track varies from the standard track in that it has high grousers for additional traction."

DRIVER'S STATION

The Panther tank *Fahrer* (driver) sat in the left front hull of the vehicle on a padded leather seat that could be moved forward or backward and came with a fold-down backrest. He steered the vehicle with two levers, one on either side of his seat. The levers pulled upward toward the driver and operated hydraulic pressure to the steering brakes. The pressure was supplied by twin swash pumps, one for each steering brake, located under the turret basket on the left hand side. The pumps were driven from the power take off.

An American tanker who drove a captured Panther tank commented on the ease of steering the vehicle in a wartime report: "Boosters on the steering laterals of a Mark V [Panther] make it much easier to drive them than our own tanks."

On the floor in front of the Panther driver were the accelerator pedal on the right, the clutch pedal on the left, and the brake pedal in the middle. The driver's hand brake was located on his extreme left and had an exposed toothed rack.

The gearshift handle was to the driver's right. It had two triggers, one at the top and another lower down. Lifting the first trigger was necessary to select first gear and lifting both together was necessary to select sixth or seventh and reverse gear. The triggers controlled the amount of side movement of the gear lever when in neutral. At the bottom of the gear lever was a spring level plunger which when pulled out toward the driver allowed the gear lever to be moved to either a vertical or horizontal position. When in the vertical position, the sixth and seventh gears were not accessible.

The driver's instrument array, which was located to his right, consisted of two panels mounted on a bracket attached to the transmission housing. The lower panel contained the tachometer and speedometer, while the upper panel contained the ignition key slot with the starter button located just above it. Also found on the upper instrument panel were the headlight switches, an oil gauge, an ammeter, and an engine fire warning light. Just above the upper instrument panel were the vehicle's fuse boxes.

A German wartime training pamphlet described the duties of a driver on a Panzer IV, (which would be the same for all German tank drivers), translated in a publication titled *Intelligence Bulletin*, dated December 1942:

"The driver operates the vehicle under the orders of the tank commander, or in accordance with orders received by radio from the commander's vehicle. So far as possible, he assists in observation, reporting over the intercommunication telephone the presence of the enemy or of any obstacles in the path of the tank. He watches the fuel consumption and is responsible to the tank commander for the care and maintenance of the vehicle. "

The downside of allowing the driver to look out over the top of his overhead hatch on the Panther Ausf. G tank was the need to duplicate his controls so he could continue to operate his vehicle from his second higher-positioned seat. The complicated mass of levers and controls that resulted is seen in this picture taken inside a Panther Ausf. G tank. *(Tank Museum, Bovington)*

Before starting the Panther tank engine, the driver would check the fuel level as well as the engine oil and water levels. He would then check to see that his gearshift handle was in neutral and the steering gear levers were pushed forward. He would also check to see that his handbrake was on.

To turn on the Panther tank engine, either the driver or another crewman first had to turn on the master switch located in the left hand rear corner of the tank's fighting compartment and the fuel control switch located on the left side of the engine bulkhead. The fuel control switch had three positions: main tank, auxiliary tank, and off. The driver or another

This picture shows the open radioman's hatch, and the locking-in-place arrangement for the hatch, on a Panther Ausf. A tank. This same arrangement is found on the Panther Ausf. D tank. Staff members of the Military Vehicle Technology Foundation who worked on restoring the driver's and radioman's hatches on a Panther Ausf. A found them poorly designed and fragile. *(David Marian)*

crewman would set the fuel control switch to the main tank and then prime the engine with a few strokes of his primer control. The driver would then insert and switch on the ignition key and press the starter button. Before driving off, the Panther driver would check the engine oil pressure and the charging rate.

A U.S. Army wartime report described the American impression of the driver's position on the Panther:

> "The main criticism that may be made of the driving compartment was that made of the fighting compartment; namely, there is inadequate room for the crew members. The driver is particularly cramped and a large man is at a great disadvantage in trying to operate this vehicle where frequent steering is necessary."

Vision for the driver on the Panther Ausf. D and Ausf. A tanks was provided by two overhead fixed periscopes and a small horizontally oriented rectangular vision port, fitted with replaceable ballistic glass, directly in front of his seat, which was protected by a rectangular armored shutter that was opened and closed with a internal spring-lever lever operated by the driver from within the vehicle.

With the introduction of the Panther Ausf. G tank, the driver's vision port and two overhead fixed periscopes were deleted and replaced by a single overhead 360-degree rotating and tilting periscope.

The backrest on the driver's seat on the Panther Ausf. D and Ausf. A could be folded down, and the driver then could stand on the backrest to project his head and upper torso out over the top of his overhead hatch. However, he could only do this when the vehicle was parked.

While the drivers on the Panther Ausf. D and A tanks did not have provisions for raising their seats to look out over the top of their overhead hatches, that ability was provided for the driver on the Panther Ausf. G tank, beginning in December 1944, with a complex arrangement involving an upper and lower seat and duplicated controls. This layout is described in a 1947 British Army document titled *The Motion Studies of German Tanks*:

A close-up picture of the radioman's hinged overhead armored hatch on a Panther Ausf. G tank. The entire hatch could be unhinged from the inside of the tank if it became jammed. Notice the thin metal post attached to the bottom of the hatch, which was used to close the hatch by the radioman. *(Andreas Kirchhoff)*

"The upper seat is positioned by hooking its forward end on to the top of the lower backrest, and the upper backrest onto the hull roof. By adjusting the angle of the lower backrest, the upper seat can be moved forwards and backwards correspondingly. The arrangement is simple and efficient and allows the upper seat and backrest to be completely removed when not required …. The seat and position are comfortable and easily accessible and the large hatch allows the driver considerable body movement …. The driver's controls (except for the choke control) are either adapted or duplicated for both positions. In both positions, the steering levers are on each side of the driver's legs. They are easily operated. When the engine is running, the steering is hydraulically assisted and quite easy to control."

OVERHEAD HATCHES

The overhead armored hatches for the Panther driver and the radioman in the Panther Ausf. D and A tanks would swing out on a pivot and on the upper hull armor plate of the vehicle. This was done with the aid of large hydraulic rams operated by oil force pumps controlled by a handle located behind the driver. Once opened, the hatches were locked in place with small clamps. The hatches also could be locked shut when closed from within the vehicle by the driver and radioman.

A German field report indicated that the drivers and radiomen on the early model Panther tanks sometimes left their overhead hatches open in combat for fear they might be trapped inside their vehicles if they became jammed.

In the Panther Ausf. G tank, the driver and radioman hatches were improved by making them hinged to swing up and then lay down on the upper hull plate. However, it was awkward to close them quickly because the driver or radioman had to expose their entire upper torso in order to close the hatch.

British military studies on the Panther Ausf. G tank found a novel feature that allowed the driver and radioman to completely remove their overhead hatches if the need arose by simply rotating overhead wing-nuts on either side of their seats. This feature would come in handy if the overhead hatches became damaged and the driver and radioman needed to leave the vehicle quickly. According to researcher Thomas L. Jentz, this ability to jettison the driver's and radioman's overhead armored hatches began appearing on the Panther Ausf. G tank in August 1944.

PANTHER TANK RADIOS

Yuri Desyatnik, a communications equipment restoration engineer at the Military Vehicle Technology Foundation, described in an interview with the authors the radio and intercom system inside the Panther Ausf. A restored by the foundation:

"The Panther Ausf. A was equipped with the Fu 5-Fu 2 radio/intercom system. Panthers that were designated as command tanks were equipped with both the Fu 5 and the Fu 8 systems both of which boasted additional radio equipment that provided a link to headquarters. The Fu 5 system was comprised of the Ukw.E.e (Ultra-shortwave receiver) and the 10W.S.c (10 Watt Transmitter). The Fu 2 designation simply describes a single Ukw.E.e receiver. Therefore, the Panther Ausf. A was equipped with two Ukw.E.e receivers and one 10W.S.c transmitter. For the crew to communicate inside the tank, an intercom box called the Kasten Pz. Nr. 20 was used. This box was a complex and versatile device, which allowed both the radio operator and tank commander to communicate with their tank-mates and other tanks. The "Kasten 20" was fully integrated with the radio system.

The Fu 5 system was developed in 1939 by Telefunken, and was the first ever tank-based radio station, designed for tactical military integration, which was defined by its ability to configure two station presets and to provide radio access to most of the tank's crew.

The Fu 5 set used AM to communicate. In contrast, the Americans used FM in their SCR-508 tank-based radio sets. The advantage of the AM method is the reduced power needed to transmit over longer distances. The disadvantage of AM is the static noise that's difficult to filter out. FM completely removes the noise and makes for a very clear signal, however more power is needed to transmit over the same distances that AM can transmit using less power. To compensate for this, the BC-604 FM transmitter of the SCR-508 station produces 30 Watts of power, which is three times the output of the German 10 Watt AM transmitter. Americans borrowed from the German original two station preset design, by building the SCR-508 with ten presets. This allowed for more complex and sophisticated tactical operations by enabling any American tank, equipped with the SCR-508, to become a platoon leader."

RADIOMAN'S POSITION

A key member of the Panther tank crew was the *Funker* (radioman). He sat in the front hull to the right of the driver's position. The driver's and radioman's positions were separated by the centrally mounted front hull transmission. The tank's radio was mounted in a bracket that itself was mounted to the left of the radioman's padded leather seat on the transmission housing. The seat for the Panther tank radioman could be moved forward and backward, but he could not raise his seat to look out over the top of his

overhead hatch. The backrest on the radioman's seat could be folded down, and he could then stand on the backrest to project his head and upper torso out over the top of his overhead hatch.

A German wartime training pamphlet describes the duties of a radioman on a Panzer IV (which would be the same for all German radiomen). The description was translated in a publication titled *Intelligence Bulletin*, dated December 1942:

" The radio operator operates the radio set under the orders of the tank commander. In action, when not actually transmitting, he always keeps the radio set at 'receive.' He operates the intercommunication telephone and writes down any radio messages not sent or received by the tank commander. He fires the machine gun mounted in the front superstructure. He takes over the duties of the loader if the latter becomes a casualty. "

TYPES OF MOBILITY

Unlike most who would consider the only type of mobility that was important to a tank's design to be battlefield or tactical mobility, those at the highest levels in the military consider that when it comes to the designing of tanks that strategic or operational mobility is just as important as tactical mobility. It is crucial to be able to get them were they are needed to win battles and wars.

Tactical mobility generally describes a tank's ability to operate on the battlefield in a variety of terrain and weather conditions. The things that come into play with tactical mobility are the speed, maneuverability, and cross-country performance of a tank. Within the parameter of speed are things like engine power, acceleration, average speed, and creep speed. Maneuverability includes a tank's braking capability, pivot turns, and steering gear ratios, while a tank's cross-country performance includes fording depth, vertical obstacles, ground pressure, and grade climbing ability. In the case of the Panther tank, its tactical mobility surpassed the Sherman tank and that of the T-34 tank series.

Looking into the radioman's position on a Panther Ausf. A tank the breech end of the glacis plate mounted MG34T 7.92-mm machine gun is visible as well as the tank's radio gear mounted on the transmission housing. In theory, the MG34 machine gun had a rate of fire between 800 to 900 rounds per minute. *(Michael Green)*

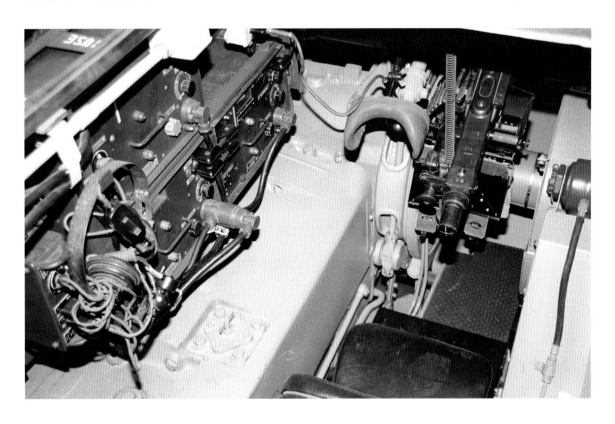

Operational mobility is concerned with how an army masses its tanks in the rear areas and how it moves them toward a combat area (by sea, rail, or on their own power) in sufficient numbers within a certain time frame to influence the course of events in their favor.

The things that come to play with tanks in regard to operational mobility include their weight and dimensions, cruising speed, radius of action, and rail and road transport issues. It is here that the Panther tank, with its gasoline-powered engine, pales in comparison to the T-34 tank series with its diesel engine, which increased the radius of action compared to the Panther tank. Add to that the T-34 tank series general mechanical reliability versus the mechanical unreliability of the Panther tank and one can see how that Russian tank allowed the Red Army to prevail in World War II, more Panther tanks being lost to mechanical breakdowns than combat action. According to a German wartime report, it was recommended that Panther tanks be transported by rail when traveling farther than 62 miles (100 km) due to the wear and tear on the suspension system, especially during the winter months.

While the gasoline-powered versions of the Sherman tank lacked the wide radius of action of the T-34 tank series, it shared the important factor of reliability, and that, in conjunction with the combined arms approach to combat practiced by the Western Allies during World War II, allowed them to generally prevail on the battlefields of Western Europe over the much smaller number of Panther tanks encountered.

CHAPTER FIVE

VARIANTS

In order to keep research and development costs to a minimum and to make as much use as possible of existing chassis in order to simplify training and spare part supplies, the German Army used the standard Panther tank chassis as the basis for several variants. These included an armored command version, an armored recovery version (ARV), and a turret-less tank destroyer version. A Panther turret-based pillbox also was employed during World War II.

The German Army proposed many more Panther variants during World War II, including a *Panzerbeobachtungswagen* (armored artillery observation vehicle) as well as a number of artillery and antiaircraft vehicles employing a Panther tank chassis. However, the sorely strapped German military-industrial complex was too hard-pressed to build even enough standard Panther tanks to meet the need of the German tank troops to consider diverting any of them for conversion for other purposes.

ARMORED COMMAND VEHICLES

Of the assorted variants of the Panther tanks produced, the least modified was a command version, known to the German Army as the *Panzerbefehlswagen* (armored command vehicle). It had to be as similar in

Pictured is a restored *Panzerbefehlswagen* (armored command vehicle) Panther Ausf. A tank belonging to the German Army Tank Museum, Munster. The *Sternantenne D* (star antenna) on the rear hull marks it as a Sd.Kfz. 267 equipped with a Fu (radio) 8. *(Thomas Anderson)*

appearance to the standard Panther tank to avoid early detection and destruction by enemy forces on the battlefield. Command variants were built for each version of the Panther tank, for a total of 329 units between May 1943 and February 1945.

Changes to the command Panther tanks included the elimination of the coaxial machine gun, which resulted in the opening on the right side of the gun-shield being closed with a welded plug. Main gun ammunition storage in the command Panthers was dropped to just sixty-four rounds to make interior room for additional radios and their associated equipment such as transformers, rectifiers, and generators.

Two slightly different versions of the command Panther tanks were fielded, each with its own vehicle ordnance inventory number. The more common of the two came with the vehicle ordnance inventory number Sd.Kfz. 267 and was employed from company to regimental level in Panzer units. It had two *Funkgeraete* (radios), the first being the standard Fu 5, a 10-watt transmitter and ultra-short wavelength receiver. Instead of leaving the Fu 5 in the front hull as with the standard Panther tank, with the command Panther tank (Sd.Kfz. 267), the Fu 5 was moved inside the turret and mounted at the loader's position. The second radio was the Fu 8, a 30-watt transmitter and medium wavelength receiver. It was mounted in the front hull in place of the Fu 5.

The Fu 5 had a maximum voice range of 1,640 yards (1.5 km) when the vehicle was moving. When stationary, the maximum voice range of the Fu 5 went up to 1.9 miles (3 km). When parked and using Morse code, the Fu 5 could reach out to a maximum of 2.5 miles (4 km). The Fu 8 had a voice range of roughly 12 miles (20 km) when stationary and a Morse code range of about 25 miles (40 km).

The command Panther tank (Sd.Kfz. 268) was intended as an air–ground liaison vehicle for coordinating tactical air support for panzer units. Besides a Fu 5 in the turret, it also had a Fu 7 in the front hull. The Fu 7 was a 20-watt transmitter and ultra-short wavelength receiver. It had a maximum

Two antennae can be seen on this *Panzerbefehlswagen* (armored command vehicle) Panther Ausf.A. The *Sternantenne D* (star antenna) mounted on the rear engine deck identifies it as a Sd.Kfz. 267 with a Fu (radio) 8. Also visible is the *Stebantenne* (rod/pole antenna) on the rear turret roof for the Fu 5 located in the turret. *(Patton Museum)*

range of about 31 miles (50 km) when using voice and stationary. When stationary and using Morse code, the Fu 7 could reach out to a maximum range of about 43 miles (70 km). However, the aircraft it was in contact with had to be flying at an altitude of 1,650 feet (500 m) or higher.

The typical command Panther tank mounted a rod antenna on the right rear of its turret for its turret-mounted Fu 5. The *Sternantenne D* (star antenna) for the Fu 8 typically was mounted on a large porcelain insulator protected by an armored cylinder and sat on the center upper rear hull deck. At the top of the star antenna were five radials emanating at 130-degree angles from the main rod/pole. In place of the star antenna on the command Panther tank (Sd.Kfz. 267), the command Panther tank (Sd.Kfz. 268) mounted a *Stabantenne* (rod antenna) on the center upper rear hull deck for its Fu 7.

If a Panther unit could not acquire a command Panther tank in a timely manner, a kit was available to convert a standard model Panther tank into a command Panther tank.

Parked in a French town is a *Panzerbefehlswagen* (armored command vehicle) Panther Ausf. A. The *Sternantenne D* (star antenna) identifies it as a Sd.Kfz. 267 with a Fu (radio) 8. However, the star antenna on this particular vehicle is mounted not on the center rear of the hull where it is supposed to be. Instead, it is mounted at the left just behind the turret where a *Stebantenne* (rod/pole antenna) typically should be. *(Frank Schulz Collection)*

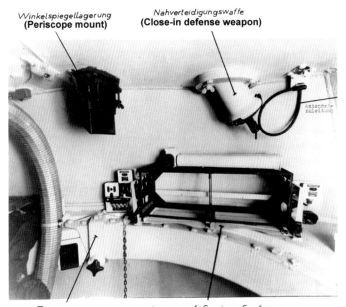

Winkelspiegellagerung
(Periscope mount)

Nahverteidigungswaffe
(Close-in defense weapon)

Antennen-zuleitung

Turmzurrung
(Turret azimuth lock)

Lagerung f. Sender u Empfänger
(Mount for radio transmitter / receiver)

LEFT

An interior photograph of the turret of a *Panzerbefehlswagen* (armored command vehicle) Panther Ausf. A tank. Visible is the bracket on the right side of the tank for mounting a Fu (radio) 5 for operation by the loader. Every standard Panther tank had a Fu 5 in the front hull. *(Patton Museum)*

BELOW

This picture shows the interior of a *Panzerbefehlswagen* (armored command vehicle) Panther Ausf. A tank. Notice the rectifier on the right side of the main gun in place of the normal MG34T coaxial 7.92-mm machine gun. *(Patton Museum)*

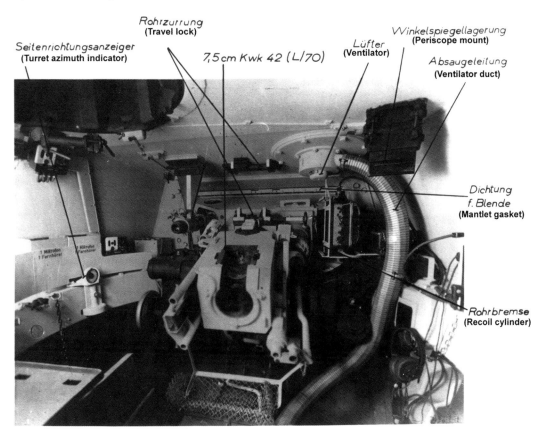

Rohrzurrung
(Travel lock)

Seitenrichtungsanzeiger
(Turret azimuth indicator)

7,5 cm Kwk 42 (L/70)

Lüfter
(Ventilator)

Winkelspiegellagerung
(Periscope mount)

Absaugeleitung
(Ventilator duct)

1 Mikrofon 1 Fernhörer

Dichtung f. Blende
(Mantlet gasket)

Rohrbremse
(Recoil cylinder)

ARMORED RECOVERY VEHICLE

The two studded plates attached to the lower front of the *Bergepanther* (Recovery Panther) seen in this picture were used for anchoring a large wooden beam employed for pushing disabled vehicles. This restored vehicle belongs to the German Army Technical Evaluation Center and is based on a Panther Ausf. A tank chassis. *(Andreas Kirchhoff)*

Few vehicles suffer the wear and tear that tanks do in wartime. Not only do they operate in extremes of terrain and weather, but they also are subjected to varying degrees of abuse by a wide assortment of weapons, ranging from antitank mines to antitank guns, all of which are designed to render them useless. However, short of complete destruction, tanks often can be repaired and placed back into service. The key is to be able to recover them off the battlefield and return them to a rear area where the restoration process can begin.

Unfortunately, as the Germans rushed the 56-ton (51-mt) Tiger Ausf. E heavy tank and the 50-ton (45-mt) Panther tank into production, they failed to anticipate the need for a more powerful recovery vehicle than their existing unarmored halftrack designated the *Zugkraftwagen* 18 ton (16 mt) and built by Fahrzeug und Motoren-Werke (FAMO), a German vehicle manufacturer.

The raised box-like superstructure seen on top of this restored *Bergepanther* (Recovery Panther) consisted of a lower all-steel structure, which supported another structure made of steel-framed wooden planks that could be folded down if the need arose. *(Andreas Kirchhoff)*

This failure would result in countless numbers of Tiger and Panther tanks being either abandoned or destroyed by their own crews rather than letting them fall into enemy hands for lack of a suitable recovery vehicle. In order to rectify this shortcoming, the German firm of MAN supplied the German Army with twelve turret-less Panther Ausf. D tanks, in June 1943 to be used as armored towing vehicles.

In July 1943, the first true armored recovery version of the Panther tank, named the *Bergepanther* (Recovery Panther), starting coming off the

Visible in this picture of a restored *Bergepanther* (Recovery Panther) is the large spade on the rear of the vehicle for anchoring the vehicle when the powerful winch was being employed to retrieve disabled tanks. Also visible is a lifting derrick. *(Andreas Kirchhoff)*

A very large wooden beam was carried as standard equipment on the left side of the raised superstructure of every *Bergepanther* (Recovery Panther). That wooden beam can be seen in this picture of a restored example based on a Panther Ausf. A tank chassis. *(Andreas Kirchhoff)*

Henschel production line. Using the Panther Ausf. A tank chassis, the new Recovery Panther featured a powerful winch, crane, and large spade at its rear hull. It went into field use beginning in August 1943. Follow-on deliveries of the vehicle were based on the Panther Ausf. G tank starting in October 1944. German industry managed to complete 297 units of the Recovery Panther before the war in Europe ended. The vehicle's ordnance inventory number was Sd.Kfz. 179.

From a U.S. Army report dated March 2, 1945, appears this description of a captured Recovery Panther:

"A German Panther recovery tank, 'Bergepanzer Panther,' was captured in Belgium. The vehicle consists of a turret-less Pz.Kpfw. Panther Model D, with a winch installed in place of the turret and a large spade hinged to the rear of the tank. The winch mechanism is installed in the original tank fighting compartment and is enclosed by a box-like structure above the superstructure of the tank. The

An early production unit of the *Jagdpanther* (Hunting Panther) Ausf. G1 can be identified by the single-piece 8.8-cm (88-mm) Pak 43/3 L/71 gun barrel, the twin periscopes for the driver, and the welded-on cast-armored *Geschuetznische* (gun recess) fastened to the glacis plate by internal bolts and studs. *(Patton Museum)*

On display at the French Army Tank Museum, Saumur, is a *Jagdpanther* (Hunting Panther) Ausf. G1. Beginning in June 1944, an armored plate was welded over the opening for the driver's second periscope, as seen on the vehicle pictured, and covered by *Zimmerit* (antimagnetic mine paste). *(Christophe Vallier)*

winch has a capacity of 40 tons (44 US tons) on a straight pull and 80 tons (88 US tons) using a pulley in the line. It is driven through a transfer case in the driveline from the engine. "

From the same U.S. Army report appears this description of how the Recovery Panther was employed:

"The recovery vehicle is brought into position about 10 yards from the tank to be recovered and the winch is used to lower the spade. The engine must be stopped before engaging the dog clutch of the winch. Both ends of the tow cable are attached to the vehicle to be recovered and the cable is placed over a loose pulley. To winch in the disabled vehicle, the brakes of the recovery tank are set, the winch brake released and the clutch lever placed on the 'on' position. "

A British military report dated August 9, 1945, outlined three conclusions based on testing of a Recovery Panther:

"The Panther is a very useful and serviceable recovery vehicle.

The winch, through complicated, is satisfactory and with its pull of 40 tons, is capable of dealing with all AFVs of the type and weight produced by the Germans.

It is capable of being operated by two men in an emergency, with the assistance of the crew being recovered. "

The building of enough of the specialized winches for the Recovery Panther was a continuing problem as is described in *Panther and Its Variants* by Walter J. Spielberger.

"The construction of this high-strength winch was plagued with difficulties, since manufacturers in possession of the necessary machinery and knowledge were already involved in armament production and were already working beyond their capacity. It was therefore not possible to equip all Bergpanthers with winches. "

TURRET-LESS TANK DESTROYER

In August 1942, the German Army decided that a dedicated Panther tank-based *Panzerjaeger* (tank hunter), mounting the newest version of the powerful 88-mm-gun designated the 8.8-cm Pak (antitank) 43/3 L/71, would be an optimum solution for replacing some of the earlier less capable tank hunter. Plans called for series production in July 1943. Numerous delays

This *Jagdpanther* (Hunting Panther) has a two-piece barrel (introduced beginning in April 1944) and a cast armored *Geschuetznische* (gun recess) bolted to the vehicle glacis plate from the outside. The thick armored lip on the gun recess shown in this picture began appearing on the Hunting Panther Ausf. G2 beginning in October 1944. (David Marian)

resulted in the first Panther-based tank hunter prototype not coming off the factory floor until October 1943 and the second unit the following month.

A modified version of the 8.8 cm Pak 43/3 L/71 first appeared on a tank hunter originally named the *Hornisse* (Hornet) and later called the *Nashorn* (Rhinoceros) by order of Hitler on February 27, 1944. A modified version of the 8.8 cm-Pak 43/3 L/71 gun also would go into the Tiger Ausf. B heavy tank, the first of the series production vehicles coming off the production line in February 1944. German references give the 8.8 cm-Pak 43/3 L/71 gun the ability to penetrate almost 203 mm of armor at 109 yards (100 m) and 165-mm of armor at 1,093 yards (1,000 m).

Although originally referred to as the 8.8-cm *Sturmgeschuetz* (assault gun), by the time the first series-production unit of the new Panther tank-based tank hunter rolled off the factory floor in January 1944, it was named the *Jagdpanther* (Hunting Panther). The vehicle's ordnance inventory number was Sd.Kfz. 173.

Belonging to the U.S. Army Ordnance Museum is this *Jagdpanther* (Hunting Panther). A German wartime report reminded everybody that the lack of all-around fighting capability of the vehicle and limited vision meant that it needed to be protected by supporting tanks or infantry whenever possible. *(Christophe Vallier)*

A close-up picture of the thickened cast armored *Geschuetznische* (gun recess) bolted to the vehicle glacis plate from the outside on a *Jagdpanther* (Hunting Panther) Ausf. G2 built sometime after September 1944. *(Andreas Kirchhoff)*

Initial German plans had called for the delivery of 150 Hunting Panthers per month by the factories assigned to build the vehicle. However, an Allied bomber raid on the German factories building the vehicle and their subcontractors, as well as the German transportation infrastructure, caused so much destruction and disruption that the zenith of production occurred in January 1945 when seventy-two rolled off the assembly lines. Total production of the Hunting Panther is estimated to have been around 413 units before the firms building them were overrun by the Allies in April and May 1945. There was also a command version of the Hunting Panther built.

OPPOSITE
A knocked-out or abandoned *Jagdpanther* (Hunting Panther) sits forlornly in a village square someplace in Western Europe. It features the new *Geschuetznische* (gun recess) introduced in June 1944, which was bolted to the vehicle's glacis plate from the outside rather than fastened to the glacis plate by internal bolts and studs. *(Frank Schulz Collection)*

VEHICLE DESCRIPTION

At 51 tons, the Hunting Panther was 22 feet 9 inches (7 m) long, excluding the main gun and 32 feet 4 inches (10 m) long with the main gun fitted. It was 8 feet 3 inches (2.5 m) tall and had a width of 10 feet 9 inches (3.3 m). A British Army report listed as Appendix J to *War Office Technical Intelligence Summary No. 142* and dated September 6, 1944, on the Hunting Panther provides additional comments on a late-model captured example of the vehicle:

"The unit consists of a normal Panther chassis with a superimposed superstructure, which is virtually a Panther glacis plate and sides extended upward to form a spacious fighting compartment, with and sloping rear plate. A noticeable feature is the amount of room available in the fighting compartment to enable the gun to be easily serviced, and the fact that all the elaborate observation facilities are on the roof plate, there being no vision openings at the front or sides of the vehicle except for the driver's episcope periscope."

The same report goes on to detail the Hunting Panther's operational characteristics:

On the roof of a *Jagdpanther* (Hunting Panther), one can see on the left side of the photograph the very top portion of the vehicle's commander's scissor-type telescope designated the S.F.14Z Gi. The commander's overhead armored hatch is directly behind the periscope heads. On the right side of the picture is the opening for the gunner's overhead periscope gun sight. *(Andreas Kirchhoff)*

❝This was basically a 46 [British long] ton vehicle with performance as follows Max. speed 18½ mph [30 km/h]; on road 15½ mph [25 km/h]; cross country 9 mph [14 km/h]; radius of action on roads 87 miles [140 km]; on average country 68 miles [109 km]; on difficult terrain 50 miles [80 km]; trench crossing 8 feet [2.4 m]; step 2'11" [64 cm]; uphill gradient 30 degrees; downhill gradient 40 degrees; fording 5'11" [1.6 m].❞

Glacis armor on the Hunting Panther consisted of RHA, 80-mm thick sloped at 55 degrees, while the superstructure's sides were 50 mm thick sloped at 30 degrees. The superstructure rear, hull sides, and the rear superstructure were 40 mm thick. The hull bottom plates were 30 mm thick. The vehicle's superstructure roof plate was originally only 16 mm thick, on the first fifty Hunting Panthers built. Thereafter, the armor thickness for the vehicle's superstructure roof plate went up to 30 mm.

IDENTIFYING FEATURES

Like the Panther tank series, the Hunting Panther went through a constant stream of changes, both internally and externally during its production run. The Germans designated the original series production units of the vehicle,

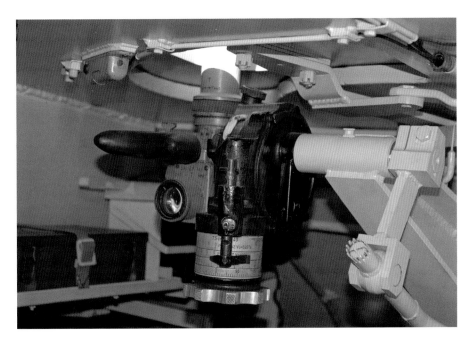

Rather than the direct telescopic articulated sights used on Panther tanks, the gunner on the *Jagdpanther* (Hunting Panther) employed the periscope Sfl.Z.F.1a *mit Zieleinrichtung* 37 (seen here), which extended through the roof of the vehicle and traversed with the main gun. *(David Marian)*

From the rear, this *Jagdpanther* (Hunting Panther) can be identified as an Ausf. G1 by the arrangement of the exhaust pipes, which comes from the Panther Ausf. A tank. The large metal tube containing the main gun's cleaning brushes has been mounted on the rear engine deck of this vehicle. This was a field modification also seen on some Panther tanks. *(Andreas Kirchhoff)*

which incorporated features from the Panther Ausf. A tank rear engine deck, as the Hunting Panther Ausf. G1.

The follow-on series production units of the vehicle were designated as the Hunting Panther Ausf. G2 and incorporated features from the rear engine deck of the Panther Ausf. G tank, including the raised armored fan tower on the left side of the upper engine deck plate, which contained the crew compartment heater and smaller air-intake louvers. Research by Thomas Jentz and Hilary Louis Doyle uncovered the fact that the upper rear deck on the Ausf. G2 version of the Hunting Panther was actually a slight bit longer than that of the Ausf. G1 version of the vehicle, which resulted in the rear hull plate being both shorter and at a steeper angle than that found on the Hunting Panther Ausf. G1 in order to maintain the same overall vehicle length.

Although the majority of the changes done to the Hunting Panther occurred at the factory, a few were made by the units in the field, such as the rearrangement of the vehicle's external tool storage from the sides of the vehicle's superstructure to the rear engine deck and rear tail plate of the vehicle.

An easily spotted external change to the Hunting Panther occurred in early June 1944, with the deletion of the driver's original side-by-side periscopes with a single periscope.

Another obvious external change to the Hunting Panther also happened in June 1944, when the original *Geschuetznische* (armored recessed bracket), which surrounded the space in which the vehicle's main armament was mounted, was changed. The original armored recess bracket, which was fastened to the glacis of the Hunting Panther with internal bolts and studs, was replaced with another type of armored recessed bracket attached to the vehicle's glacis with eight large external bolts, four on the top rim and four on the bottom rim. The new armored recessed bracket measured about 49 inches by 42.5 inches (1.24 m by 1.1 m).

A second version of the externally bolted on armored recessed bracket for the Hunting Panther appeared in August 1944, with a much thicker lower armored rim that is very noticeable in pictures.

The external *Topfblende* (armored sleeve casting mantlet), which actually enclosed a portion of the main gun that protruded out from the much larger armored recessed bracket on the Hunting Panther's glacis was 3.94 inches (100 mm) thick and referred to by the Germans as a *Saukopf* (pig's head).

MAIN GUN FEATURES

The Hunting Panther originally was armed with a mono-bloc (single piece) 8.8-cm (88-mm) Pak 43/3. However, beginning in April 1944, the vehicle began coming off the production lines with a sectional (two-piece) 8.8-cm (88-mm) gun. The sectional gun was easier to build and retained the same designation as the mono-bloc gun.

Two types of muzzle brakes were fitted to the Hunting Panther main gun. The original production version was 21 inches (530 mm) long, had a maximum diameter of 12 inches (295 mm), and weighed 132 lbs (60 kg). Beginning in June 1944, a new smaller muzzle brake began appearing on the Hunting Panther that was only 17 inches (440 mm) long with a maximum diameter of 9 inches (230 mm) and weighed only 77 lbs (35 kg).

The main gun on the Hunting Panther supposedly could be elevated up to 15 degrees and depressed down to 8 degrees, depending on when it was built in the production cycle. A British Army report dated September 6, 1944, and listed as Appendix J to *War Office Technical Intelligence Summary No. 142* stated that upon testing a captured late production Hunting Panther, it was discovered that the main gun could be elevated and depressed only 12 degrees and 9 degrees, respectively, when the weapon was centered fore and aft.

This photograph shows the rear superstructure plate of a *Jagdpanther* (Hunting Panther). Visible is the large rear access hatch as well as the small spent cartridge hatch located to the right of the access hatch. *(Andreas Kirchhoff)*

OPPOSITE
Taken inside a *Jagdpanther* (Hunting Panther) is this view from the left-hand side of the vehicle's superstructure showing the massive bulk of the 8.8-cm (88-mm) Pak 43/3 (L/71) main gun, as well as the gunner's elevation and traverse hand wheels. *(Andreas Kirchhoff)*

The same report stated that its main gun could be traversed 14 degrees left or right. However, by removing 10 main gun rounds stored to the left of the driver's position, the main gun could be traversed left and right up to 15 degrees.

The same British military report stated that there was storage rack space for only forty-nine main gun rounds in the Hunting Panther, with additional

Looking through the rear access hatch of *Jagdpanther* (Hunting Panther) the main gun ammunition storage racks on the left-hand side of the superstructure are visible. *(Andreas Kirchhoff)*

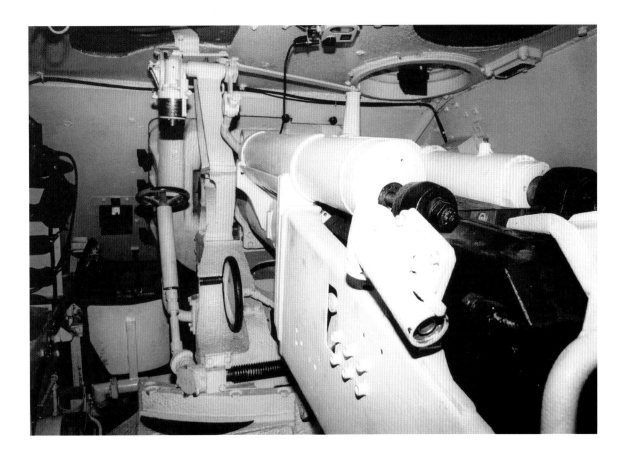

main gun rounds being stored on the floor of the vehicle. In one captured Hunting Panther the British found fifty-seven main gun rounds in the vehicle, twenty-eight being AP and the other twenty-nine HE. Another captured Hunting Panther carried sixty main gun rounds, forty being AP and the remaining twenty being HE.

SECONDARY WEAPONS

In addition to the 88-mm main gun, the Hunting Panther had a glacis mounted MG34T machine gun, in a ball mount, on the right side of the vehicle, approximately in line with the main gun. In the first thirty-one series production units of the vehicle, it had fallen to the vehicle commander to operate the glacis-mounted machine gun, since he was located in the right front-hand side of the vehicle's superstructure. This was quickly seen as an error in the crew arrangement of the vehicle, and

OVER LEAF
A rare wartime photograph taken inside a *Jagdpanther* (Hunting Panther). The vehicle had a crew of five. These included the vehicle commander and radioman on the right-hand side of the superstructure and the driver, gunner, and loader on the left side. *(Patton Museum)*

This picture shows the driver's position on a *Jagdpanther* (Hunting Panther), with his cushioned leather seat and his single replaceable periscope. As with most tanks, the driver of the Jagdpanther depended a great deal on the vehicle commander for directions. *(Andreas Kirchhoff)*

the radioman (who formerly had been positioned directly behind him) switched positions. This freed up the vehicle commander to concentrate on more important matters.

Protection from close-in enemy personnel was supposed to be provided to the Hunting Panther by the mounting of a *Nahverteidigungswaffe* (close defense weapon) in the superstructure roof. However, delays in the production of the close defense weapon meant that Hunting Panthers built before June 1944 did not have the weapon mounted. The hole in the vehicle's roof where the weapon would have been mounted was therefore covered by a bolted-on circular plate.

The vehicle commander of the Hunting Panther could talk to his driver via an intercom or in a more novel manner, which is described in a British military report listed as Appendix J to *War Office Technical Intelligence Summary No. 142* and dated September 6, 1944:

> "Apart from the usual controls associated with a normal Panther chassis there is a control resembling that of a ship's telegraph on the front offside of the fighting compartment for transmitting the commander's orders to the driver in the nearside front of the vehicle.
>
> The commands 'reverse left,' 'reverse right,' 'forward left,' 'forward right' and 'halt' may be transmitted by moving a lever opposite the required order on the

From the rear superstructure of a *Jagdpanther* (Hunting Panther) this picture was taken looking down the right side of the 8.8-cm (88-mm) Pak 43/3 (L/71) main gun. The radioman would be located far forward to operate the glacis-plate mounted machine gun. The vehicle commander's position is evident by the lower portion of the scissor-type telescope designated the S.F.14Z Gi. *(David Marian)*

Taken inside a *Jagdpanther* (Hunting Panther) from the left-hand side of the rear superstructure is a view looking to the right of additional main gun ammunition storage racks. Also visible is the interior portion of the spent cartridge case ejection port and one of the crew's overhead periscopes. *(Andreas Kirchhoff)*

commander's side, when a pointer, accompanied by a clang of a bell, points to the corresponding order on a panel in front of the driver.

The mechanism resembles that of a Bowden cable, with the operating wire running in a coppered steel pipe approximately ¼ inch in diameter. **"**

The same British military report contains some observations regarding the battlefield employment of the Hunting Panther:

"A German document states that the equipment is designed for engaging important targets at long ranges from stationary positions, and that it should not be used in support of infantry or as an 'assault' gun. It adds that unarmored targets must invariably be engaged with HE ammunition, which constitutes half the total ammunition carried. **"**

PANTHER TANK TURRET PILLBOXES

To quickly upgrade the firepower of its defensive positions during World War II, the German military began mounting the turrets of obsolete tanks, both foreign and domestic, on concrete bunkers. In October 1943, the Germans decided to use Panther tank turrets as the firepower for new portable pillboxes to be sent and emplaced wherever needed, on short notice. Hitler, who sometimes became involved with the smallest details of weapon designs, took a personal interest in the design of the Panther tank turret pillboxes.

Panther tank turret pillboxes came in various versions. The original model was known as the *Pantherturm I Stahluntersatz* (Panther turret I steel shelter) and consisted of a Panther tank turret mounted on top of a two-section prefabricated armored steel box. The Panther turret I steel shelter designed by *Organization Todt* (a civil and engineering group) could be quickly emplaced into the ground. Once in the ground, the two-piece steel box substructure of the Panther turret I steel shelter was to be surrounded by an earthen embankment under which were reinforced concrete blocks, which sloped away from the above ground turret.

The upper two-box substructure section of the Panther turret I steel shelter contained the turret basket for the crew, while the lower section contained the crew's bunks, a stove, and a gasoline-powered motor that powered an electric generator. There was also a steel armored door in the lower section that typically would connect to an ingress and egress trench.

A description of a Panther turret I steel shelter appeared in a 1944 British Army report:

A couple of American soldiers examine a knocked-out *Jagdpanther* (Hunting Panther) that has taken numerous large-caliber projectile hits on the left side of its superstructure. The preferred engagement for most tanks is to strike at your opponent thinner flanks. *(Frank Schulz Collection)*

The Germans developed a specialized defensive system that incorporated modified Panther tank turrets. These turrets were to be mounted on portable steel shelters, as seen here, which could be transported to a battlefield area and quickly emplaced to stem an enemy's offensive operation. *(Patton Museum)*

"Panther turrets were first met in the Hitler Line (Italy) and were in fact the salient features around which the other defenses were built up. They are actual tank turrets, though perhaps of a slightly earlier vintage than those now on tanks. They are mounted on a turret ring fitted on an armored box built up of welded plate about 2.5 inches thick. The whole of the box is sunk into the ground and earth is banked up close to the turret so that it is just cleared the gun at depression and yet offers some additional protection to the base of the turret skirt. Traverse is by hand only and no power is supplied."

In 1944, a new technical directive appeared regarding the construction of the Panther turret I steel shelter. Instead of surrounding the upper portion of the two-section prefabricated armored steel box, which the turret sat on with reinforced concrete blocks, covered by earth, it was decided to encase the entire below ground substructure within concrete. This was a trend that had begun in Italy with the building of the Hitler Line in early 1944. The new designation for the revised setup was known as *OT Stahlunterstand mit Betonummantelung fur Pantherturm* (Organization Todt Steel Shelter with concrete surround for Panther turret).

In Neil Short's book *Tank Turret Fortifications*, there is a description of the discussion that went on among the German military on the new mounting configuration of the Panther turret. The gist of that discussion was that the general in charge of engineering works and fortification believed that it made much more sense to use concrete (which was relatively plentiful) than steel in bunkers featuring Panther tank turret due to its continued shortages of steel.

Another problem that bedeviled the employment of the Panther turret and its supporting steel substructure was the logistical burden of transporting and erecting the components that were both heavy and bulky. By 1944, the railroad system in Germany and the occupied countries it controlled were overtaxed and constantly under threat of attack from Allied aircraft. Even when delivered to the desired location, the Panther turret and its supporting steel substructure overwhelmed the Organization Todt units responsible for moving the components to the selected sites, as they lacked a suitable number of heavy-duty trailers and tractors to complete their tasks.

With the many concerns and difficulties incurred in the continued use of the Panther turret and its supporting steel substructure in the field, Hitler decided in May 1944 that the steel substructure could be dispensed with and that the Panther turret could be mounted directly onto concrete shelters. In this configuration a new designation came about: *Regelbau* (standard design) 687 or *Pantheturm II Betonsockel* (concrete body).

On display at the Westwall Museum, Pirmasens, Germany, is this example of one of the few surviving specialized Panther tank turrets modified to serve as a pillbox during World War II. Most such artifacts were cut up for scrap in the years right after the conclusion of World War II. *(Pierre-Olivier Baun)*

As the German military was being pushed back on all fronts in late 1944, the planned building of large numbers of the Panther turrets on concrete body fell by the wayside. The next variation of the Panther pillbox theme occurred in November 1944, when the decision was made in the name of expediency to do away with the time-consuming process of building concrete shelters and mount the Panther turret onto a wooden substructure buried in the ground. This new configuration became the *Holzunterstand* (wooden shelter). Other designations included the *Schnelleinbau* (rapid installation) or *Pantherturm* II or A.

Panther pillbox turrets consisted of those turrets directly off the production line and originally intended for mounting on the Panther Ausf. A tank chassis or refurbished Panther Ausf. D tank. A specially designed turret also was intended for use as a Panther turret whose main external spotting feature was the replacement of the vehicle commander's cupola seen on the standard Panther tanks with a low-slung hatch incorporating an overhead 360-degree rotating periscope.

An American soldier looks over a knocked-out Panther tank turret pillbox. Whenever encountered, the Panther tank turret pillboxes almost always took a heavy toll of those attempting to destroy them. However, once their position was identified, it was certain death for the crew. *(Patton Museum)*

INDEX